BEYOND THE CLASSROOM:

WHAT THEY DON'T TEACH AT BUSINESS SCHOOLS

A. NAG

ATLANTIC
PUBLISHERS & DISTRIBUTORS (P) LTD

ATLANTIC
PUBLISHERS & DISTRIBUTORS (P) LTD

7/22, Ansari Road, Darya Ganj, New Delhi
Tel.: +91-11-4077 5252, 2327 3880
E-mail: orders@atlanticbooks.com
Web: www.atlanticbooks.com

Published by Atlantic Publishers & Distributors (P) Ltd 2024

Disclaimer

- The author and the publisher have taken every effort to the maximum of their skill, expertise and knowledge to provide correct material in the book. Even then if some mistakes persist in the content of the book, the publisher does not take responsibility for the same. The publisher shall have no liability to any person or entity with respect to any loss or damage caused, or alleged to have been caused directly or indirectly, by the information contained in this book.
- The author has fully tried to follow the copyright law. However, if any work is found to be similar, it is unintentional and the same should not be used as defamatory or to file legal suit against the author.
- If the readers find any mistakes, we shall be grateful to them for pointing out those to us so that these can be corrected in the next edition.
- All disputes are subject to the jurisdiction of Delhi courts only.

Printed & bound in India by Atlantic Print Services

To

All those who have attended
the Business School
and also
All those who have not attended
the Business School

Preface

From What They Teach to What They don't Teach at Business Schools

Introduction

Business schools have been set up to impart business education, i.e., to offer or teach courses which prepare the students to get closer to realities of business and management, and, to become good or successful managers. But, the question has arisen: do the business schools offer the right modules? It is widely agreed, after many years of business school education, that a distinct gap exists between what business schools teach and business or corporate realities. This gap should be addressed or filled. The present book is an attempt in this direction. *This is the first book of its kind in India.*

Objective

The objective of the book is to discuss subjects in business and management which are not taught in business schools, but, which are closer to the realities of business management and corporate career. In other words, the objective is to bridge or reduce the gap between what they teach is business schools and what companies do.

Approach

The approach follows from the objective. The book does not explain any management theories. Those are given in textbooks. The book deals with application of theories and models to actual business situations or companies. The book also analyses topics which are not covered in textbooks but which are pertinent to business and management—the ins and outs of everyday business.

Book Design

The book has been developed in three parts:

Part A: What They Don't Teach at Business Schools

Part B: Lessons from What They don't Teach at Business Schools

Part C: The Epilogue

In Part A, the book covers 20 important topics in corporate or general management, marketing, selling and entrepreneurship. These are covered in four sections and 20 chapters.

More important topics discussed under corporate or general management (Section I) include decision making at corporates, staff-line relationship, informal management, climbing the corporate ladder, how to be a successful manager, corporate culture and values, excellence in management etc.

Topics covered in marketing (Section II) are: important marketing laws, marketing myopia and major marketing sins and a marketing epilogue.

Topics covered in selling (Section III) are: why sales people fail, and success in selling.

In entrepreneurship (Section IV), entrepreneurship and business success have been elaborately dealt with including start ups.

In Part B, twenty important lessons, mostly derived from the text, have been presented or prescribed pertaining to different vital areas in business, management and corporate career. These include the ABCD principle, job hopping for career growth, the best organisation to work with, growth in an organisation, professionalism and success, efficiency, managerial mistakes, compromises in management etc.

In Part C, the Epilogue analyses the state of management education today in terms of industry-institute interface, faculty, course curriculum and a perspective for the future.

Emphasis/Focus

Throughout the book, the emphasis or focus has been on company thoughts, practices, experiences, successes and failures.

Latest thoughts and developments have been incorporated as far as possible. These give more relevance and significance to the topics discussed in the text which are not taught in business schools.

Many feel that the best lesson anyone can learn from business school is an awareness of what it can't teach you—all the ins and outs of everyday business life. The book focuses on these 'ins and outs' of business and management.

For Whom

The book is intended for all final year (Fourth Semester and Sixth Trimester) and just passed out MBA/PGDM students, working managers, business professionals, organisational libraries and business school libraries.

A. NAG
anag_123@rediffmail.com

Contents

PART A

WHAT THEY DON'T TEACH AT BUSINESS SCHOOLS

Section I
Corporate Management

1 Decision Making at Corporates

Decision making is the heart of corporate management.

Decision making takes place almost everyday in corporate functioning. Some are operational decisions relating to routine functions. Some are strategic decisions pertaining to market share management, profitability, growth and diversification. Operational or routine decisions are taken quickly. Strategic or difficult decisions are taken with planning, care and caution. Some CEOs take intuitive decisions. But, all decisions should be taken timely.

Correct and timely decisions lead a company to more success and greater heights. Wrong decisions may result in instability, downturn or downfall. This is corporate reality. What is important is how critical are the decisions which have gone wrong. In professional companies, right decisions outweigh or, rather far outweigh, wrong decisions. These are characteristics or virtues of successful companies.

Sometimes, an apparently bad or questionable decision works; and, sometimes, a good decision fails. Mark McCormack, CEO and Chairman, International Management Group (IMG), a great decision maker himself, observes: “A lot of questionable decisions have worked, because, the people who made them were determined to make them work; and, a lot of good decisions have failed because the people who made them never got over their doubts.”[1]

Corporate decision making involves many factors or dimensions. Five essential aspects or dimensions are:

1. Who should make the decisions,
2. Which factors should govern decision making,
3. To delegate or not to delegate,
4. Whether to centralise or decentralise decision making,
5. Decision making by committees.

WHO SHOULD MAKE THE DECISIONS

Should all decisions be taken by the CEO of the company, i.e., at the top level? Or, decisions can be or should be taken at other levels also?

The obvious answer may be: "The person most qualified to make it." It still begs the question: "Who is most qualified?" This has an answer. The manager who is most informed about the situation, and, particularly aware of the outcome or possible consequence of the decision. For all decisions, he need not be the CEO.

A general prescription is: in operational matters, the manager at the desk should take the decision and be responsible for it. All strategic or long-term decisions will be taken by the top management or CEO. The Board of Directors may approve some such decisions.

Be it middle-level manager or the CEO, the decision maker must have the initiative and courage to make the decision and resources to implement it. *In some sense, implementation makes a decision complete*. In some decisions, follow-up is required. In such cases, follow-up is as important as implementation. It has been observed in many companies that some good decisions have not produced results because of poor implementation and follow-up.

Some CEOs think the CEO should take all the decisions himself (herself). The logic is: the CEO is running the company and is responsible for its performance. So, what better to ensure consistency than to make every decision himself (herself)? Quality may also come from attention to nitty-gritty. The organisation also needs consistency of decisions and results.

But, this may not be the most preferred course for decision making. Some CEOs feel this very strongly. Thomas Horton, CEO of American Management Association (formerly IBM Senior management) observes: "If there were a Management Hall of Shame, it would be filled with statues of those who dedicated their business lives, and, their every waking moment to minutiae to deciding *everything*."[2]

This may appear to be an exaggerated statement or observation. But, this is the decision-making style of autocratic CEOs. More CEOs are democratic where many decisions are delegated, and in more professional organisations, delegated to right levels.

WHICH FACTORS GOVERN DECISION MAKING

Should a business decision be intuitive or based on facts and information? Should the decision maker consider different alternatives before taking the final decision? Should a manager or CEO should follow some "Dos" and "Dont's" for better decision making? These are the factors which commonly influence or govern business decisions.

Choose the Best Alternative

Some say it is motherhood that the best among the alternatives should be chosen. But, it is not so simple or straightforward. It is not always easy to determine which is the best alternative.

It is true that a manager (also CEO) should consider different available alternatives and choose the best one. But, how to decide the best alternative? Is it only on the basis of outcome or result of the decision? Or, a manager (CEO) should consider the cost-benefits of every alternative because every decision involves a cost in terms of resources—financial or non-financial or both. Experience of most companies shows that both result and cost-benefit analysis are important. The final decision may be based on balancing the two.

Managers can take advantage of game theory for choosing among alternatives. Management games are played (computerised) to evaluate the alternatives with different scores and choosing the best alternative on the basis of total score of each alternative. New quantitative techniques are also emerging in the field of management.

Management game or quantitative decision results should be backed by manager's or CEO's personal judgement. According to me, the judgemental factor should finally prevail. Many may agree with this. In fact, the best decisions are most often guided by the judgemental factor than by quantitative techniques.

Past experience can sometimes help. Past decision under similar situation can be chosen. But, *using past experience may sometimes mean repeating the past mistakes*. This is the danger of extrapolating the past.

Situations (environmental factors) are hardly same or similar during two time periods. Therefore, assumption of same situation may often be faulty. Past experience and decision can, at best, be used as rolling benchmarks or approximations.

Intuition or Facts?

A story about intuition versus facts is told like this: Ford Motor Company asks every candidate during interview for managerial position whether he puts salt and pepper in his food before he tastes it. The theory or assumption behind this is that such a person is likely to make a decision before knowing all the facts. In reality, this may not have much to do with decision making because many successful decision makers like spicy food, and, many bad or poor decision makers like non-spicy food.

This leads us to the main discussion or debate: should decision making be intuitive or based on enough facts and information? Management experts and decision makers have differing views on this.

Managers and CEOs who depend heavily on data/facts often suffer from the "desire to know too many facts, their theory being that if you have enough facts, the decision will make itself." Then, you don't need the manager, let alone the CEO. Also, in reality, all facts are hardly ever known.

Also, the reality is that facts are nothing more than a decision maker's "tools." Those are only as useful to a manager or CEO as his ability to interpret or analyse them. Interpretation and analysis differ depending on the interpreter or personality/individual concerned. *Facts, by themselves, do not make any decision. Neither it substitutes intuition or judgements.*

According to many, "decision making is more an intuitive process than an analytical one, and, no amount of market studies, focus groups, and research reports is going to change that fact. The danger is that the more data people have to chew upon, the more likely they are to underestimate the importance of intuition (or judgement)."[3]

Legendary Dhirubhai Ambani (Reliance Industries) was more an intuitive decision maker. L.N. Mittal (also known as Arcelor Mittal), the creator of a global steel empire, was also guided more by intuition or gut feeling than fact. So, is Azim Premji (Wipro) and Kiron Mazumdar Shaw (Biocon). These are entrepreneurial CEOs. CEOs in more professionally managed companies (mostly multinationals) like GE, 3M, IBM, UNILEVER, HUL, P&G and ITC make a good blending of intuition and facts/data for decision making, may be, bending more towards the latter used as base for decision.

In all these CEO decisions, the organisational system or culture becomes the guiding factor. That makes the decision more meaningful because decisions are always taken for an organisation.

Decision Maker's "Dos" and "Don't Dos'?

Decision makers will do well to follow some "Dos" and "Don't Dos." These are cautions, safeguards or inspirations.

Three Important "Dos"

1. Take decision with courage and honesty or integrity;
2. Take the support of your senior/boss while taking a decision;
3. If a decision goes wrong, use it as an input or lesson for future decisions.

Three Important "Don't Dos"

1. Do not take decision in baste. Every decision should be well thought out.
2. Do not keep pondering over a decision—whether it is right or wrong. Take the decision and move forward.

3. Do not break down if there is a wrong decision. Even the best decision makers have sometimes made a wrong decision.

TO DELEGATE OR NOT TO DELEGATE

Decision making implies delegation—of authority and responsibility. Delegation is top-down—the CEO or boss delegates to subordinate managers. According to some CEOs, one skill or characteristics which distinguishes leaders from others is their ability to delegate. Some other CEOs may have a different view.

How Much to Delegate?

"Don't delegate—do," "don't do—delegate"; these are two extreme positions sometimes taken by the bosses or CEOs. In the first case, the (autocratic) boss would like to retain all formal (and informal) controls and decision making with him. The subordinates, like soldiers, should carry out instructions and deliver the goods. In the second case, the CEO or boss is like the king. The subordinates would have almost all the autonomy to plan, decide and execute (this signifies more an informal delegation system), and, give the credit of achievement to the boss.[4]

Sometimes, the most promising fast-track manager can get quickly derailed by delegating too much or too little. An insecure first-line manager may fail to delegate because of fear of failure. A general manager with an engineering degree may find it hard to let others make technical decisions howsoever competent they may be. Chief executives who consider themselves marketing experts may under-view their brand managers. Some CEOs convinced that they are utterly irreplaceable are reluctant to retire, i.e., do the ultimate act of delegation.[5]

Between these polar positions, lie the more normal situations in the reality of corporate environment in which the boss both "does" and "delegates" in different degrees depending on a whole host of factors—personal as well as organisational.

A simple management rule or principle is that decisions be pushed down as far as possible and be taken as close as possible to the action to which they apply.

The management charter of GE (USA)'s Lamp Division almost echoes this by saying: "All authority not expressly and in writing reserved to higher management is granted to lower management." In other words, the decision which a manager is not entitled to take within his delegation of powers should always be spelt out; for all others, he should be supposed to have the delegation, authority and responsibility.

Let us also listen to the subordinates' cry—their lamenting experience of what delegation means in practice. A group of junior and middle-level managers was attending a workshop on delegation. They came from wide range of backgrounds and industries—heavy industry, public utilities, electronics, insurance, local government and manufacturing. At a warm-up session, they were asked to describe, from their own experience, what delegation meant to them. Here are some of their responses:

> "I get the boring and dirty jobs my boss doesn't like dong." "...When I was given really interesting assignment that was in my speciality, the boss was on my back the whole time telling me how to do it. I don't really get a chance to get my teeth into it."
>
> "Every so often I get a heap of papers through the internal mail, mostly routine returns and requests which have sat on my supervisor's desk until he's noticed the deadline is long overdue and somebody had better done something about it—that's usually me, and, I'm on a Chiding to nothing before I even start."
>
> "I don't know—boss keeps everything to herself. I don't even know what she does most of the time."

Delegation: Ins and Outs

Lee Iacocca, whose initials are often jokingly said to stand for "I Am Chairman of Chrysler Corporation of America," was dabbling with design even at the age of 66. According to a recent news report:

> Many Chrysler executives, engineers and stylists complain that many of the company's car and truck models have sold poorly in recent years because of changes and delays ordered

by Mr. Iacocca. The designers in particular, roll their eyes when describing, how Mr. Iacocca, with a wave of his cigar, has forced them to submit long, boxy designs and plenty of chrome, when rounder, cleaner models were clearly winning customers.[5]

We may or may not regard Iacocca as a great CEO, but, his record as a delegator was not good. In contrast, PepsiCo's Wayne Calloway is regarded by his people as a great delegator.

To become leaders, more so successful leaders, CEOs should abandon the attitude: "If I want anything done right, I must do it myself." The fact may be that there are managers in the company who may be able to do many things better. CEOs/Managers who do not appreciate this may limit their ability to lead. "Those who fail to delegate because of fear of failure increase their probability of failure."

A CEO, however, cannot and should not delegate everything. The CEO, for example, should not delegate the strategic task of planning for growth and diversification or crisis management. Delegating these tasks may put the CEO's own career and even the company at risk. In fact, in planning for the future projects, the CEO's leadership vision, he has to formulate strategies for realising the vision.

For delegation to work and succeed, relationship between the two parties in delegation is important. This almost goes without saying. Unless the relationship is based on mutual understanding and trust, delegation cannot work. Both parties should have confidence in each other, particularly the one who is delegating.

This also implies that delegation cannot work without clear and open communication between the two parties. "You need to know where things stand, and, your people need to know where they stand." This transparency is vital. Many delegations have failed because this factor was absent.

These can be expressed in terms of two common reasons why delegation fails. First, the person who is to be delegated is reluctant to take the responsibility (sometimes task or responsibility is almost forced); second, the person who is delegating wants to secretly keep authority or responsibility with him. More often it is the latter. This can be a delegation killer. It has been rightly said: "Though you cannot delegate your personal accountability, you can make others accountable for their results. But, only if your are willing to give them your authority—and live with their results."

Delegation and Team Building

Delegation is not always a solo act (one-to-one). It can be through team. Delegation is a way of team building for better corporate governance. Many companies have realised and implemented this.

The CEO has to select the players of his team based on homogeneity of thought, discipline and commitment. After this, the process of team building starts. One can say that *team building is a process of managerial transition.*

A Harvard Business School study shows that more successful CEOs are effective in building trust among their team members. Once trust is developed, the team members understand each other better, and, there is also mutual respect. With such a team, the CEO can take better decisions than he can make on his own.

Robert Crandall, CEO of American Airlines, is known to be a highly effective decision maker. But, he relies strongly on the views of his team. Every Monday, Crandall calls a meeting of his Planning Committee consisting of eight senior executives. Such meetings go for long hours. Crandall says: "I think you have to accept the notion that at the senior levels of any big company, you rarely know what the outcome of any decision going to be. When we are making a decision, we do our best to elicit all the views about how the decision might come out. And, we debate those views rigorously."[6] During such sessions or meetings, strong teams are being built.

Team vary in size, composition, attitude, perspectives—and efficacy. According to some CEOs, more diverse the team members, more effective is the team because the members give diversity of perspectives. The CEO's job is to ensure cohesiveness or strike unity in diversity. If this can be successfully done, then this will be teamwork at its best.

The Japanese decision-making system is a great example of the team approach.

CENTRALISATION VERSUS DECENTRALISATION

Decentralisation in decision making is another name for delegation. Decentralisation, in some sense, can also be a form of delegation.

Among others, Peter Drucker highlights the role of decentralisation—"decentralisation is the cornerstone of good management." According to him, decentralisation helps an organisation to know exactly what lines of manufacturing or production are profitable and which are unprofitable. In a centralised system, unprofitable lines of the production would have continued for years alongside profitable ones. Drucker's view may be long past now.

Today, centralisation versus decentralisation is more like a debate or discussion in corporate management with advantages and disadvantages of both. Companies and CEOs have different views and experiences on this.

Let us start with decision making in the Japanese management system. The Japanese companies are known to adopt team approach and decision by consensus which imply decentralisation of decision making. But, this does not eliminate the role of centralisation in the Japanese decision-making system.

The Sony System

I shall illustrate this with the example of Sony and its founder, CEO and Chairman Akio Morita. Morita says: "If may sound like a contradiction to say that Japanese companies, as opposed to Western companies, are run by consensus in light of what I have already written about the individuality we prize at Sony and other Japanese companies such as Honda, Matsushita and some others, where a strong central figure traditionally makes bold decisions, seemingly all by himself. But, it is not a contradiction ."[7]

Morita explains: "The concept of consensus is natural to the Japanese, but, it does not necessarily mean that every decision comes out of a spontaneous group impulse. Gaining consensus in a Japanese company often means spending time preparing the groundwork for it, and very often, the consensus is formed from the top down, not from the bottom up... While an idea may arise from middle management, for example, top management may accept it whole or revise it and seek approval and cooperation all down the line. When I pulled my bluff on the Walkman, threatening to resign, my colleagues knew that I was ahead of them, that I was using all my experience and knowledge of marketing and consumer psychology in making my decision. And, because of it, they committed 100 per cent to helping make the project a success. If we had failed with the Walkman, I could not have pointed to any market research as the cause of its fiasco."[8]

Spatial Decentralisation

Decentralisation has a spatial connotation. Corporate headquarters decentralise authority and responsibility to the regions. In multinational companies, the parent company decentralises authority to the subsidiaries in foreign countries for their local business decisions—Siemens, GE, Procter & Gamble, Nestle, Honda, Coca-Cola, Pepsi and many others.

Let me narrate the GE way of decentralisation in India. According to GE, the idea of the command-and-control system is gone. GE thinks itself as a flat organisation. The CEO won't be the power base any longer, Jack Welch, GE's CEO of the Millennium, says: With increasing transparency brought about by the Internet, the CEO will increasingly be the orchestra leader of very bright people, doing their things."[9] Welch says further: "I and Scott Bayman, GE India CEO, work together. We don't have a lot of people telling us what to do. He pretty much has his own head. And, so by the nature of having many direct reports, you automatically give lots of freedom to the people."[10]

Spatial decentralisation is typical in all multinational companies with fully owned subsidiaries. In partly owned subsidiaries, decentralisation is even more.

An Unresolvable Conflict?

Some feel that centralisation versus decentralisation is an unresolvable conflict or debate. This may continue and centralisation and decentralisation may coexist.

Konosuke Matsushita, founder, CEO and Chairman, Matsushita Electric Company (maker of National Panasonic brands) was one of the first to recognise that centralisation versus decentralisation may be an unresolvable conflict, but, great organisations must have both. This is based on his own experience.

The divisionalised system in Matsushita is known to be of "extraordinary efficiency." But, in spite of this, "Matsushita continually tinkered as a way of ensuring his organisation's vitality." Yasan Okamoto, an authority on Matsushita, writes: "When we look at the overall characteristics of Matsushita's structure, we see decentralisation and centralisation revolving in a kind of spiral. That is to say, it's not that decentralisation replaces centralisation and then reverses itself again, but, rather that the two forms of organisation swing back and forth in an ever more complex marriage."[11]

To many decision makers, this may appear to be a very realistic model with suitable adaptations to their own companies.

DECISION MAKING BY COMMITTEES

Sometimes, organisations refer decision making to committees usually for strategic reasons. The purpose is to infuse objectivity in the decision and make it less subjective.

Team and Committee

Distinction should be made between a "team" and, a "committee" although many use these interchangeably. A team is formed to take a decision; but, more often, the team is formed to perform a task or execute a project. Sometimes, inter-disciplinary teams are formed for better execution of projects. A committee is formed only to take a decision and not to execute. Decisions which involve high stake for the organisation (like diversification), the CEO may not like to take all on himself, and, may refer these to committees of business planning experts in the organisation. The CEO will also have his inputs in these.

The difference between a team and a committee may appear very fine or delicate, but, the distinction exists.

Committee Formation: Do and Don't Do

Here are some advisories on forming and not forming committees:

- Form a committee if you do not want a decision; do not form a committee if you want a decision.
- Form a committee if you want to put the gun on others' shoulders and fire; do not form a committee if you want to face or fire yourself.
- Form a committee if you want to defer a decision; do not form a committee if you want to act now.

These give different perspectives to committee formation. These also happen in reality.[12]

Here is an example of how a committee is sometimes used by the CEO/Chairman. This relates to MMTC, Nava Ratna public sector company. Chairman SVS wanted to promote some managers out of turn (normal promotions are based on seniority cum merit). To get managers of his choice promoted, SVS appointed a committee of experts. Probable candidates were called for an interview. Needless to say, the committee promoted those managers SVS wanted along with some others.

SOME WISE OBSERVATIONS

Given below are three wise observations on what is good corporate decision making:

> "A decision is a choice between alternatives, but, rarely a choice between right and wrong. It is much more often a choice between two courses of action neither of which is probably more nearly right than the other. Nor is it based merely on facts. In real life, a fact is often in the eye of the beholder. Decisions, on the other hand, are largely based on opinions."
>
> —Peter Drucker, Management Expert

> "To make right decisions, you need facts, unshakable facts. You need self-confidence. And a conviction that the decision is yours to make. You need to confer with other people and inform still others. But, the really difficult decisions require something even more: guts."

—T.R. Horton, CEO, American Management Association

"Sound corporate decision making is a constant process of staying current, of perceiving how new information can alter old decisions, (and) of anticipating the future."

—Mark McCormack, CEO/Chairman, International Management Group (IMG)

So, corporate decision making has no rigid frontiers. Boundaries of decision making have to be defined by the decision makers. But, every decision should have logic and an objective—the objective of productivity and results.

2
Line-Staff Relationship

"Staff" Serves; "Line" Controls...?

Much has been written and said about "line" and "staff." According to some, there probably is no other area in the field of management which has evoked as much discussion as this subject. It is probably also true that many of the difficulties and frictions encountered in the daily life of an organisation is because of line and staff problems. Misconception and lack of understanding of what "line" and "staff" are is probably the source of many bickerings, conflicts, disunity, duplication and loss of production or sales even in companies that are generally known to be well-run.

It is understandable that there is confusion about "line" and "staff" functions among the practitioners of management. But, what is not so easily understandable is that much confusion exists even among the management scholars and writers.

NATURE OF "LINE" AND "STAFF"

As in other institutions, staff in business has grown by evolutionary stages, both within individual companies and in business as a whole. Because of the growing complexity of the technological aspects of business and industry, there is a definite trend for staff to become increasingly specialised; but, at the same time, to associate itself more closely with line in the accomplishment of the organisational objectives. On the one hand, this has led to greater opportunity for significant staff accomplishment; on the other, it has resulted in added confusion and friction.

In the attempt to clarify the difference between line and staff, one of the most frequently found explanations is that "line" refers to those functions which have *direct responsibility* for achieving the major objectives of the enterprise and "staff" refers to those functions that *help the line* in achieving the primary objectives of the enterprise—activities which are *indirectly related* to the major objectives. Some enterprises treat line and staff designations as a way of distinguishing between productive and non-productive efforts of the company.

Let us consider the contention that "line" are those who are engaged in the primary activities that are necessary to reach the stated corporate objectives, and, "staff" are those who only indirectly contribute to these objectives. This approach to "line" and "staff" leads to difficulties because of differences in objectives and characters of enterprise. Because the objectives of companies differ, the nature of those activities which directly contribute to the major objectives will also differ. Therefore, in some companies such as a manufacturing company, the manufacturing function is line; in others, manufacturing and sales are line, and, in others, engineering (civil construction, project and engineering consultancy) and finance (financial institutions or organisations) may also be identified as line. Traffic and transportation are generally assigned to a staff function. Transportation, can, however, be a line function in the operations of an integrated oil company.

Louis Allen explains the difference between "line" and "staff" in terms of differentiation of the assignments or roles: "At any time, two or more people work together, the distinction is a means of determining who makes decisions directly related to the attainment of end results and who provides advice and service in making those decisions. 'Line' refers to those positions and elements of the organisation which have responsibility and authority and are accountable for accomplishment of primary objectives. 'Staff' elements are those which have responsibility and authority for providing advice and service to the line for the attainment of (corporate) objectives."

This can be stated in a direct way in terms of a line manager and a staff manager. A "line" person is defined as "any individual who gets results directly or through other individuals reporting to him." A "staff" person is "an individual who gets results through someone who does not report to him."

It is convenient, at times, to refer to one department as staff department, and, to another, as line department. It is also common practice that certain activities and functions in today's enterprises are normally undertaken in staff capacity within the organisation structure. This applies most often to personnel departments, public relations, industrial relations, legal departments and such others. Typically, line functions are manufacturing or selling. Other functions in an organisation are staff functions—finance, personnel and administration, R&D, quality control, legal and secretarial, public relations, corporate planning, etc.

According to some, line and staff are characteristics of authority relationship and nothing else. Therefore, the only way one can determine whether a department is related to the organisation structure as line function or in staff capacity is to examine the intentions and actions of the delegating manager. It is he who, following managerial principles, will confer upon a certain department line authority or place it into staff capacity. Staff is not inferior to line authority; it is of a completely different nature. The objectives of the staff elements are, of course, ultimately the same as those the line organisation is pursuing, namely, the achievement of the enterprise's goal.

The Scalar Principle

Another group, led by James Mooney, one of the pioneer writers on line-staff relationship, holds a different view. Mooney points out that, in all organisations, there is a gradation of authority as an uninterrupted series of steps. This principle is described as the *scalar principle*. Wherever there is line function, there is a superior and a subordinate with a direct line of authority running between the two. The scalar principle states that, within an organisation, there is a line of superior-subordinate relationship which runs from the top of the organisation to the bottom. Staff is auxiliary in nature and helps the line executive in many ways. It provides counsel, advice, and, guidance, but, it does not issue orders and commands. In Mooney's thorough analysis, he points out that because staff is purely auxiliary in nature, one cannot look at the structure of the organisation as if it were a double track railroad consisting of line and staff as the two tracks or coordinates.

Mooney goes further to state that "the structure of organisation is single-track only, and, can never be anything else. What is known in military organisation as line is synonymous with what we have called the scalar chain, and, there can be but one chain of line authority. Any work or function in the organisation which cannot be identified as an actual link in the scalar process is an auxiliary function, adhering to the line like sidings along the main track. This means that every staff function must adhere to the line in some dependent relation, and, could not otherwise exist."

This line of thinking, however, is being debated today, if not challenged. In the modern management system, with manufacturing or selling as the core line function, most of the functional growth has been in staff departments, as stated above. It may not be correct to say that all staff functions are auxiliary in nature. Functions like personnel and administration and budgetary planning are definitely mainstream functions. In general, it may be said that staff functions are gaining more control today.

Personal Staff

Finally, a word about personal staff. Much criticism has been levelled against the use of personal staff. Frequently, a personal assistant (or an executive assistant) has become sign of prestige. In some companies, there has been a proliferation of assistants who, in turn, have acquired their own personal staff adding ultimately to the administrative hierarchy. The personal (or executive) assistant is shown in the organisation chart above almost everybody else, and, undoubtedly in day-to-day operations, he is exceedingly close to the boss. Due to this closeness, he would undoubtedly become familiar with the ways, methods and many major decisions of the boss, and, because of such familiarity considerations—whether they are erroneously created or justifiably so—he may exercise undue influence on subordinate line and staff managers, and, also, on visitors to the boss. We know of an executive assistant to a chief executive who would interview every visitor, and, in the process confuse him, before he is let in. This bossing practice continued till he interviewed the boss's wife and was reprimanded. Such black spots bring the entire personal staff community to disrepute.

LINE'S COMPLAINTS: STAFF'S COMPLAINTS

The problem of line-staff relationship started with the introduction of various management practices more than half a century ago. But, even today, this continues to be a typical problem in most of the organisations so much so that some have contended that *line-staff relationship in most organisations are like proverbial mother-in-law and daughter-in-law relationship*—very prickly. Line has many complaints against staff; staff has many counter-complaints against line.

One of the line management's most common complaints is that staff does not know its place and wants to assume line authority. Line management frequently feels that staff elements encroach upon line management's duties, responsibilities and prerogatives.

Another common complaint of line managers is that the advice of staff is academic, theoretical and unrealistic. It is contended that since staff is not responsible for final results, staff people, at times, have a tendency to propose and suggest untried and untested new ideas. Line management would sometimes willingly put these ideas into practice if staff would take time and make efforts to discuss and explain such ideas to line management properly. Such discussion and explanation, however, may become difficult for line to understand at times because of the academic, professional or technical jargons used by the staff.

Another complaint is that staff thinks in a vacuum and does not see the total corporate scenario. Line management thinks that the staff specialist is so involved with his own speciality that he thinks only of the objectives of his speciality instead of the objectives of the enterprise as a whole. This complaint is very common and, at times, quite in order.

Another very common criticism about staff is that when a project does not become successful, line management is blamed for its failure (wrong implementation); but, whenever a project is successful, staff will try to take the credit (for right advice and project formulation).

If one enquires with staff elements about the causes of conflicts, one will hear a completely different story.

One of the most commonly heard complaints by staff is that management resists new ideas and is not willing to go along with rapid progress of a particular speciality or area.

Another common complaint is that line does not make proper use of available staff; it is felt that those line officers who are in most need of specialised advice most often hesitate to ask for it. Such line officers might feel that asking for advice of the staff is admitting ignorance or defeat. To this, the line officer might reply that the staff could not have been of much effective assistance anyhow.

Again, staff often complains that some line managers, after going through the motions of asking for advice, will reject the suggestions either because they did not really want to ask for the advice or because they distrust the advisor. Both are bad for the organisation.

Another frequently heard complaint by staff is that they do not have enough authority. They often feel that if they have arrived at the best solution, they should be allowed to put it into action.

"SERVE" AND "CONTROL" CONTROVERSY

This brings us to the "mother-in-law" and "daughter-in-law" or "serve" and "control" controversy proper. But, who is mother-in-law and who is daughter-in-law?

The historical antecedents of staff functions, according to Koontz and O'Donnel, lie in the formation of the papal bureaucracy. Many centuries ago, a very learned group of monks, the Monks of Benedictine, formed a cell. They specialised in a vast range of subjects, and, the church directed the clergy that if it ventured on any project, the relevant monk must compulsorily be consulted. The church, however, went on to add that it was not necessary to fully follow or implement any advice or suggestion. Hence, the philosophy developed whereby the Monks of Benedictine had only the "right to be listened to." They existed to serve.

Staff people in most organisations have been following the above concept of "service" for long. However, in some organisations, the staff function becomes a controlling authority. Experience has shown that either of these two philosophies or approaches tends to generate conflict and affect smooth line-staff relations.

Balancing 'Serve' and 'Control'

There are companies in which line functionaries seem to ask the question: "Is staff here to serve us or control us?" The reply most staff functionaries give is: "How do we serve or control people who do not report to us? We do not have any power over them." There is truth in both the question and the answer. These imply the need for balancing between "serve" and "control."

As organisations grow and newer areas of specialisation emerge, it is necessary for them to find a balance between service and control within the staff function. The staff has to be a group of people who both control and serve the line to achieve corporate objectives. How is this balance to be brought about? How can one have a staff function with a "high control-high service" orientation?

For an answer to this, we may use the managerial matrix developed by Mouton and Blake. Mouton and Blake's original (9 × 9) matrix analysed managerial behaviour in terms of concern for production or results and concern for people. Using the same approach, it is interesting to analyse line-staff relationship. The row (horizontal axis) in the matrix, in this case, would show "concern for control" "(different concerns for control shown on a 9-point scale) and, the column (vertical axis) would show concern for service" (9-point scale). Managers, by and large, fit into one of the five dominant styles depicted in the matrix, viz. 1/1, 1/9, 5/5, 9/1 and 9/9. We discuss these styles below.[1]

- *The 1/1 Staff:* Low concern for control/low concern for service. The staff put forth just enough to get by. They go along with facts, beliefs and positions given by line, keeping their own counsel but responding only when asked. They avoid taking sides by not revealing their opinions, attitudes and ideas. They stay out of conflicts. They let line to make decisions or come to terms with whatever happens and avoid giving feedback to line.

- *The 1/9 Staff:* Low concern for control/high concern for service. This category of staff initiates action that help or support line. They only look for facts, beliefs and positions that maintain "all is well." For the sake of harmony, they are inclined to accept opinions, attitudes and ideas of line even if they have reservations. They avoid generating conflict with line, but, when the conflict arises, they try to soothe feelings to contain the situation. They search for decisions that maintain good line-staff relations, and, encourage line to make decisions whenever possible, praising line, when something positive happens, but, avoid giving negative feedback.
- *The 5/5 Staff:* Medium concern for control/medium concern for service. These staff maintain a steady pace, taking line people more or less at face value, and, check facts, beliefs and positions only when obvious discrepancies appear. They express opinions in a tentative way, and, when conflicts arise, try to find a reasonable solution and workable decision that line accepts. They give informal or indirect feedback regarding suggestions for improvement to line.
- *The 9/1 Staff:* High concern for control/low concern for service. These people drive themselves and line, and, investigate facts, beliefs and positions of line so that they are in control of any situation and assure themselves that line is not making mistakes or acquiring ascendancy. They stoutly defend their positions even if it means rejecting line's views. When conflict arises, they try to cut it off or win their point, placing high value on making their own decisions, and, are rarely influenced by line.
- *The 9/9 Staff:* High concern for control/high concern for service. This is thought to be the ideal style for

staff. Such staff make vigorous efforts and line joins in enthusiastically. They search for and validate information that line provides, inviting ideas and suggestions from line even if they are different from their own. They review and evaluate line's beliefs and those of their own on a continual basis, and, consider it necessary to express their own concerns and convictions. They respond to ideas sounder than their own, even if they emanate from line, by changing their mind. When conflict arises with line, they look for underlying causes, placing high value on arriving at sound decisions, and, encouraging two-way feedback to strengthen operations.

Most managers will generally recognise the staff functions in their own companies in one or more of the above categories. (The skeptics say that the 9/9 style hardly exists in reality.)

To achieve an optimal blending of service and control, staff should develop their knowledge or expertise base in such a way that line seeks their service and accepts their control. Lack of such knowledge or expertise base may lead them to either a 9/1 style of attempting to bulldoze line or a 1/9 style of placating line, or worse still, a 1/1 style: "To hell with it—let line do what it wants."

There are numerous such examples in every organisation, but, dealing with such manifestations or problems in isolation will not help; one may have to dig deep to search for and validate underlying causes in a 9/9 way. This should be the goal. In this context, one sees little relevance today in the theory of the Monks of Benedictine or the proverbial mother-in-law controlling and the daughter-in-law serving.

BEHAVIOURAL AND APTITUDE FACTORS

We should also emphasise the role of behavioural and aptitude factors in line-staff relationship. We have just talked of different "serve" and "control" styles. These styles have a behavioural base—behaviour based on certain assumptions.

Mouton and Blake contend that assumptions guide behaviour. Everyone of us tends to respond to circumstances in the light of our assumptions, since these assumptions control our view of others' behaviour. Such assumptions constitute our personal theory of behaviour. For example, say Mouton and Blake, a manager assumes that several people are slacking off; so he takes action to push the slackers. They resent it and slow down. The manager's assumption is verified and he pushes harder, both the lazy ones and others. A slow-down or sit-down protest confirms his belief that people will do anything to get out of work. The manager may never think that his assumption that "people are lazy" may have caused the "sit-down process."

The dominant "serve" and "control" styles depicted above, are, in fact, based on five sets of dominant assumptions regarding line's behaviour or line's response to staff behaviour (or line's reactions to staff action).

The personnel departments in some companies are prone to work on a 1/9 (low control/high service) set of assumptions where they find it easy to settle the demands of the union by purchasing peace at exorbitant prices. Or, let us take the case of quality control department passing a slightly defective product by succumbing to line (production department) pressure, thereby abdicating its control function. Or, the maintenance engineer letting the production manager run a machine beyond stipulated hours to enable him to reach production targets, again, giving way to line's pressure based on some implicit assumption about line's reaction or behaviour if he does not agree.

Many feel that, in any company, the chief executive's own set of assumptions regarding line-staff relationship should be clarified first. One often sees the chief executive in a company using internal audit in the 9/1 (high control-low service) manner. In such cases, the control element plays such a dominant role that compliance over a period of time tends to stifle initiative. For instance, in one company, overtime is not given, even for an important job, only because "we may be questioned by audit." A paltry sum of overtime which could have saved or made a couple of thousands for the company. Such matters are normally never reported and one can imagine the massive wastage that can occur—normally hidden costs that the chief executive never gets to know about.

From behavioural factors, we move to aptitude factors. Some managers show a natural aptitude for staff functions—more specialised and less supervisory; others have a natural flair for a line function—less specialised and more supervisory in nature. It is like a student showing an aptitude for art, science or engineering; or, a more closer comparison, a postgraduate opting for MBA programme for a business career or a research career in his own area of specialisation.

If a manager with "line aptitude" is posted in a staff capacity, his approach towards line-staff relationship would be different than if a manager with a "staff aptitude" is placed in a line function. For example, a manager with line aptitude, if posted in a staff cadre, is likely to demonstrate more concern for control than service (9/1, 9/2, 9/3, . . . , etc.). On the other hand, if a manager with staff aptitude is appointed in a line position, he is quite likely to show more concern for service than for control (1/1, 1/2, 1/3, . . ., etc.).

TODAY'S "STAFF" TOMORROW'S "LINE"?

All this indicates that, sometimes we tend to blow up too much line-staff relationship problems or conflicts. Inherently, there may not be much conflict. The difference between the two may be more of degree than of order. The difference in relationship may be a matter of posting particular personnel in particular positions, assignment of particular jobs and responsibilities, and functions and authorities resulting from them. May be a manager has an aptitude for line and he has been posted as a staff or vice versa.

Span of Control

A comparative study of a number of industrial organisations in different European countries points to possible interchangeability of line and staff in connection with span of control. In some of the organisations studied, staff assistants have been used to relieve line managers to widen the span of control. "In practice, they may function as an intervening level of management, although this is rarely shown in organisation charts,"[2] the study points out.

Another study[3] mentions that "it is at times difficult to determine whether a position or a function in an enterprise is line or staff. This confusion is more prevalent since what is line in one company may easily be staff in another depending upon the authority relationships within that particular enterprise. An example of this is research. There are many companies where research is staff, providing advice, guidance, and, counsel to the line managers. On the other hand, there are companies where research has changed to line. An excellent illustration of this is the Du Pont Company in USA, where until 1921, all of the company's research was conducted by a chemical staff. However, with the reorganisation in 1921, the management decided that each general manager of an industrial department should not only have a manufacturing and sales line but also a research division. (This structure continues even today.) The only way one can determine whether a department is in a line or staff relation is by actually examining the actions, intentions and delegations by the operating executives."

In many public sector undertakings (may be almost all), there is a system of rotational transfer of managers—transfer from a trade or a commodity seat to personnel and administration and vice versa (to the extent feasible). Such rotation is based, among others, on the assumption that a manager is as good or as bad for a line function as for a staff function, and such rotation has been an established culture of such undertakings or corporations.

In many organisations, there are precedents or cases of staff managers being shifted to line functions based on their aptitude, and company's assessment of their potential or calibre. In public sector corporations like MMTC, a number of managers from the Research and Management Services Division have moved to general cadres and have turned out to be quite successful, some even moving to Board level positions.[4]

I joined MMTC in staff function as Economic Adviser, and, was later moved to line function as General Manager and moved further upwards in line capacity. During an intervening period, I served in staff cadre in corporate planning. This makes "staff" and "line" roles almost interchangeable.

In the private sector also, many successful line managers—the so-called "gold collar" managers of today—were staff managers yesterday. Dr. A. Ganguly, Chairman, Hindustan Lever Limited, is one of the most glaring examples. What is more interesting is Dr. Ganguly saying, "If I had to begin all over again, I would go back being a research scientist." This easily makes it an interpenetrating staff-line cycle. There are other cases also.

CHRO TO GLOBAL CEO

$ 10 billion French luxury group Channel (which competes with L'Oreal, Gucci, Hermec, etc.) has appointed Leena Nair, Chief Human Resources Officer (CHRO) of Unilever, as its Global CEO. This brings CHROs, conventionally perceived as staff specialities, to the forefront of leadership candidatures.

Announcing Nair's decision to leave Unilever, CEO Alan Jope said: "Leena has been a pioneer throughout her career at Unilever, but, no more so than in her role as CHRO, where she has been a driving force on our equity, diversity and inclusion agenda, on the transformation of our leadership development and on our preparedness for the future...."[5]

A Channel release said: The new 'partnership' between company's Global Executive Chairman, Alain Wertheimer, and Global CEO, Nair "Will further ensure long-term success as a private company, believing in the freedom of creation, cultivating human potential and acting to have a positive impact in the world."[6]

LINE-STAFF RELATIONSHIP: CONCLUSIONS

One is almost led to the conclusion that both "line" and "staff" should "serve" as well as "control." They are two sides of the coin; they should reinforce each other and the coin—the organisation. This should be the ideal line-staff relationship. But, this may not be true in all organisations or even in the large majority of the organisations.

To more realistically cover or represent all or most of the organisations, two conclusions may be more logical. This may be called the 75 : 25 pattern:

1. In conventional management system which is followed by about 75 per cent of the companies, staff-line relationship is about "serve" and "control" controversy, mutual rivalry,

bickerings and often conflicts. Some say that line cadre managers are like IFS and IAS; the staff cadre or managers are like allied services. Such observations may perpetuate in these companies.

2. In selected progressive or forward looking management system which is practised by about 25 per cent of the companies, line and staff managers are viewed as mutually compatible and complementary to each other for achievement of organisational objectives or goals. Good examples are MMTC in the public sector and HUL, Unilever, Channel, etc. in the private sector. In the private sector, these trends are more exhibited by global companies.

3 Informal Management

Every organisation has an organisational system or structure. This is the conventional or classical formal organisation. This is what is always talked about. But, "There is much more to organisations than is portrayed in management charts, that are published"—that is informal management. Surprisingly, no company or management talks about the informal management system. Neither the textbooks on organisational system or strategic management mention about this. But, managers, at all levels, including CEOs, make use of this or practise this in different degrees in all organisations.

WHAT IS INFORMAL MANAGEMENT

In every organisation, there is a formal organisational structure and reporting system. This is shown in the organisation chart. But, there is also an informal system. *The formal system and the informal system run parallel to each other.* Informal management practice exists both in the public sector and the private sector, more in the public sector.

I shall give a classic example from MMTC to explain the concept and practice of informal management. MMTC has foreign offices. One foreign office is/was in Rumania. A DGM-level manager was to be posted there. The posting is decided by a committee of chairman and directors. A meeting was convened in the chairman's office. Chairman (SVS) was holding office then. All the directors assembled. Each director obviously had a candidate to push. Chairman (SVS) told the directors: "I have to go for a meeting. But, I have told Doshi (name changed) that he will go. You can discuss and decide", Chairman (SVS) said this and left. The directors were numb. The matter was processed on file and the posting was recorded as a unanimous decision of the committee.

This story was told to me by one of the directors. This is informal management. In informal management, a decision is taken by a senior/top executive and it is given the disguise or form of a formal decision. This means that the informal system undermines the formal system or it prevails over the formal decision-making system.

Informal management system operates in every organisation, with difference of degrees. Higher the level of management more is the use of the informal management practice, the maximum being at the highest level, i.e., the CEO or the CMD.

FORMAL ORGANISATION VERSUS INFORMAL ORGANISATION

An organisational system with the formal organisation and the informal organisation can be conceptually presented below:

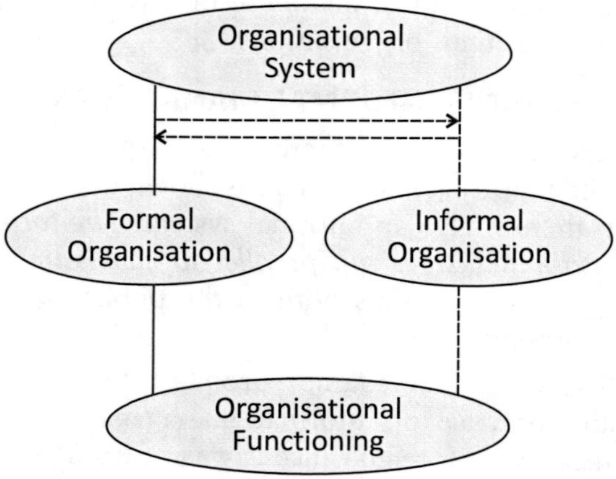

The formal organisation in a company has different structural forms. These are discussed in any standard book on strategic management. The formal organisation can have entrepreneurial structure, functional structure, divisional structure, SBU structure, matrix structure, project-based structure, team-based structure, network structure, holding company structure, and intermediate structure.[2] Each of the structural form indicates a particular hierarchical system.

More common structural forms are functional structure, divisional structure, SBU structure and matrix structure. A particular company may decide to adopt any of these structural forms based on its corporate philosophy or goals, organisational concept of control, centralisation/decentralisation and the nature of business or business strategy.

The informal organisation does not have any hierarchical system. It is an "unstructured organisation." It is embedded in the nature of organisational functioning. Managers, at different levels, in every company have a tendency to cut across formal channels in the hierarchy and communicate informally within the organisation.

Some of them also tend to form small informal groups. They are influenced or inspired by leaders who have been granted some formal authority by the management to perform their functions or tasks.

Informal organisation may be specially important in very large organisations. This may help to address or correct the damage which might be caused by specialisation, compartmentalisation and mechanisation of work or functions.[3]

DIFFERENT FORMS OF INFORMAL MANAGEMENT

Informal management thrives for different reasons or in different forms. A particular senior executive may not be in the good books of the boss (for non-performance reasons, although as a manager, the particular executive has an excellent track record) and the boss likes him to be overshadowed; or, the boss likes a manager (or the manager manages to make himself likeable) and, he wants to highlight him. In either case, the normal or formal hierarchy is subdued. This can be called "management by personality" (MBP) substituting for "management by objective" (MBO).

In a second situation, a particular manager might have reached the level of incompetence and does not perform; but, the company, for various reasons, may not be in a position to do a golden shakehand; the manager is sidetracked or fixed in a corner, and, therefore, the normal reporting pattern does not prevail. This commonly happens in the pubic sector.

A variant of this happened in MMTC. It involved me. I was then GM, Bombay. We also had a CGM (Western Zone). His job was to oversee the functioning or operations of the Western Zone of MMTC, but, primarily Bombay. Dir. (RG) did not have much confidence in him. Therefore, he used to operate mostly through me. He even remarked: "If I send a query letter to Nag, I get the reply in one day; but, if I send the same letter to Nehra (name changed), I receive the reply in one week". So, Dir. (RG) used to communicate directly with me sidetracking him.

This had a fall out. Because Dir. (RG) was meting out discriminatory treatment to him, Nehra was displeased with me for no fault of mine or for wrong reason. He, along with Dir. (SKA), even went to the extent of trying to block my career. Incidentally, Nehra's strength in MMTC was not his work or performance (as you might have guessed) but his godfather in the commerce ministry.

Nehra is only one example. You will find many such personalities or characters in the public sector. Such people, instead of trying to improve themselves, take the revenge route. How do you like that!

Let me now turn to another situation in informal management. A functional or divisional head may promote an informal system within the division to establish his (her) supremacy or ascendancy. The divisional head would generally like to operate through his "confidants" undermining the levels; and, in the process, he (she) would be mostly overshadowing the next immediate senior executive who is a potential threat to his ascendancy particularly if the immediate subordinate is a brilliant performer. The system becomes functional or remains functional because the CEO accepts or allows the system to operate. But, with the change of the CEO, the entire informal pattern of management may change. The divisional head himself may be overshadowed or changed. And, so the informal system perpetuates.

During the crisis management period in MMTC, I also used to often operate through my confidants. Although we had hand-picked the managers, there were differences in performance level and confidence level. I had very old confidants who, I knew, would deliver the way I wanted. I had a DGM but he was rather slow and, not fully oriented towards the new management style. So, I had to often overshadow him for faster result and use my confidants. I realized that more the stake in a decision or result, more is the tendency, one can also say need, to operate through your confidants. *The practicality of management justifies informality*. In such case, it is difficult to say whether it is good or bad practice, but, definitely it helps to produce results.

The Reverse Flow

Informal management can also be said to take the form of reverse flow—the reverse flow of the management process or the decision process. It is common in many organisations that the CEO (or the director or the divisional head) delegates authority down the line, but, continues to take the decision himself. In a large number of privately owned companies or even in publicly owned companies which are run like privately owned companies, important decision making is often done like this. You may call it autocratic management if you like.

More typical of the reverse flow are situations where the CEO may be autocratic in decision making, but, formal decision process will have the disguise of democracy. A live case will illustrate the point. The CMD of a public sector company (with corporate headquarters in Delhi) wanted a particular godown space to be acquired in Bombay. Instead of issuing a corporate directive for acquiring the space, informal direction was passed on to the regional head to prepare a case and send a self-contained proposal to corporate office for approval. The regional head, with his blood pressure mounting, had to perform the act for his survival and growth. Later, there might be audit, and, even enquiry on this.

Promotion Committee

Another situation of informal management in the public sector relates to promotion—more specifically, promotion committees. Committees are set up to promote a particular manager or managers. Let me give an example. This happened during Chairman (SVS). He wanted to promote some particular managers at senior level. It was difficult to promote them within the normal promotion rules—mostly seniority cum merit (CR). So, he appointed Vaidynathan (name changed) Committee to interview eligible candidates, and, recommend a panel of three candidates for promotion. Needless to say, Vaidyanathan and other members of the committee were confidants of Chairman (SVS); and, therefore, they recommended only those three names whom Chairman (SVS) wanted. On paper, it was a democratic procedure, but, informal instructions prevailed over the formal system. There was resentment among the managers who were overlooked or ignored. But, Chairman (SVS) was not heartless. He informally sent feelers to the deprived managers not to lose heart and wait for their turn which might come soon.

We also have the story of a young executive—a specialist. A company appointed a young vigorous executive as its chief publicity officer. Soon after, an advertising agent approached the bigger boss with some publicity material. The boss, after some discussion, approved them. After the advertising agent left, he suddenly thought of the young publicity officer. He called him and told him (a little guiltily) that he had approved some publicity material, and, did he not think it was rather good? The executive smiled politely and said: "of course, Sir it is splendid. But, if you will permit me Sir, I will quote you a saying: If you engage a dog, why do you have to bark yourself?"

Well said, young executive! what else could you have done?

INNOVATIVE APPLICATION OF INFORMAL MANAGEMENT

I now turn to a new type of application of informal management—use by a team instead of an individual. The informal management system can be used by a team to expedite decision making, i.e. to minimize response time within otherwise slow and rigid procedural and accountability system. This is a very positive use of informal management. We can also say that this is a very innovative use. This is how we used informal management in MMTC to implement the crisis management strategy.

Let me explain this with reference to aluminum purchase by SAIL through MMTC. In this case, international procurement and domestic sale to SAIL had to be finalized/executed within a single day. This was not possible within MMTC's normal procedural and accountability norms/standards. We innovated an expedient. We discussed the entire deal (both purchase and sale) informally among ourselves including Dir. (RK) and executed the transaction on time. Then, the formal note with necessary documentation, was properly prepared on file during next two three days and put up with a slip attached: "Sign with date—." After all concerned had signed with due date, the slip was removed. The file is complete as per the organisational and accountability requirements. This is a *good marriage between informal management and formal management.*[4] I wish more public sector companies and senior executives use informal management like this.

IN CONCLUSION

I have explained above various forms or applications of informal management with special reference to MMTC and also my role. To summarise or to conclude:

1. Formal management is mostly bottom-up; informal management is mostly top-down.
2. Informal management and formal management run parallel to each other in an organisation.
3. Informal management system undermines or prevails over the formal system. But, this is done in the disguise of democracy.
4. More aggressive or powerful or autocratic a leader/CEO/CMD is, more is the use of informal management.
5. Informal management is used more in the public sector than in the private sector.
6. Informal management is normally used by an individual senior/top executive; but, it can also be used by a team in a more positive or productive way.[5]

Every company should recognise that informal management exists. It cannot be eliminated. Some even feel that it is a "pre-requisite for effective management."[6] It is not a question of whether it is moral or immoral. Organisational practices show that formal management and informal management are almost inseparable. This is the corporate reality.

I wish more managers, particularly at senior level, adopt informal management mechanism for the sake of fast decision making and productivity whenever the formal system gets chocked. This is quite ethical.

4 Management by Obstruction

Obstruction is almost inevitable in work and life....
Our attitude determines how we look at obstruction. To a positive thinker, it can be a challenge or a stepping stone to success. To a negative mind, it can be a stumbling block.

—Shiv Khera (Adapted)

Management, as is commonly understood and practised, is management by obedience to instructions (of seniors). But, in the conventional process, "obstruction" can creep in. This makes the management process often lengthy; sometimes complicated, unproductive or ineffective or inefficient.

WHAT IS MANAGEMENT BY OBSTRUCTION

What is management by obstruction? If you read Harrison's *Management by Obstruction; or How to Save Your Organisation from Needless Efficiency*,[1] you get to know its nature and different forms or manifestations. The essence of management by obstruction, in Harrison's own words, is: "Problem solution is the root to recognition, promotion and prestige. So, for the present-day manager, proper application of the techniques described in this text will prevent his problem stream from ever drying up. He will be able to generate all types of problems and then leap in and come up with positive solutions—thus gaining recognition, promotion and prestige."[2]

Harrison states further: "A close examination of any manager's job reveals that the average 'good manager' spends approximately 80 per cent of his time solving problems, while the other 20 per cent is spent getting haircuts, playing golf, completing expense accounts or generating memoranda and policies that create problems for subordinate managers. Thus, if there were no problems to solve, there would be little need for managers."[3]

In many cases, management by obstruction stops with generation of problems or obstructions and do not go to the solutions. Later discussions and examples will make this clear.

MANAGEMENT BY OBSTRUCTION IN OPERATION

Harrison mentions 26 obstructive management techniques. He has talked about techniques like Innovative Complacency, Democratic Favouritism, Flexible Rigidity, Magnanimous Autocracy, Dynamic Lethargy, Dramatic Negativism, Conscientious Incompetence and Diligent Indecisiveness. We shall explain six of these techniques—considered more relevant—here to make applicability or practice of management by obstruction more clear. The six techniques are:

1. Strategic myopia
2. Democratic favouritism
3. Dynamic lethargy
4. Diligent indecisiveness
5. Affirmative abandonment
6. Innovative complacency

Strategic Myopia

The first obstructive management technique mentioned by Harrison is *strategic myopia*. We are all familiar with strategic myopia. Strategic myopia is: securing immediate personal gain by completely disregarding long-term implications or interest of the company. We can also call it deliberate management short sightedness. This is commonly practiced in many organisations.

Democratic Favouritism

Democratic favouritism is like informal management. To use democratic favouritism is "to build a formal organisation with well-established reporting relationships, and, then superimpose on it an informal organisation which represents the true power structure".[4] This can be expressed in different ways or forms. Some of these were mentioned during the discussion on informal management in the previous chapter.

Dynamic Lethargy

Dynamic lethargy relates to the lethargy of the leader. Dynamic lethargy, as an obstructive technique, "creates an environment in which the doing of the work is more important than the output of the function. Work is carried out at a dynamic, fast moving pace, but, due to the lethargy of the leader, no significant accomplishments are ever produced".[5]

As there are aggressive leaders, there are also lethargic heads—leaders who are slow in execution with no focus on results or attainment of the objective or goal. Such people do exist in organisations and they continue till they are superseded or changed.

This usually happens in departments which are not of much consequence in relation to the mainstream operating or functional departments. Harrison explains this technique with reference to the Analysis and Development department. This can happen also in Research and Development (R&D).

Diligent Indecisiveness

Diligent indecisiveness is almost the opposite of dynamic lethargy. In this obstructive technique, things happen only at the level of the leader or the highest level. Diligent indecisiveness creates a "working environment in which subordinate managers are diligent in the pursuit of routine tasks yet totally indecisive" when faced with a situation to take a decision. It slows down or stops operations or progress because "workers and low level managers live in constant fear of making a wrong decision". Decision is taken only by the top man or the leader.

Harrison explains this with the story of the Big Boy Boiler Company. One morning, as the work in the plant was about to start, one worker made a shocking discovery. He found, in the main assembly room, a huge hole in the centre of the floor. He immediately called other workers to come and have a look at the hole.

Because they did not know what to do about this, they promptly called the foreman. The foreman saw the hole and was also puzzled. He almost exclaimed: "I have never seen such a thing. We have to do something about this. I must call the shift superintendent". So, he called the shift superintendent.

The shift superintendent came and found all the workers and the foreman crowding around the hole very anxiously. He looked perplexed and almost exclaimed: "I have never seen such a hole inside the plant area. I must bring it to the notice of the plant manager". So, they called the plant manager.

The plant manager almost came rushing to the spot and had a bewildering look at the hole. He saw the workers, the foreman and the shift superintendent all looking at him anxiously for guidance or a decision. He paused for a while. Then, he also sounded a disappointing note. He said: "That hole is much too large for me to cope with. I am sure the Vice President of manufacturing better be told about this". So, the VP, Manufacturing was called.

The VP, Manufacturing was not in office. He was in a nearby town. But, he came promptly. He saw the hole. He could guess/measure the gravity of the situation with all helpless people standing around and looking up to him. He was known to be a decision maker. He responded to the situation with authority: "Fill the damn thing in". He also overviewed the implementation.

This story explains a typical operation of the diligent indecisiveness technique. As an obstructive management technique, this can "completely stifle an organisation's ability to make decisions except at the highest level." Our experience shows that this can happen in many organisations. Managers at different levels have a tendency to pass on the buck particularly in the public sector. In public sector, not taking a decision is often safer than taking a decision. There is also hardly any motivation or reward for taking a decision.

Affirmative Abandonment

This obstructive technique means that a manager should affirm his "absolute leadership position", and, then totally abandon his function of leading.

In conventional management, managers are supposed to act as leaders who resolve conflicts and give decision. Too much of these can lead to needless management efficiency. Obstructive managers have developed the technique of affirmative abandonment to combat such "dangerous situation."

Affirmative abandonment can give a manager many advantages. First, it makes him free from all major activities he is supposed to perform or manage. This gives him enough free time to engage in office/company politics. This may help him to get promoted to higher or more attractive positions where he may be able to practice other obstructive techniques to his advantage. Second, the function or department he has abandoned will be struggling to increase its output or efficiency. This way the threat of over-efficiency may be successfully centralised.

Innovative Complacency

This is a planning strategy which creates the illusion of innovation, but, in reality, sticking to status quo. This strategy is recommended whenever pressures for change are building in the company.

The "innovative complacency" manager should correctly foresee a signal of change in the company functional system and act accordingly. For example, an aggressive sales manager, an MBA, may suggest that company policy should be realigned from product orientation to customer satisfaction. The innovative complacent manager's immediate target would be to fire the aggressive sales manager if he can. A more practical or wiser method would be to adopt the innovative complacency strategy which should result in the eventual promotion of the sales manager to a position of incompetence or impotence. This makes the technique successful.

Resistance to change is common in many companies. "Innovative complacency" rightly emphasises this.

All the 26 'Management by Obstruction' techniques classified by management functions of planning, organising, controlling and evaluating are presented in the Annexure.

MANAGEMENT BY OBSTRUCTION IN COMPANIES

In an organisation, management by obstruction is generally prevalent in departments of finance, law and HR. In public sector companies, this is also found in the "Please speak" syndrome.

I shall first talk about law and HR and then discuss obstructive finance and the "Please speak" syndrome with special reference to MMTC. The discussions will show how these had an impact on the company's business and my role or functioning and how we tried to handle it or overcome the obstruction.

Law, HR and Finance are all staff functions. Because they are not in mainstream "line" functions, and, not accountable for corporate results, they can create obstructions. This is one way to assert their presence or existence, and, also create enough nuisance value for receiving attention.

Law and Obstruction

Law, as we all know, is, by definition, a slow process, and, by its nature, obstructive. This is true in most of the organisations, public or private. If a matter is referred to the law department for examination or advice, it takes its own time. They are known to "sit" on the file. They hardly make recommendations which are positive or in conformity with line's thinking. This delays or blocks decision making. Ideally, they would like to take over a matter/case and commence the legal process which ends in litigation. This means that the matter is blocked for years. In many such cases, an out of court settlement may be in the best interest of the company, but, they never agree with or support such solution.

In the process of the legal battle, the company may end up spending more money than the amount at stake. This happened in a case in Bombay Regional Office of MMTC when I was GM there.

The law professionals should not take exception to or offence in this because this is embedded in their profession. It is not always easy to digest the truth.

Obstructive Role of HR

HR, in its conventional form, can create obstructions in recruitment/appointment, positing and transfer. Recruitments or appointments are decided by the selection committee in which

HR may have a representative or member. Besides this, HR is an important segment or link in the entire recruitment loop. So, also, in positing or transfer. HR's obstructionist role can and does come here. Delay or obstruction can be caused in processing of papers or matters related to recruitment, posting and transfer.

Sometimes, obstruction can be caused in the form of incompatible or irrational posting. I wish to give here an example from MMTC. We had recruited (I was also a member of the selection committee) some MBAs from IIMA, IIMC, and IIMB. Each of them had given choice or preference for areas or departments—marketing/sales, finance, HR—in which he (she) would like to be placed or posted. But, CGM (HR) made the postings disregarding the area/department choices or preferences. Young MBAs from such top business schools resented and expressed their disappointment and frustration. Some of them came and met me also. I could foresee the consequence of such anomalous posting—some of them may leave soon. Our objective was the opposite of this. We wanted to infuse new blood in the management/company. So, I decided to take up the matter with Dir. (P), Dir. (RK) and Dir. (F). The postings were finally rationally done.

In MMTC, HR also played an extended role in processing/finalizing housing loan for managers/staff. I shall give an interesting example of HR's obstructionist role in this. The matter/case involved me. I had bought a flat in East Delhi (Trans—Jamuna) by availing housing loan from MMTC. I wanted to sell the flat and buy a bigger and better flat in South Delhi. For this, I had to inform the office and repay the outstanding loan amount. I did not inform MMTC about my plan to purchase a new flat. I did not have to do that (as per rule).

I had sent a letter to CGM(P) expressing my desire to sell the flat and repay the loan amount. Through this letter, I had sought MMTC's approval for this. But, CGM (P) raised objection to this. His argument was very strange: "Housing loan is given for a social need or cause. Therefore, employees cannot sell their houses". I was surprised. I spoke to some GMs/CGMs. They were also surprised. Some even laughed.

I had to take up the matter with Dir. (P). He called CGM (P) to his office and asked him in my presence: "What exactly is the reason for your objection to this?" CGM (P) repeated his argument: "Housing fulfills a social need—a shelter. We should not allow employees to sell this." Dir. (P), rather annoyingly remarked : "Mr. Suri (name changed), Dr. Nag must be having a plan to buy a bigger or better house. But, that is not in our purview to ask or discuss here."

Not to give up, CGM (P) referred the matter to Dir. (Vigilance) hoping that he would get some support or protection there. Dir. (Vigilance) remarked (on file): "This does not have any vigilance angle". He additionally commented (on file): "We should be happy that Dr. Nag is repaying the loan so fast. Some managers and staff default in repayment of loan".

A disheartened CGM (P) had to finally succumb, and, my proposal was approved. We lost sometime in the process. According to me, this is almost a classic case of obstructionist HR policy. An obstruction without any substance.

Obstructive Finance

Unlike law, the finance process is not slow, but, like law, finance is obstructive. This happens because their general approach to management is negative—to negate or put a rider on "line" proposals. This is the way they feel they can best demonstrate their knowledge and expertise, and, also play their role as the "guardian" (self-assumed) of finances and general interest of the company.

In public sector, "Associate Finance" can typically play an obstructive role. Because AF is associated with almost every line decision, they can play such role. Some AF managers are positive or progressive (I had one such GM(F) working with me), but, they are more like exceptions. AF managers can play their obstructive role because they have only to make observations or comments and are not under any pressure to perform.

I shall give two examples of obstructive Associate Finance. Both are related to MMTC. I was involved or associated with both the examples or cases. I shall explain how Associate Finance created obstruction and how we overcame it.

The first example or story related to determination or fixation of selling price of non-ferrous metals. This was the month of March—financial year ending. We had high inventory of one metal (nickel) and we wanted to liquidate the stocks to end the year on good note. It was, therefore, necessary to fix a very aggressive or competitive selling price so that the inventory could be liquidated.

In non-ferrous division/profit centre, we had constituted a pricing committee for every metal. The composition of the committee was: Manager (Product, i.e. the concerned metal), Manager (Market Price) and Manager (Finance, i.e. Associate Finance). Manager (Market Price) would give the input on prevailing market price—national and international. For determination of selling price of any metal, the three would meet and discuss possible pricing keeping in mind the inventory level, profitability and the market situation. They would then come and discuss the pricing with me before finalizing the price. This is how I used informal management for price fixation.

If all the three managers/members agree on a particular price, the matter is straight forward and simple. But, if they have disagreement among themselves, I would have to intervene. In the present case, i.e., nickel pricing, Manager (F) had disagreed. He argued: "At the price suggested, we are not making any profit." I had to explain to him: "The objective in present pricing is not profit, but, liquidating stocks. If we cannot sell the metal at the price you are suggesting, the cost of carrying the inventory will more than offset the possible profit that may accrue". Manager (F) still seemed adamant. I then used a weapon. I told him: "Alright, we will agree to the price you have suggested. But, we will make you a member of the selling team. By the end of the month, you have to show that the inventory is liquidated". He paused for a moment and said: "I agree with the price". The sales team went full steam and we could liquidate almost the entire inventory.

In the second example/case, the obstruction by Associate Finance was a strange action. In this case, it was GM(F) associated with non-ferrous division. In the previous chapter, I had explained innovative use of informal management for selling aluminum to SAIL. The innovative informal approach was discussed with all concerned including GM(F). But, when the file was put in circulation for signature, suddenly, the file was missing. Manager (Product) went around and asked everyone involved in the matter including GM(F). But, the file was not traceable.

I had to inform Dir. (RK) also about this. I was sitting with him. He told me: "Dr. Nag, I know who has done it. Just wait and see". He called GM (F) and told him in my presence: "Mr. Dhulati (name changed), you are aware that we are not getting this file. If you know where the file is, let us know. Otherwise also we will find it out. Once we find it, the person who has done it will have to face the music. We will enter the remark in his CR that he was deliberately obstructing important official work. It will become an adverse remark". With these words, he asked Dhulati to leave. Next morning, when I came to office, I found the file lying on my table.[6]

Obstructive role of Finance can be seen in the private sector also. I observed this in Hindalco Industries (Copper Unit) where I had worked as a full-time Adviser. VP (Finance) was diligently laying his obstructive role. Strangely enough, he was later fired from the company because of his corruptive practices earlier in a group company.

The examples given above amply demonstrate that obstructive management does exist in different forms in corporate functioning. More important than that, the examples show that obstruction can be overcome if we adopt the right approach or strategy to overcome it.

"Please Speak" Syndrome

A unique obstructive behavior/posture in the public sector exists in the "Please speak" syndrome. I did not have any personal experience or involvement in this, but, I thought you may like to read or know this as a possible technique or mode of management.

"Please speak" is used by senior managers under three situations. First, when a subordinate manager puts up a matter/file, the senior manager is not very clear about what the subordinate manager wants to say or mean. Instead of writing something in the file on presumption, the senior manager feels that it is better to clarify the contention or issue, and, then, record his views. It may also be possible that the subordinate needs to provide more input (data/information) supporting his view or proposal. This is professional or positive use of "Please speak".

In the second situation, a senior or top manager uses "Please speak" as a disguise for informal management. The senior/top manager wants a particular decision to be taken, but, he (she) does not like to record it himself (herself). He (she) wishes to give it the flavor of a team or group decision. So, he (she) tells the subordinate manager to put up the matter in a particular way, i.e. putting his (her) decision in the subordinate's words. This can often happen in companies.

In the third situation, "Please speak" is used as an expedient by senior/top managers who suffer from work avoidance or indecision complex. They are work/decision avoiders. They are not very competent also. They want to avoid their work or decision through "Please speak" as far as possible. Through "Please speak", the decision on or movement of the file can be postponed for some time. So, they can have one or two paid holidays. This typically happens in the public sector. Because they have job security, they are not very concerned or worried also.

I wish to narrate here a "Please speak" story from MMTC. A GM, exhibiting *dynamic lethary*, was postponing decision through "Please speak" mode. If a file reached him during the day, he would keep it till 5 pm (office closing time is 5:30 pm). At 5 pm he would write on the fire "Please speak" and send it back to the submitting manager. If he receives a file after 5 pm, he would keep it for the whole of next day and, dispose it of at/after 5 pm. One subordinate manager had piled up few such files. He then initiated a note: "Sir, I have piled up few files with your remark 'Please speak'. Please indicate a time when I can come and discuss these files with you". The note reaches the GM at 5 pm. He immediately sends back the note with his stamp: "Please speak".

What does the manager do now? Please help him if you can.

In my functioning in MMTC, I was using a substitute for "Please speak" as a method or mode for the first two situations.

If I do not agree with or I am not satisfied with the way the matter/proposal has been put up, instead of writing "Please speak" I would call the manager, I would explain to him (her) how the proposal should have been put-up in a more logical/ professional way (not informal management). The manager changes the note and resubmits the file. This fosters better inter-personal or "boss subordinate" relationship and also makes the system more transparent.

ANNEXURE

Twenty-six 'Management by Obstruction' Techniques of Harrison:

Section I—PLANNING

1. Strategic Myopia, 2. Long-Range Discontinuity
3. Innovative Complacency, 4. Cognitive Discordancy
5. Calculated Reactionism, 6. Prolific Ponderousness

Section II—ORGANIZING

7. Democratic Favoritism, 8. Flexible Rigidity
9. Concentrated Decentralization, 10. Expeditious Filtration
11. Synergistic Regression, 12. Synchronized Discontinuity

Section III—CONTROLLING

13. Free-Flowing Censorship, 14. Affirmative Abandonment
15. Magnanimous Autocracy, 16. Dynamic Lethargy
17. Concentrated Constructionism, 18. Dramatic Negativism
19. Conscientious Incompetence, 20. Consequential Retaliation
21. Diligent Indecisiveness, 22. Exuberant Demoralization
23. Polished Pompousness

Section IV—EVALUATING

24. Probabilistic Implosion, 25. Effective Devaluation
26. Objective Introspection

5 Managing the Boss

Rule 1: Boss is always right.
Rule 2: If boss is not right, see Rule 1

One of the many manifestations of manager's job in practice is his relationship with the boss. "Familiarity (with the boss) breeds promotions," "what separates management winners from management losers?—it is the relationship with the boss," "the boss can be the best prophet of your future." Such and other sayings about the boss make the "Boss-box."

BOSS IS ALWAYS RIGHT

The foremost saying from the "Boss-box" tells us: "The boss is always right" (although in practice, the boss can be wrong many times), or, we can say: "The boss can do no wrong" like "The king can do no wrong." Such pronouncement, however, is more normative than positive—more a corporate slogan than a principle of management—more an advice to an individual manager than a tenet of professionalism.

We sometimes find the top man taking the decision about transfer of a peon. And, a junior officer loses his sleep worrying about the loss of morale in the organisation. Right decisions taken at wrong levels (or wrong decisions taken at right levels). But, take it easy, because your boss has taken the decision, and, the boss is always right!

One theory of management tells as that as one moves higher in an organisation, there is need to acquire a higher and higher level of tolerance for ambiguity. High level jobs are often supposed to be more abstract. Many executives stretch this tolerance for ambiguity too far so as to be comfortable with indecisions and indecisiveness in themselves. Your boss may be one such executive.

But he is your boss!

One of the strategies available to decision makers (or decision avoiders?) is the reference method. Under this, almost every problem gets referred to others—sometimes to individual managers, sometimes to committees, although many of such cases could have been disposed of by the boss himself. Search for a way out of the impasse, but, do not revolt; because he is your boss!

Ten Commandments

We should all try to remember the following ten commandments of boss administration:

1. The boss is always right.
2. The boss is never late; he was at a meeting.
3. The boss never leaves work; perhaps his presence is required somewhere else.
4. The boss never reads newspapers in the office; he keeps himself informed.
5. The boss does not sleep in the office; he unwinds.
6. The boss does not drink; but, he must entertain.
7. The boss does not become familiar with the secretary; he orients her.
8. The boss does not change his mind; he reviews his decisions.
9. He, who enters boss's office with ideas of his own, should leave with those of the boss.
10. The more one thinks with the boss, the more one gets ahead.

BOSS-SUBORDINATE RELATIONSHIP

From sermons and slogans, we now turn to more serious business related to the boss phenomenon, the foremost being boss-subordinate relationship. Boss-subordinate relationship matter may not be as perennial as husband-wife relationship, but, certainly not less delicate.

Boss-subordinate relationship revolves around matters related to the classical principle of span of control, and, as a corollary, man management, and as a modern extension of this, manners management and all that.

One of the most fascinating aspects of management is the art of dealing with people, either individually or in groups, and those who are skilled in this can contribute enormously to effectiveness of management. The chief executive or the boss must adjust his actions to a variety of people in a variety of circumstances. Some subordinates, for their own good as much for that of the company, require to be controlled with a tight rein; others may produce their best only if given a lot of freedom including the freedom to make some mistakes. This is one way of creating confidence. Here the boss has to decide how much freedom should be given to such men. Unless they get enough freedom, they may be frustrated and, may become inefficient. If they are given too much freedom too often, there is the risk of their making serious mistakes. And, the correction of subordinates who make mistakes calls for different treatments. Some executives respond best if spoken to in a tough, uncompromising manner; with others, the iron fist in the velvet glove is the correct prescription.

There should, however, be no misunderstanding that the iron fist is often needed in business to get results. Success often comes most readily to those iron men who are most determined to win it—to those who, when faced with difficult situations, have the grim determination to keep going "through muck or nettles."

Span of Control

We now turn to span of control proper. Graicunas' mathematical formulation of the principle of span of control is based on the idea that there is one main limitation on the number of subordinates who can be effectively supervised. The supervisor must keep in mind not only the direct relationship between himself and each subordinate, but, also his relationship with different groupings of the subordinates and the cross-relationships among all the subordinates. ("Subordinates" stand for only supervisory and executive personnel). He calculated that with four subordinates, the number of group and cross-relationships is 44, but, with six subordinates, it increases to 222. Urwick contends that it is doubtful if any individual can keep track and understand the relationship involved of more than five, or, at most six, direct subordinates, and, that such understanding is necessary if a man has to lead and not merely administer.

Graicunas stated that where there are few working contacts between the subordinates, the relationship will be less complex. In confirmation of this, Urwick added to his principles, the modification "subordinates whose work interlocks." He suggests that stores, and, departments within one store, may be examples of little interlocking, and, hence a much larger number of subordinates can report to one chief. This could explain the wide span of control in the Sears Roebuck organisation, the large American chain store, often quoted as an example of the fallacy of the principle of span of control.

A number of studies of span of control in practice shows that it varies widely between companies. The average span of control of senior managers in the companies studied is wider than that given by Urwick and the range is much larger.

An American study examined the span of control of the chief executive of 620 manufacturing companies in Ohio with 100 or more employees. (Chief executive also included managers of branch offices/plants.) These companies covered a very wide range of industries. The study showed that the average span of control of the chief executive increased as the number of employees went up. In the firms with 1500 to 3000 employees, the most frequent span was eight subordinates; in firms with over 3000 employees, it was nine. In these firms, over 60 per cent of all the main plant executives had a span of seven or more subordinates. In the plants with less than 1500 employees, the most common spans were four, five or six subordinates. The span of control was also found to vary according to the type of industry. Higher spans were more common in the main plants of paper, and, allied products of petroleum and coal; and, in branch plants they were more common for stone, clay and glass products, primary metal products, electrical machinery, equipment and supplies, and, miscellaneous manufacturing.

Another American study of the number of executives reporting to the chief executive in 100 companies employing over 5000 people, yielded similar results. All the firms included in the study were described by the American Management Association as having good management practices. The average (median) number of subordinates was between eight and nine and the range between one to twenty-four. The chief executives of twenty-four firms had thirteen or more subordinates reporting directly to them.[1]

One of the jobs of a senior executive is to decide when to act on his own initiative and when to act through a committee. In some circumstances, it is necessary to be immediately decisive; to give an immediate decision which may be 90 per cent correct rather than to delay matters until a committee is constituted which may give a solution which may be 100 per cent correct. Where speed of decision is important—and, in business it often is—individual action is generally the best course. It is also the cheapest.[2]

Whether a manager's subordinates are individuals or teams makes little or no difference in the span of managerial control or responsibility. However, a team should always have a small number of members. One of the largest functioning teams found in business is the Board Directors of Standard Oil, USA. It is a Board composed exclusively of full-time officers of the company, and, it is actually the world's largest, most extensive, most complicated and most successful business. Hence, its membership of fourteen does not seem excessive. Still, a team so large as this can function if it strictly disciplines itself. The Standard Oil Board, for instance, never takes a decision except unanimously. For general purposes, however, this procedure is too elaborate. Teams should normally not exceed five or six in number; and, they work best, as a rule, if they have three or four members.

Upward and Downward Relationship

Coming back to boss-subordinates nexus, the relationship between higher and lower manager is not just the downward relationship expressed in the span of control. It may not even be a two-way "top-down" or "bottom-up" relationship. According to some, it has three dimensions: a relationship up from the lower to the higher manager; a relationship of every manager to the enterprise; and, a relationship down from the higher to the lower manager.

Every manager has the task of contributing to what his superior needs to attain organisational objectives. This, indeed, is his first duty. From this he derives the objectives of his own job.

Secondly, he has a duty towards the enterprise. He has to analyse his own tasks, and, spell out the activities required to attain corporate objectives. He has to establish the management jobs these activities require, and, he has to help his managers to work together and to integrate their own interests with those of the enterprise.

Finally, the manager has responsibilities downward to his subordinate managers. He has first to make sure that they know and understand what is demanded of them. He may have to help them set their own objectives. Then he may have to help to reach these objectives. He has to help with advice and counsel. He has, if need be, to teach them to do better.

If a one-word definition of this downward relationship is to be given, "assistance" would come closest. In fact, several successful companies—notably International Business Machines (IBM)—have defined the manager's job in relation to his subordinates as that of an "assistant" to them. Their jobs are theirs—by objective necessity. Their performance and results are theirs, and, so is the responsibility. But, it is the duty of the superior manager to help them—to assist them—to attain their objectives.

Blake and Mouton's new managerial grid depicts the downward relationship sometimes as assistance, sometimes togetherness, sometimes motivation and communication, sometimes team management, sometimes authority-obedience, sometimes tough mindedness—depending on various (9×9) combinations of concern for production or performance and concern for people. The boss decides his behaviour based on his relative concerns for performance and people and that fixes his downward relationship with the subordinates. Some of the resulting grid patterns are: impoverished management (exertion of minimum pressure on people to get work done), country club management (satisfying subordinate relationships leading to friendly organisation), team management (interdependence through a common stake), authority-obedience (efficiency with minimum tolerance for human relations). Different postures of the boss evoke different reactions from the subordinates: sometimes apathy, sometimes friendliness, sometimes total commitment, sometimes submission, sometimes passive resistance, sometimes open resentment.[3]

DISAGREEING WITH THE BOSS

Can we disagree with the boss? Or, should we disagree with the boss? The professionalist's prescription is: *Don't disagree if it is a matter of opinion, but disagree if it is a point of principle.* For example, a difference of opinion might arise if the boss wants to paint all the doors green, whereas you think muted colours would be more appropriate. In such a case, one might argue briefly and drop the issue. A matter of principle might arise if the boss insists that all painting contracts be given to a particular party ignoring the offers of others, more competent and cost effective. One would be justified in giving battle in such cases especially if substantial matters or stakes are involved. This is a principled fight and may not be given up. Also because many such matters may have integrity and ethical implications.

But, it is easier said than done. Even if matters of managerial ethics are concerned, one may have to be bold or tangent enough to carry the fight to the boss's camp.

A boss has many claims upon the subordinate. He may be an elder, more experienced and, has more power. He can be a protector; he can be a killer also. We shall state here how Thomas Beckett (in T.S. Eliot's *Murder in the Cathedral*) was killed by his boss, Henry II. Beckett had risen from humble origins to chancellorship; along the way, he had become Henry II's confidant and companion even in adventures not fit for publication. But, eventually, upon being made Archbishop of Canterbury, Beckett felt obliged to take a stand against his king. The rewards were death—and immortality and canonisation as a saint. In business life, we do not expect such drama, but, career killing is not very uncommon.

How to Disagree

How then does one disagree with the boss? Disagreement through persuasion and tact has been the traditional advice. This means that one may argue in private with the boss until a decision is taken; thereafter, one must close ranks to implement the decision (theorists refer to this as the ethics of structure) or resign where the occasion demands. This, however, may not always find universal application. The resignation of a middle-level manager (or sometimes even of a higher level manager) may go unnoticed and the point may not be made. So, it may be necessary to fight evil from within. Simple tactics such as stalling or asking written instructions have many times proved remarkably effective.

An illustrative situation is given below of when and how to disagree. Robert McNamara (head of the World Bank sometimes ago) was once President of the Ford Motor Company. He was member of a group of analysts who sold themselves to Henry Ford II to cure his giant, ailing business. Subsequently, to cut costs, large Ford plants in Massachusetts and Texas were shut down. McNamara called a meeting of top executives to consider further closures. No one could really find fault with the impressive recommendation before the even more impressive boss. Finally, a veteran joked "why don't we dose down all the plants and then we will really start to save money?" There were no more closures and the company went to a new peak of performance.[4]

This illustrates not only when to disagree but, also how. There could be other times and ways also. A freshly articled clerk was asked by a senior, under pressure of time, to sign off on his section of an audit before he was satisfied. "After all," he said, "I am finally responsible for even your work." The Eichmann trial being still fresh in the articled clerk's memory, the boss was shaken when told by him that the Nuremberg doctrine did not allow him to abrogate all responsibilities on his instruction. (At Nuremberg, international jurists condemned Nazis who had committed atrocities, rejecting the defence that they had acted on instructions from superiors.) The articled clerk got away by working all night to beat the deadline. But, the principle is defensible: one can never wholly avoid individual responsibility,[5] and, this may lead to disagreement with the boss.

The lesson is: Disagree with the boss when you must; give up when you can; let morality and ethics keep a low profile in all this.

MANAGING THE BOSS

If the lesson just given is sermonised, managing the boss may be one of the most delicate jobs in the corporate world.

"Managing the boss" as a proposition, may appear incongruent because, the boss manages, and, he is not managed. But, "managing the boss" really means understanding the boss—his approach, his attitudes, his strengths and frailties (the subordinate may do a short mental SWOT of the boss)—and orienting or adjusting one's own style to match his.

If you ask an Indian manager about his boss, he will quite often express his ambivalence, if not dissatisfaction, with him. Very few have positive things to say about their bosses, and, most find them less than competent. This happens because "they would like the boss to be a textbook model, not only in his technical ability but also in his personal behaviour." Because, there is an illusion (although misplaced), disillusionment becomes high. One may call this the boss-complex.

But, one has to come out of the shell of complexity to the reality of boss management. Negative or tangent feelings about the boss is not going to improve one's relationship with him. The energy spent in complaining about or in highlighting the shortcomings of one's boss can be gainfully used in improving one's rapport and communication with him.

Common Thinking

A common thinking is that the boss would take the initiative with his subordinates and, not the other way round. This is a misplaced thinking. One should not always wait for the boss to make the first move. A good subordinate is one who is always willing to initiate, and even, pre-empt if the situation demands.

"In order to take the initiative, one must pay attention to the way the boss perceives his world: the way he articulates his views; influences others; reflects his attitudes, his interpersonal style and relationship. If one gives attention to these things and tunes one's communication to his wavelength, a boss will listen, respond, explore and resolve."

The subordinate should try to win over the boss, but, he should not venture a reformist approach; for to be sure, he cannot change much of his boss's behaviour. He can, however, try to influence boss's behaviour or actions by employing various strategies. If the boss is moody and sometimes irrational, one should focus on the times when he is not so. If the boss is curt and impatient, you employ the virtues of softness and patience. Changing one's own behaviour is always easier and more effective than trying to get your boss to change. Although it is easier said than done, this is perhaps the best alternative for a subordinate particularly if he aspires to continually taste success.

Confrontation with the Boss

We must remember the fundamental principle that *the boss must be recognised*. The boss may and will have weakness, and, those may provide the best platforms for you. If you can handle those matters which he does not handle or are irritants for him, he will feel that he is being helped. So, contribute where your boss is weak. But, if you try to undermine him or confront him or sabotage him, you are challenging his authority and legitimate power. And, this may mean some writings on the wall.

I had virtual confrontation with my immediate boss (CGM) when I was GM, Bombay in MMTC. But, my boss's boss, i.e., Director was fully supporting me. He was not liking the CGM. The CMD was with the Director. The system was functioning smoothly. My 'today' was well protected. But, this could not protect my 'tomorrow.' There was change in the organisational setup. The CMD left and a new CMD (Acting) (earlier Director) took charge. I did not have much of equation with him. CGM quietly established rapport with him; a result. I became at the receiving end.

The whole episode shows that the boss may not be able to do good to you. But, he can harm you. This means that confrontation with the boss should be avoided because equations in the organisation may change; and, confrontation with the boss (open or silent) may have adverse impact on your career and growth in the organisation.

So, confrontation should be avoided as it causes a strain that can be detrimental in the long run.

Giving Credit to Boss

The opposite route is too common for elucidation. Some subordinates avoid all confrontation with the boss. According to knowledgeable sources, this type can be seen in Iacocca who took every humiliation Henry Ford II dished out—with the expectation that he would one day be crowned king.

A clever variation of this strategy was used by an executive assistant to a top Tata executive. He found himself run ragged by doing the boss's errands and trying to maintain independence, (there was no time left for family and friends) until one of his predecessors advised him, "put the boss first. If he says top priority ignore all else. After all, he knows something and can protect you from others. Further, give him credit for all your initiatives. It will give them momentum, and, in any case, he does radiate good ideas." He and his two predecessors have grown to be managing directors, without the ulcers to prove it.[6]

Giving the boss credit is a particularly good technique if the boss enjoys generating ideas and being complimented on them. A bright spark we know has a boss of this kind. He gave the boss all credit in public and hired assistants to do the boss's bidding. He himself did as he pleased and said as much in private. His latest reward has been a lucrative overseas posting with potential for further growth.

Mutual Acceptance

Another variant of managing the boss is through mutual acceptance. This is illustrated through the story of an expatriate boss and a professional subordinate. The expatriate's attitude was colonial, but he knew his job and, he knew the subordinate knew his job too—he had hired him. Being competent professionals they learnt to live with each other—a kind of peaceful coexistence. There was no personal fondness, but, there was good working relationship. The moral is: "Even if one does not like one's boss as a person, if you accept each other professionally, a boss can be managed."[7]

So far so good. But, what happens if your boss does not believe in mutuality, is rugged and is not willing to forget the past (occasional bickerings). This may happen sometimes if your erstwhile colleague becomes the boss. We have the story of a senior colleague becoming the boss, and, again, a professional (academics) being the subordinate. "As a colleague, I had occasions to critique his projects one of which was most disappointing. He never forgot it and, from the day he became my boss, we were at loggerheads. He found it difficult to accept me and I reciprocated the feeling. After some months, I made a profit and loss analysis and decided to quit. He was surprised at my decision, and, tried to persuade me to stay, but, I was convinced that leaving would do both of us good."[8]

Such boss-subordinate mismatches develop in corporate life (peers becoming bosses and even otherwise) and not too infrequently. In such situations, the subordinate has two alternatives; either to fight to the finish (through the boss's boss, may be) and, establish his credentiality in relation to the organisation (because, in the final analysis, the organisation, and, not the boss, is supreme) or quit in search of a better boss.

These steps are extreme options. These should be mostly avoided. There are ways to manage a difficult boss suggested by practising experts. All subordinate managers would like to know them.

MANAGING DIFFICULT BOSS

Conventionally, *managing is a top-down process, but, managing a boss, particularly a difficult boss, is a "managing up" process.*

The crux of "managing up" is understanding the operating system of seniors or the boss, "The workaholic, the micro-manager, the narcissist, the 'ghost' or the gas-lighter"—dealing with any kind of boss becomes easier if a subordinate understands their operating systems.

Different people and bosses have different operating systems. These depend on the types of bosses—their personalities and behaviour patterns.

Some bosses are "introverts"; they tend to keep to themselves. But, this does not mean that they don't care about things. They watch you and can also be difficult sometimes. You have to understand their 'silent' or unspoken postures.

Then, there are "extroverts" who are always in your face and talking things through. There are also "advancers" who want to make things fast. There are "evaluators" who are detail-oriented and want to get things right in all respects. Some bosses are "harmonisers" who are generally nice and conflict-averse, but, conflict may arise and you should be good at conflict resolution. Some are "energisers" who incorporate lot of passion and new ideas, and, expect you to catch up with those ideas.[9]

You may have bosses who are more difficult. You might have a micro-manager; a "ghost" boss who is never around; a workaholic who is very impulsive; a "seagull" boss who swoops in and takes projects away; or, a "narcissist" or a "gas-lighter". Whichever kind of boss you have, you need to understand what drives their behaviour or operating systems[10] and act or manage accordingly.

Virtual work environment, mostly caused by the pandemic has given a new dimension to managing the boss. Many managers and bosses are resistant to virtual work management because they do not believe or trust that subordinate managers know how to manage virtually effectively. You may have to have a conversation with your boss, and, decide or agree on how virtual management is going to work, how to implement it to the satisfaction of the boss. Review this regularly and stay on the radar. This is also a way of managing a difficult boss but the virtual mode.

HOW TO IMPRESS YOUR BOSS

Impressing the boss is an extension of managing the boss. "Managing up" can be used as a strategy for impressing the boss.

A manager can adopt many methods for impressing his(her) boss. These may depend on his(her) aptitude, skill and capability for "managing up" and earning trust and confidence of the boss given the boss's operating systems and personal preferences. Based on these factors, one or more of ten methods are recommended. These are:

1. Paddle in the same direction
2. Be sure of 'what, how and when'
3. Do before being reminded
4. Adapt to your boss's style
5. Suggest options/alternatives
6. Do not spring surprises
7. Communicate dispassionately: state facts
8. Keep building trust
9. Volunteer for workload sharing
10. May I help you, boss?[11]

Paddle in the Same Direction

A manager should ensure that he(she) and the boss are working towards common objectives and priorities. A manager may be making many "micro-decisions" everyday on how to allocate time and energy to the tasks assigned/to be performed. Every manager should share or review his(her) to-do list (may be every morning) with the boss to make sure that his(her) work priorities are aligned with those of the boss as far as possible, if not completely.

Be Sure of 'What, How and When'

You must make sure that your boss has complete details of your work including time plans (dates) of the tasks assigned to you particularly new allocations or assignments. Do not hesitate to seek clarifications/guidance. Timely discharge of functions or fulfillment of tasks is critical to keep the boss satisfied. This also serves the organisational purpose.

Do Before Being Reminded

A reminder from the boss means that half your reputation as a performer or credibility is lost. Do not allow this to happen. If you think, for some reason, you cannot deliver on time, be proactive and explain this to your boss and seek some time. *A proactive approach is always better than a reactive approach.* This saves you from a reminder and your reputation remains intact.

Adapt to Your Boss's Style

Every manager has a style of functioning. So has your boss. Try to adapt to his(her) way or style of working.

Some bosses may like a one-page write-up or note; some may prefer a short oral presentation; some others may like presentation on Power-Point slide desks; some may even have some delicate way or style. Try to adapt to also this even if you have to compromise some values. Adaptation to boss's style is important.

Suggest Options/Alternatives

You may sometimes approach your boss for guidance on an issue. But, do some groundwork yourself before you go to him. You should present your thoughts on possible options or alternatives. This will show that you have done some good base-work, and, seek the final direction from the boss. This will save time for your boss. He(she) will definitely appreciate this and be glad to give his(her) considered view or decision.

Do Not Spring Surprises

Do not spring surprises with your boss. If it is a good news, it may be an exception. This is a pleasant surprise.

But, never surprise your boss with a bad news. His(her) immediate reaction will be on you. Avoid that. The old adage says: "Tell me early, I am your friend; tell me late, I am your critic." But, this is for general developments, and, not for bad or disheartening news.

Communicate Dispassionately: State Facts

Have you got a bad boss? Relax. Don't get upset, your boss may be imposing too much of workload on you. He may be switching tasks or assignments frequently, changing decisions, springing last minute surprises, etc. Sometimes, he(she) may be doing it unknowingly or unintentionally; he(she) may not really be aware of the amount of stress he is causing to you. But, do not react suddenly. Communicate your concerns dispassionately to him—objectively by stating facts. Your boss may change his behaviour or work allocation or delegation style.

Keep Building Trust

Trust building is a continuous process—you can build trust everyday by managing up effectively or intelligently.

Trust can be built through major performances or achievements, and, also through small moves or actions. Integrity is very important. Integrity builds trust. Once the "trust bridge" is built between you and your boss, he does not have to micromanage you. He may start giving you bigger responsibilities. This may brighten your career growth prospects.

Volunteer to Share Workload

Companies often work with leaner staff and sometimes even in emergency mode. This increases workload of everyone including your boss. You may stretch yourself and offer to take some work off your boss's plate. This gives your boss some welcome break or relief and he(she) will definitely appreciate this. This will give you exposure to higher-level work and more visibility.

May I Help You boss?

This is a logical extension of sharing workload of boss. But, it can have a different context.[12]

You may observe that the boss is looking absent-minded or "frenetic or inconsistent." May be work pressure is telling on him—pressure of managing other subordinates, some peers or seniors. If your boss look overworked or overwhelmed, try to ask: "Can I help you boss?" This posture may go a long way in building your relationship with the boss. This is also an innovative way to impress the boss.

A TURNING POINT?

Many feel that there is also a turning point—a turning point in boss-subordinate relationship. There may be good reasons for this.

Spirit of Times

One important factor is the spirit of times. Today's scenario is in marked contrast to the straight-jacketed environment of even ten years ago when crossing swords with the superior would have meant instant relegation to the company's back-yards. The spirit of change seems to be catching up with the bosses also.

In conflict management, the parties to a conflict have some sort of relationships if only for the purpose of the conflict or the dispute. And, whatever that relationship is, it could probably be better. So, also in boss-subordinate relationship. A good working relationship should enable them to deal effectively with the disagreement, large and small, that may inevitably arise in any complex interaction in business organisations. This may sometimes presuppose a well-designed conflict resolution process in a broader sense.

Transition Process

Equally important is the fact that, in the increasingly competitive arena of the corporate world today, top management can no longer take anything for granted, least of all, their subordinates. "The present brat-pack is supercharged, super confident. And, armed with their MBAs and CAs, they are increasingly questioning the boss, proving him wrong, and getting away with it."[13]

The reason for this is easily comprehensible: job mobility. The new generation of subordinates are professionally and intellectually as qualified as the boss; some are even more so. Many of them can walk out of a job into another, may be a change for the better. Job security, as such has no great relevance any longer. These new breeds or high fliers are definitely demanding to be heard.

SRF has gone so far as to circulate among staff what it calls an "opinionaire" once a year to elicit subordinates' perceptions about their bosses. This is apart from the regular open-house sessions where differences are thrashed out. SRF's opinionaire has not only helped the company's top management understand their subordinates better, but it has also given the latter a confidence to play a more participative role.

Many companies are no longer interested in pure "yes-men," says Anand Shome, general manager, Personnel and Administration, Ballarpur Industries: "The boss being always right is more of a joke than anything else now. In fact, at BILT, we are encouraged to differ from our bosses. The days of unilateral decision-taking are over."[14]

The transition process is aided by another development: emergence of bosses younger than their subordinates. It's a common feature in many companies now. The age factor has contributed substantially to the informality in the boss-subordinate relationship. Ten years or so ago the general manager and other senior executives of the company were 50 plus. Now, not only are these posts occupied by executives in age group 35-40, but there are also situations where a boss is younger than his subordinate.

Some of the older companies may be bending backwards to create the informal environment, but, the comparatively new ones have it on their straight course. According to Dilip Piramal, Chairman, Blow Plast, "there hasn't been much change in the boss-subordinate relationship in his company because communication has always had this culture," says Piramal. Piramal Group, even held regular open-house sessions between bosses and juniors in order to iron out differences until three years ago. "They were discontinued as we found there was no need for them any more," says Piramal.

Although an increasing informality may be making inroads into marketing and service departments, manufacturing units generally tend to stick to the rigidity of old hierarchies. For example, superiors at Maruti's Gurgaon factory tend to keep their distance. The same is true in SRF units, too. "The set-up is such that here are more levels and they have and follow an older legacy. But there it's a question of discipline more than anything else." It is also understandable because on the shop floor, there may be need for more of control than management.

Another significant fact about the development of the boss-subordinate relationship is that the changes so far have been noticeable in the middle and not-so-senior levels, the levels in which the new generation managers are consolidating. Things till seems to be quite different in the rarefied atmosphere of the very top. *Changes are always harder to come by in the bottom and top levels, the proverbially inelastic levels.*

All this notwithstanding, the emerging fact is that bosses are learning to bend with the winds of "glasnost" that is sweeping the corporate world. The old chestnut who thought he was always right is cracking or would be cracked. A new parity or order is looming large. Change is coming. In some companies, it might have already come.

Turning points are always welcome. Those soften or melt the highpoints in boss-subordinate relationship.

We, however, would like to conclude like this: *The boss-subordinate relationship is a fundamental fact in corporate management. This will continue to evolve in its own way. Evolution is always for the good. It would also depend a lot on a particular organisation. Organisations are so diverse.*

6
Climbing the Ladder

Every manager wants to climb the corporate ladder. Every manager dreams to be the COO and ultimately the CEO of the company. If there was a prescribed guidebook or roadmap, every manager would have moved to the top or become the CEO. Then, companies would be full of CEOs and there won't be any manager to serve. This is obviously not true. The realities are different.

With similar backgrounds and capabilities, some managers move straight to the top while there are many others who languish in the middle manager level. Why so?

Some explain this in terms of knowing the difference between capabilities or *efforts* and *results*. Efforts may lead to efficiency, but, this does not necessarily ensure result or success. This is the reality of life and the corporate arena.

An MBA can land you at the doorstep of your career, but, after that, the journey is all yours. Business schools cannot help you. "Getting ahead is one of those real-world concerns of everyday business life that no textbook can prepare you for."

THE MANAGEMENT GAME

In some sense, the race for corporate ascendancy is like playing a management game. The managers are the players. According to some: "...it is several games all going on at the same time."

The managers have to play the game to the best of their capabilities, and, use the right strategies or tricks. Sometimes, the game is played openly or transparently, but, more often, it is played secretly (there is no level playing field). The winners go ahead. The losers languish.

THREE BASIC RULES

To be a winner, every manager must follow the rules of the game. Three basic rules or factors are:

1. The company has a system
2. Peers are your natural competitors
3. The boss matters

The Company has a System

Every company has its own systems and procedures. We can call these the organisational boundaries. In some companies, the management gives plenty of freedom to individual managers. In some others, the management is more boss-centric or CEO-centric. There are others who adopt a middle course. So, every organisation is unique in its own way.

Managers working in the organisation have to understand this uniqueness. Every manager has to identify himself (herself) with the organisational system and follow it. Then only he(she) becomes an insider and can contribute. Otherwise, he(she) becomes a misfit let alone contributing and getting ahead.

Let me give an example. In MMTC, we had recruited some MBAs from IIM(A) and IIM(C). They thought they are high-flier MBAs and they should work on strategy making for the company. But, they knew nothing about the organisation. Then, whom would they develop the strategy for? One of them was posted in my department. I called her and told her: "If you prepare a strategy paper now (without knowing anything about MMTC), you will only be reproducing your strategic management textbook. But, the company does not want that. In fact, no company in reality wants that."

The public sector may have some commonality of system(s), but, in the private sector, companies are more diverse in terms of their corporate policies, organisational structures and operating systems. Hindustan Unilever (HUL) has its own system; ITC has its system; so has Procter & Gamble, Larsen & Toubro (L&T), RIL, TISCO, Tata Motors, Wipro, Infosys, so on and so forth.

If, as a manager, you want to serve the organisation and grow, you have to become an insider in the company and work "within it or through it or around it". Only this will pave the way for your internalisation and growth in the company.

Peers are Your Natural Competitors

Peers in the company are natural competitors of a manager because all are vying for the same pie or ladder. The race is sometimes open, often hidden. Every manager wants to take a march over the others.

Some, however, feel the opposite. They say that peers are natural allies of a manager in the corporate race. They even go to the extent of saying: "If you alienate your peers, you won't need any other corporate enemies."[1] In the tactical battle for ascendancy, alienation of peers may be an automatic or natural process.

Apparently, peers and managers are all allies in the daily working environment in the company. Sometimes, peers and managers also work as teams. But, the competition for the ladder remains. Some peers may be strong competitors, few others may be the most immediate or strongest competitors. But, this may not be always visible. Invisible move also includes stabbing at the back. This is not uncommon in the corporate race.

The Boss Matters

We have discussed above (last chapter) boss management and its various configurations. The discussion clearly shows how important is the boss in the career building of every manager.

If you want to climb the organisational ladder, *you have to carry the boss with you or the boss has to carry you with him*. There is no short-cut or alternative to this. If you do not realise this or fail to put this is practice, you get stranded or stagnated, or, you may crawl like a crocodile.

Some bosses may matter more, some may matter less. *More friendly the boss, less he matters. More difficult the boss, more he matters. In either can, the boss matters*. This applies to even so-called professional bosses.

If the boss is very difficult, you can try to establish equation with boss's boss, build bridge between you and him and seek his support. But, this may be bit of a complicated proposition, and, should be generally avoided. This indirectly means confrontation with the boss. It has its own risk.

TWELVE IMPORTANT STEPS

Three basic rules or factors mentioned above are the stepping stones. We can call these the base or foundation. These are necessary, but, not sufficient. Managers have to build on these bricks. They have to infuse sustainability in the journey, that is, build growth on growth. In other words, it should be sustainable growth.

Twelve steps or factors are mentioned below. Every manager should follow these steps, practise and try to perfect them to win the race. Slippages may be there; those may be unavoidable. I, like many others, have experienced this. But, managers have to recoup and get quickly back on track. This is the name of the game.

Twelve steps or factors are:

1. C.A.D.I.F (commitment...)^2
2. Don't change the system
3. Mistakes not to be committed
4. Discipline yourself
5. Build trust
6. Loyalty is very important
7. Making impressions
8. Go beyond job description
9. Using tricks of the trade
10. Learn to wait
11. Self-analysis or assessment
12. Survival of the fittest

C.A.D.I.F. (Commitment ...)

C.A.D.I.F. stands for 'commitment: Attend to details: Immediate follow-up.' These are almost like basics.

Your *commitment* to the job should be total. If you deliver less, this will be noticed and your sincerity may be questioned. Don't allow this to happen.

In our chase for big things (tasks or targets), we tend to neglect or ignore small things or details. We assume that those will take care of themselves or some others will take care of those. This is a common tendency among managers. This should be corrected.

We must remember that taking care of details is very vital for completion of bigger tasks. So, enough *attention* should be paid to *details*.

Some action or decision requires *immediate* or timely *follow-up* for best results. It should be done forthwith. This may appear to be an insignificant issue, but, it can become significant in many cases.

Don't Change the System

We had mentioned in three basic rules that every company has a system. As a manager, you should understand the system and work through it. Don't try to change the system. *You better change yourself*. This is the practical course.

Managers often complain about the company's system—difficulty of working with it, "things don't get done", etc. Some also try to fight against the system to break the stone wall. This is a futile exercise and can also be counter productive. Don't try this. If you find the system too difficult to work with, you can leave the organisation and go to another organisation. But, you may face the same problem there. Be prepared for it.

Another aspect is office politics. Let us see this: "Lee Iacocca, a business superstar rising shifty through the ranks, worked in a Fortune 500 corporation for thirty-two years, was clearly destined for the top spot until at the age of fifty when he was abruptly fired and his executive vice-president named CEO."[3] Is this office politics? Many think so.

Most people think that workplace politics is a pervasive phenomenon. Walter Vieira, based on his long consultancy experience, observes: "It can be found in the public sector with its additional groups of bureaucrats and politicians who wield influence. It prevails in large public limited companies where senior directors and managers operate like they owned the place and follow the pattern of Japanese warlords with their own private zones of influence. It also holds sway in private or family companies where different family members may provide foci for group formations and subsequent group or family rivalries."[4]

Is there really no escape from office politicking? There may be difference of view on this. I personally feel that it is possible to sail through without involving oneself inside politics. My experience says so. Also, if you involve yourself in office politicking, you may sometimes become a bigger victim of this.

Smart and intelligent managers do not try to fiddle with the company system, and, do not waste time and energy in office politicking. They internalise fast, *use or exploit the system* and grow. Aspiring managers should try to establish wavelength with such managers, align with them and follow their course. This will make it easier for them to climb the ladder.

Mistakes not to be Committed

Mistakes can happen in life and business. Mistakes can happen at different levels. Even the CEO can make mistakes. It is correctly said that mistakes are unavoidable in corporate management.

Of course, managers should try to minimise mistakes if not eliminate them. They should try to avoid certain mistakes, and, not repeat the same mistakes.

More probable mistakes, not to be committed/repeated, with some suggestions for corrective postures, are mentioned below:

(i) *Don't rub your senior (includes boss) on the wrong side*: Be manipulative;

(ii) *In a discussion/meeting, don't force your argument on others*: Try to listen; then others will also listen to you;

(iii) *Do not pose very serious in office*: Brace a smile from time to time; a sense of humour relieves stress and pressure;

(iv) *Do not work on wrong wavelength*: Establish the right wavelength with seniors, peers and also subordinates;

(v) *Do not criticise your peers, or even subordinates in public*: Do it privately and settle between you and him(her);

(vi) *Never take a decision when you are in stress or angry*: Good decision presupposes calmness and temperament.

Discipline Yourself

Not committing mistake indirectly means disciplining yourself. Discipline your work, discipline your personal life because both are mostly interrelated.

Disciplining means casting yourself properly in different situations, and, exercising control over yourself in difficult or crunch situations. This also means being smart or street-smart. You should not only think that you are smart or street-smart, you should actually be so. There is often a large gap between number of managers who think they are smart and those who are really so. Those who fall in the "difference category" are quite likely to languish in the lower-middle or middle management cadres.

Discipline means using instincts in the right manner. Are you instinctive? All of us are instinctive. But, how we use our instincts is important. We, as managers, should be able to say something when it should be said and not earlier or later. That is using the right instincts. Otherwise, you are showing lack of discipline.

Emotion, impulse and discretion are also disciplinary traits. Business or decision situations test your emotion, impulsiveness and discretionary ability. For example, "when a business situation must be handled discreetly, how do you use your discretion? When a humorous or conciliatory remark might have taken the heat out of an exchange, how cooling was your influence or action? Did you act very impulsively, or, you used the right instincts? These are tests of a manager's disciplinary traits.

Building Trust

Needless to say, every organisation wants to have employees (managers) they can trust. Trust levels may vary though. Almost in every company, some managers are trusted more than others because of their character, judgement and credibility. Have you tried to find out your trust level in your company? You must try to do this because this may determine how much responsibility the company may entrust to you.

Trust also has an ethical connotation in the integrity sense. The managers should be honest. But, the definition or meaning of honesty is under lens. This is today's corporate reality.

Some managers manipulate their travel accounts. The allowances given by the company may not be sufficient to meet daily costs in large metropolitan cities like Mumbai and Delhi. What does a manager do? The manager may have to manipulate accounts so that he(she) does not have to leak his(her) pockets. Is it unethical? Is it dishonesty?

Let me narrate my own case. When I was in ORG (now ORG-MARG) based at Baroda (now Vadodara), I was sent to Delhi with meagre daily allowance. I sought advice from my boss who was very practical and progressive. He told me: "Show more travels during the day (there was no restriction on taxi travel)." I took his advice. This is not dishonesty. This is taking advantage of the company's travelling rules. This is being realistic. This helps to focus on work or productivity.

Let me give example of a business situation. A manager is asked to clinch a deal. "Go and get the business," says boss. The manager finds that the person on the other side (the buyer) wants to be personally pleased. Practical marketing/selling strategy envisages 3Cs: convince, confuse, corrupt. Try to convince the buyer/customer. If you cannot convince, try to confuse him and get the business. If that also does not work, corrupt him. But, get the business anyway. Most of the companies want that. We got some business for MMTC (a public sector company) like that.

Is this unethical? In today's reality in the marketplace, many management allows this. So long as you do not corrupt yourself, management may accept it. This is the real test of trust.

Loyalty is Very Important

Loyalty is another name for trust. Every company wants that all its employees should pledge 100 per cent loyalty to the company. This should be the commitment level. If you want to climb the ladder in this company, you should not only realise this, but, also practise this, and prove it to the management. All aspiring managers should look for opportunity to do this.

This does not mean that managers should not do job hopping. But, there is a way to do it. Some managers trade off loyalty for a small gain in another job. This is a very short-sighted view. First, if you do this, you are showing to the present company that you have no loyalty. Second, you are not realising that loyalty pays, but, it takes time. There are cases where a person joined as an induction level manager and climbed to the position of chairman of the company. For example, Ashoke Ganguly of HLL (now HUL). Such can be the reward for loyalty.

Loyalty can, however, be traded if the alternative is very lucrative and may turn your career. The future is uncertain including your future in the present company till you have actually achieved something. So, resign and go. Even if the present company offers to retain you, politely decline. They have already noted that you are trading your loyalty. Go and focus on your career in the new company. Work on building loyalty there. Forget the past company. Dump it. This is my policy.

Some may call it "rolling loyalty", but, sometimes, this may have to be traded with "life-long loyalty" for career building.

Making Impression

Making impression means, in other words, creating an impact. It should be visible. Of course, there are some silent workers (managers) who also contribute, sometimes even effectively. But, they may not appear to make much impression or create impact.

The impression a manager makes in the company and business depends on various "conscious and unconscious" statements and postures he makes. "The way you dress, your phone manner, your efficiency, the way you phrase a letter, the way you greet people, the way you deliver"—all affect the impression you make on others—your subordinates, peers, seniors, business associates, customers and other stakeholders.

Smart or effective managers sometimes impress in "unobtrusive" ways. It may be a simple gesture or action; if it is not made, this may never be noticed. But, if it is made, it is noted, quietly acknowledged and kept in mind.

Making impression can sometimes be subtle. Creating impression often demands "conscious connection" between the impression you want to create and the impression you actually create. Some managers think that they are impressive, but, they actually create bad or wrong impression or no impression at all. This suitability factor should be clearly understood. Otherwise, it may have the opposite effect.

The impression a manager creates makes his(her) perfect or imperfect depending on his(her) management style. "If you can take advantage of all the little opportunities to create an overall ongoing impression of competency, effectiveness, maturity and fair-minded toughness"—the kind of manager most organisations like, then the company may overlook your occasional "transgression" or "out-of character" because their overall impression of you is a favourable one.

Creating impression also relates to emotion management. Emotion often overtakes us. If a big business talk or negotiation has fallen through, the disappointment usually carries to the next person you talk to. If you are feeling harassed, irritation or impatience can creep into a meeting or phone call. Some have suggested "compartmentalisation" as a solution, i.e., having the emotions of a situation to the confines of that situation. It is easier said than done. The temperamental manager should try to achieve it.

Creating impression has both short-term and long-term implication or impact. In the short-term, you must realise that "you get along by getting along". If an incidence of mistrust has taken place, the manager should bury the hatchet by admitting that to be his(her) own mistake.[5] This will pave the way for long-term impression or impact. This way the manager builds his(her) reputation for long-term trust worthiness. This should be the final objective for creating impression.

Go Beyond Job Description

Every manager is assigned certain duties and responsibilities in the company. These are his(her) routine or day-to-day functions. This is almost constant. Do you go beyond the "constant" to prove yourself? If you do, your performance or distinctiveness will be noticed. Every manager should aim for this.

In a company, most jobs or positions are 75% "functional", meaning set responsibilities and duties which come with these, and, 25% "personal style," that is, how you deliver or excel in your job or responsibility. The degree to which you can stretch this 25% is the degree by which you will stand out in your company. So, stretch this 25% with your capability, dedication and innovativeness as far as you can. Then, your performance becomes more and more visible or distinct.

You may come to office earlier (5 to 15 minutes) than your peers and others. You may leave office after they leave. You may spend more time at your desk and less on lunch and tea breaks. If your boss asks you to complete a task in two hours, try to complete it half-hour earlier. If you are asked to come to office on an off-day or holiday, show your response smilingly. All these go beyond your job description. These help you to climb the ladder.

Using Tricks of the Trade

In addition to going beyond job description, the aspirant manager should use some tricks. We can call these tricks of the trade. These tricks embody a manager's management style or style of functioning. These consist of some "Dos" and "Don't's". Six major identifiable tricks are:

(i) *Don't get stuck in routines*: Try to find time for new things;

(ii) *Do not try to influence your boss*: Politely make a point of disagreement, but, the boss should prevail;

(iii) *Try to be fair and transparent in whatever you say or do*: This improves your image;

(iv) *Build your imaginative power to anticipate trouble or error:* Try to take pre-emptive action;

(v) *Keep a brief note of what you have said over the telephone*: For important matters, follow this up with written confirmation;

(vi) *Observe people in the organisation who have risen quickly through the ranks*: Try to follow them.

Learn to Wait

Patience is the name of the game. Some people become restless, may even be frantic, to achieve the target or reach their goal. Sometimes they succeed. But, more often they fail. Speed does not always ensure victory. We all know the rabbit and tortoise story.

It has been proved many times, even in business and management, that time or waiting solves many problems. McCormack observes from his experience: "It is still amazing to me how the simple passing of time can totally alter a situation, solve problems, render other problems meaningless, cool down confrontations, and, add a whole new perspective."[6] This may not happen always. But, the waiting game pays.

Finding an opportunity in life mostly means waiting for it. This applies to career management also. Learning to be patient or learning to wait has led to many successes, and, the lack of it has resulted in failure. McCormack observes again: "...in our twenty-odd years in business, 90% of our businesses have involved some way the need for patience, and, 90% of our failures have been caused in part because of lack of it."

How frequently you expect your promotion or raise in pay? For promotion, three years are conventional. It can come before or after. Show patience. Don't ask for it. It will come to you. Indra Nooyi, CEO, Pepsico (former), never asked for a raise in her career in Pepsico. She says: "I've never never asked for a raise."[7] But, she got many raises till she became the CEO of Pepsico. There is a lesson for all of us in this.

In MMTC, Raghaven, CMD, gave many promotions. In one round, some managers missed their turn. They aired their reactions. Raghavan said: "Don't lose patience. Your turn will come soon. They got their promotions. So, even if you have missed a bus, show patience. Rewards, sometimes, can be a waiting game. So, learn to wait.

Self-analysis or Assessment

Self-analysis or assessment has two aspects or dimensions; first, SWOT analysis of the self and self-assessment for career building.

SWOT Analysis for the Self

SWOT stands for strengths, weakness, opportunity and threat as explained below:

S = Strength **W** = Weakness	Internal competence factors
O = Opportunity **T** = Threat	External or environmental factors

SWOT analysis is commonly done for organisations or companies. Companies have been using SWOT analysis for long for business growth or expansion or diversification.

Like an organisation, SWOT analysis can also be usefully utilised by individuals. He(she) should identify his(her) or major strengths and try to match or balance them with opportunities. He(she) should work on converting some of the weaknesses into strengths with intelligent use of personal resources. He(she) should also endeavour to neutralise or minimise threats for achievement of goals.

Discover Your Strengths

Do we all know our strengths or full potential? I feel many of us don't really know because we have not seriously looked into them.

Different individuals have different strengths. Some strengths may be common among certain individuals; but, generally, strengths will vary from person to person because of differences in personality traits, skills and competence levels. However, we can try to enumerate certain potential strengths which individuals may possess:

Potential Strengths

- Clarity of thought
- Hard working
- Care for sentiments
- Positive attitude
- Ability to convert plan into action
- Mentally tough
- Determination
- Ability to take decision
- Resilience
- Self-motivation
- Self-confidence

Know Your Weaknesses

We are generally less expressive, may be less aware also of our weaknesses because we are often sky of thinking or talking about threw. But, more we are conscious about them the better. Certain potential weaknesses which individuals may possess are listed below:

Potential Weaknesses

- Takes life easy
- Lack of motivation
- Gets confused easily
- Lack of commitment
- Impatient
- Too emotional
- Indifferent attitude
- Lack of confidence
- Lack of determination
- Not result seeker
- Poor decision-making
- Do not coordinate plan and action

A close look at the potential strengths and weaknesses shows that, with some efforts and application, certain weaknesses can be converted into strengths. For example, 'lack of motivation' can gradually, but surely, change to 'self-motivation' with some motivational counselling and/or courses. 'Indifferent attitude' can also be transformed into 'self-confidence' if a person is determined to improve himself(herself). The same can be true of transition from 'lack of commitment' to 'determination' to success.

Opportunities in life, business or profession can be many and in different ways or forms. At macro level, it depends on the country or economy in which we are living. For a particular individual, it would also depend on his(her) objective or pursuit. For example, if you want to become a cricketer, your country should be a cricket playing country and cricket coaches and academies should be available.

However, some potential opportunities may be:

Potential Opportunities

- Economic boom
- Government deregulations
- Government incentives for new ventures/startups
- Multinational companies
- New job opportunities
- Special training institutes
- Sports facilities
- Institutes for higher education
- Loan facilities for higher education (MBAs)
- Family background

Neutralise Threats

Like opportunities, threats also can be many and in different forms. Those would also vary from individuals to individuals depending on their ambitious, academic brilliance, preparedness in life and fighting spirit.

However, some potential threats can be:

Potential Threats

- Recession/Economic downturn
- Increased government regulations
- Political interference
- Demographic shifts
- Cultural barriers
- Competition for jobs
- Competition from peers in office
- Competition in civil service examinations
- Entrance tests for medical, engineering, MBA etc.
- General unemployment

SWOT analysis enables a manager to know his(her) competitive position in career building in an organisation.

Self-Assessment for Career Building

During building our career, we should, from time to time, analyse or assess ourselves. Self-assessment gives very useful inputs on career building and progression—right steps or wrong moves, etc. A manager should sit back and reflect on his(her) career path. Since joining the present company, has my growth or progression been upto my satisfaction? Have my peers moved up faster than me? Am I feeling like lagging behind or left behind? Seek answers to such questions from your own self.

The answers to these questions will give you some direction about how to proceed further. If you closely peruse the ten steps or factors first mentioned, you may find answers to these questions. You may find some missing links. You should work or rework on these links based on your trait, style and personal characteristics. You may soon find yourself on the ascending curve.

Survival of the Fittest

The Darwinian law or principle applies to corporate survival and growth also. "Survival of the fittest" in corporate climbing means survival of the "most competent" or "most complete."

"Most complete" includes many things—the organisation's expectation from a manager, the organisation's assessment of the manager against expectations, competitive ability of the manager in fulfilling or promoting company objectives, and, based on such factors, career planning of the manager in the company. Every manager should keep the company perspective in mind and endeavour to match his(her) own perspective and planning with this. This is the way to make oneself fitter and the fittest. There is a time perspective also.

Some of the steps or factors mentioned above may be more important than others. This largely depends on the individual manager. Every manager should prioritise these factors based on his(her) background, capabilities, job profile and the organisational environment.

Finally, I should mention 'luck' as a factor. Some may contend that a person makes his(her) own destiny. This may not always happen. My personal experience says so. *The slip between the cup and the lip is explained by luck*. Many might have experienced this.

Some have suggested that we should try to know or anticipate when we would be lucky. I think that is astrology. We don't venture into that. If you like, you can.

HOW TO GO TO THE TOP

If you are one of the fittest to survive the corporate race, and, in the ascending ladder, your target is the "top". But, there is a distinct difference between getting ahead and reaching the top. Not all those who get ahead reach the top.

For reaching the top, an aspirant manager needs to have more capabilities—cutting edges. We do not also rule out your star or luck.

Parkinson and Rustoniji, in their book, *How to Get to the Top without Ulcers, Tranquillisers or Heart Attack*,[8] have mentioned twelve factors a manager should consider to move to the top. Some of these are more mandane like human relations, teamwork, ability to organise, mistakes to be avoided, preparing for promotion and moving steadily.

These factors should be found in almost all senior managers who want to move up. CEO aspirants should possess some special qualities or characteristics. Three are very important:

1. To be visionary
2. Man management
3. Leadership qualities

We may add one more factor the CEO aspirant or CEO faces or confronts:

4. The CEO Paradox

To be Visionary

The CEO aspirant is the future CEO. He(she) should be a great visionary. He(she) has not only to manage the company successfully, but, also to build its future. So, he(she) must have a vision. The right vision makes a company; the wrong vision may unmake it.

The visionaries see changes before they come. They sense constraints and possess or develop capabilities to overcome the constraints and emerge winners. When, in the 1970s, Narayana

Murthy (Infosys) and Azim Premji (Wipro) ventured into computers, computers were hardly known in India. Verghese Kurien foresaw the great potential of villagers and the cooperative milk movement in India. Kiran Mazumdar Shaw saw the emerging potential of biotechnology in India when people hardly knew about it. We all know about legendary Dhirubhai Ambani.

These are entrepreneur—CEOs or founder-CEOs. There are also many professional CEOs like Jack Welsh (GE), Indra Nooyi (Pepsico) and Y.C. Deveshwar (ITC) who have risen from the ranks and taken their companies to greater heights with their vision.

A CEO should translate vision into action and result. Thomas Horton, CEO, American Management Association, observes: "A successful CEO will describe a vision, develop a plan, create a team, and, give it perspective as well as authority. The CEO must consider his entity as a part of a large world, not as an end to itself."

Man Management

Two principles are important in man management:

(a) *Do not react to a staff member (includes managers) in any matter without fully knowing his(her) point of view.* It is always good to understand people before taking any action directly affecting them.

(b) *Do not take staff (manager) complaints or grievances personally*. These are not against you; these are addressed to the organisation. Take them objectively and try to find a solution.

Good man management goes much beyond this. Here is a very good example of how a CEO perceives successful man management. Customers of Xerox posed a challenge to the company about how quickly the copiers shipped by the company can be installed and made operational. Newly appointed CEO of Xerox, Paul Allaire, described the situation as embarrassing. He identified an experienced manager and entrusted the problem to him. The manager solved the problem by creating a team of people from all departments involved. Says Allaire: "you can't get people to focus only on the bottom line...you have to give them an objective like 'satisfy the customers' that everyone can relate to. It's the only way to break down those barriers and get people from different functions working together."[9]

Leadership Qualities

Man management is a leadership quality. But, qualities sought in a leader can be many and varied. Many books have been written on this. More books may be written on this because leadership qualities vary from one leader to another. *A new leader emerges and a new quality emerges.*

But, if we peruse through these qualities, six distilled qualities or characteristics may be found. These are:

(a) *Keeping an eye on the target of the company.* The target has to be achieved. The focus should be on productivity of the people and the leader himself (herself);

(b) *A leader should make the best use of the available resources*—both human and financial particularly human resources available to him;

(c) *A leader encourages initiative among managers.* Initiative, sometimes, is like a tender plant. It has to be nurtured properly. The leader should do this to build human capital;

(d) *A leader does not presume that he is the only person in the company who possesses all the talent and capabilities.* He recognises talent and capability of others. He also encourages teamwork whenever necessary;

(e) *A leader fully understands that things are continuously changing*—new ideas, new systems, new circumstances. He adapts his approach and strategy to changing conditions;

(f) *The leader owns responsibility for all the right things, and, also wrong things* which happen in the company. He does not shift blame to others.

A successful leader really makes things happen—make difficult things possible. As Narayana Murthy puts it: "A good leader makes the impossible possible." This is what he has himself tried to prove. Dhoni exemplified leadership in the cricket field.

Also refer “Leadership: Ins and Outs” in Ch. 11.

The CEO Paradox

CEOs are bestowed with many powers. They also have big responsibilities and tremendous pressures. How do they deal with the tricky combination of “worship” and “resentment”? How do they “juggle the apparent freedom to do anything and the burden they constantly bear: that the careers, investments, and, incomes of thousands of people depend upon their wisdom?” This is the CEO paradox.

Some senior executives/CEOs wear multiple hats, i.e., simultaneously hold more than one position. David Mathis, President and COO of Kemper Corporation, would become CEO and Chairman, but would retain the position of COO (reports *The New York Times*). Harvey Golub, Vice-Chairman, American Express, and, Chairman of its subsidiary, IDS Financial Services, has been given the additional position President, American Express. Golub added two more hats, CEO and Chairman, TRS Division, American Express (reports *The Times*). For a long time, AzimPremji was holding the dual positions of CEO and Chairman of Wipro.

Multiple position holders like Mathis and Golub are not just few. It is estimated that 15 per cent of those who head Fortune 500 companies hold all three of the top positions of President, CEO and Chairman.[10] They enjoy more powers and privileges, but, their jobs and responsibilities also become more demanding.

Thomas Horton observes: “Until those at the top perceive their accountability as a sacred trust, and, accept only the privileges they fully deserve, the troubling CEO paradox will persist.” Only those CEOs who can successfully balance privilege and responsibility can resolve the CEO paradox and stay at the top.

7

How to Be a Successful Manager

Successful managers don't do different things; they do things differently...

Everyone of us want to succeed in life. Every manager wishes to be a successful manager. Success brings recognition, reward, promotion and career growth.

But how to become a successful manager? There is no copybook or textbook formula for this. Managers have to learn it the hard way.

Is a "successful manager" same as an "efficient manager" or an "effective manager"?

Let us begin by understanding or analysing this. "To be efficient" means to be "productive"; "to be effective" means "to execute or contribute"; "to be successful" means "to produce results." What are the interrelations between these three characteristics of managerial performance? Or, what are the correlations? Does efficiency imply effectiveness? Or, does effectiveness ensure results? Or, do efficiency and effectiveness together produce result or success? Is "result" same as "success"? Or, these two are close synonyms?

These are related or interrelated questions or issues. Answers to these questions or analysis of these issues are logical steps to "how to be a successful manager."

EFFICIENCY NORMS RE-VISITED

We start by re-visiting some of the efficiency norms. Some may say that such norms are motherhoods, but, that may not be true. More than two decades ago, a management writer[1] observed: "Our knowledge about what makes for efficiency is still limited; so, there is plenty of scope for disagreement" on this. The observation holds good even today.

Some may emphasise discipline or orderlines as an input to efficiency; others may highlight flexibility of operations as necessary input; some others may envisage organisational size or structure as an important factor; many others may put forth man management and interpersonal behaviour as critical variables; there are still others who may argue that environmental factors are the most important.

But, we all agree that efficiency is synonymous with productivity. To increase efficiency, therefore, there should be improvement in managerial productivity. Traditional efforts to improve efficiency have usually focussed on finding answers to two questions:

1. How can we do a job faster?
2. How can we do the job cheaper?

But, in the effort to do the things faster and cheaper, we often overlook a third and more basic question:

3. How can we do it right the first time?

We may learn from the Japanese (who originally learnt from the Americans) that the key to higher productivity is in working *better* rather than working *faster*. Working faster and cheaper only allows one to produce the same old defects more efficiently. But, improving quality has a large number of long-run pay-offs.[2]

So, the emphasis on quality is inevitable. Efficiency or productivity is not only pure number or quantity; it is also as much a quality. *As the One Minute Manager* preaches: "Remember productivity is more than just the *quantity* of work done. It is also the *quality*.[3]

The GMP Story

We give here a GMP story[4] on quality versus quantity efficiency. Jeff, a plant manager, had an interesting philosophy about work: If you can't do your job in an eight-hour work day, then either you have too much work assigned, or you are inefficient, or incompetent. He would actually walk through the halls every day five minutes after quitting time and throw out anyone who was still working. Nevertheless, things went smoothly, the plant ran at maximum capacity and morale was excellent during the three years he served as plant manager.

Jeff was promoted and Jules was hired as his replacement. Jules' approach to work was: An eight-hour day just isn't enough time if you really want to do your job efficiently. Besides, anybody who leaves at quitting time can't be very dedicated.

Conforming to Jules' approach, people started coming earlier and leaving later, although the workload was same. Instead of arriving at 7.30 A.M. and leaving at 4.30 P.M., people started coming to work between 6.30 and 7.00 A.M. and staying until 5.00 or 6.00 P.M. or sometimes even 7.00 P.M.

A review was made after four years of Jules' plant managership and the review showed that plant production had actually declined during the last four years. The old timers say that the problems were at an all time high since Jules took over. And, when an analysis was made of why this was happening in spite of increased work hours, the reasons became dear.

Early mornings were now times for social gatherings. Instead of coming at 7.30 A.M. and getting down to business, everybody was enjoying a nice hot cup of coffee, or two or three, and, talked about what happened last night or what they had planned for the weekend. It was usually well after 8.00 A.M. that people settled down to work.

Afternoons were worse. Thirty-minute lunch breaks had evolved into two-hour marathons complete with drinks. By 4.00 P.M. when people had been at work eight or nine hours, concentration started to fade. Many turned their attention to non-job activities like making phone calls, doing homework for a night class or balancing their check-books. When Jules appeared, everybody made an extra effort to look busy and dedicated.

There was a method in Jeff's madness of kicking people out at quitting time. He forced them to become goal-oriented. Everybody knew that they had only eight hours in which to get things done, and, they developed efficient work habits. But, Jules changed the work culture from goal-oriented to time-oriented. Quantity increased, but, the quality suffered.

In spite of corporate slogans on quality, productivity, and efficiency, studies show that office efficiency consistently averages only 45 to 50 per cent. So, there is always scope for increasing efficiency or improving performance—and there is scope for improvement in every situation. In other words, there are no real limits to improvement even in the best situations. In fact, high performing organisations and managers have greater potential for still higher performance than poor performance. And, performance can be improved in four different ways: (i) decreased time, (ii) decreased resources, (iii) increased quantity, and (iv) increased quality. Every way or situation has different emphasis and thrust.

Managers often react: "I have been doing my best; in fact, better than every one else; and, still you suggest that there is scope for further improvement." A deeper involvement in the performance process, however, reveals that many important areas of performance often remain neglected even in the apparently high performance situations probably because the neglected areas are less conspicuous and visible. Efficiency, at any point of time, is relative—relative to the situation, i.e., goal or task, the opportunities and constraints.

With change of situation, the efficiency level will change. Efficiency, therefore, is a continuing process or a continuum.

"EFFECTIVENESS" RE-VISITED

Peter Drucker's *The Effective Executive*, till today, continues to be the most elaborate treatise on managerial effectiveness (burying, for the time being, the subtleties of differences between a "manager" and an "executive").

In defining or describing effectiveness, Drucker states: "To be effective is the job of the executive. 'To effect' and, 'to execute' are, after all, near-synonyms. Whether he works in a business or in a labour union, in a university or in the army, the executive is, first of all, expected to *get the right things* done. And, this is simply saying that he is expected to be effective."[5]

Effectiveness implies coping with constraints and challenges. While others complain about hindrances and stumbling blocks, and resulting from them, their inability to do certain things, the effective executives turn the stones successfully. As a result, the limitations and constraint seem to disappear. An example would be more illustrative. Everyone in the management of a major railroads company in the USA knew(?) that the government would not let the company do anything. But, then a new financial vice-president joined who had not yet learnt that "lesson." He went to Washington, called on the Inter-State Commerce Commission, and asked for permission to do a few rather radical things. "Most of these things," the Commissioner said, "are none of our concern to begin with (and, therefore, you can do them). The others you have to try and test out and then we will be glad to give you the go-ahead." This illustrates the differentiation between an effective, and, a non-effective executive.

It is not very difficult to know how to become effective, or, in other words, there is no reason why anyone with "normal endowment" should not achieve effectiveness. But, one must work for it. One must develop appropriate work habits.

Five Ways to be Effective

Drucker has prescribed five ways to become effective. (For the extraordinary executives, effectiveness may be an essential ingredient of their extraordinariness, and, therefore, may not have to be specially cultivated.) First, effective executives know how to plan and manage their time that can be brought under their control. (A lot of their time is not under their control.) Second, effective executives focus on results, and, therefore, gear their efforts to achieve results rather than do only work. They begin with the question, "what results are expected of me?" rather than with the question, "what work (not correlated with results) is to be done by me?" This way, the morning shows the day. Third, effective executives build on strengths; they do not build on weaknesses. They develop on strengths—their own strengths, the strengths of their superiors, peers and subordinates; and, the strengths of the situations or the environment. Fourth, effective executives concentrate on few major areas where superior performance will produce outstanding results. They force themselves to set priorities and stick to their priorities of decisions and actions. They know that they have no choice but "to do first things first and second things not at all." Fifth, and finally, effective executives make effective decisions. They know that effective decisions are a matter of system—of the right steps in the right sequence. They know that an executive decision is always a judgement based on "dissenting opinions" rather than on "consensus on facts." They also know that to make many decisions fast is to make the wrong decisions. What is needed are few, but, fundamental decisions. What is needed is "the right strategy rather than razzle-dazzle tactics."

SUCCESS FOR RESULTS?

"From activities to results"—it is an important slogan of the Mbo movement. Focus on results is important because all activities do not lead to results or contribute to results in equal measure.

In day-to-day management, there is generally an "activity trap." Activities involved in clearing the in-tray, or the dak, or the papers; reports and files quite often get lost in the tunnel and do not see the end of it. Odiorne has pointed out, that in a short span of time, people forget their objectives and become so enmeshed in the activity of getting there that they forget where they are going.[6]

In fact, according to the Pareto Principle, activities and results are almost inversely related to each other. The famous Pareto Principle (enunciated by renowned economist Vilfredo Pareto) envisages the 80/20 rule: 20 per cent of the inventory items often accounting for 80 per cent of the value; 20 per cent of a manager's time accounting for 80 per cent of the results. A common corporate experience is that a small number of a manager's activities usually accounts for a large proportion of his results.

Which are the activities which lead to success or results? Are success and results the same things? Some draw a finer line between the two. Results are quantifiable—measurable. Success can be qualitative; success may be equated with performance—performance as assessed by the senior's judgement. If a boss is happy with a subordinate manager in terms of performance indicators which are not necessarily physical or financial targets, the manager is considered successful. We know of an amenable manager who was managing his boss of highly volatile temperament with his ice coolness—the instrument of success in the present situation—and, he became the pick of the lot for the boss. Here, as happens in many corporate situations, quantitative indicators of success or result were playing a second fiddle.

Success: Not Result Alone

For success at the top level or for a chief executive or a CMD the indicators or configurations may be many, targetted results—or "pure profit numbers" as the Americans would put it—being only one of them.

Business World (BW) and Marketing and Research Group (MARG) has researched out eight such dimensions or configurations: leadership, innovation and entrepreneurship, strategic vision, honesty and integrity, ability to take hard decisions, industrial relations policies, ability to keep talented managers and profit orientation (result) with an overriding weight for profit orientation. The most successful of "India's best chief executives"—as the Poll would put it—have been determined by BW-MARG[7] on the basis of the opinion poll carried out among the top echelons—all executives designated as directors or vice-presidents in the top private sector and large public sector companies—of the Indian corporate world. For each dimension or parameter (call it a barometer, if you are a precisionist), a 10 point scale was used and the overall image rating was derived by averaging the mean scores received by the CEOs on each of the eight dimensions. The poll depicted the ratings and success stories of the "Overachieving Steelman" (Russi Mody, TISCO), "Father of the Equity Cult" (Dhirubhai Ambani, Reliance Industries), "King of the Road" (Rahul Bajaj, Bajaj Auto), "No-nonsense Technocrat" (Ashoke Ganguly, Hindusthan Lever Ltd.), "A Bullish Trustee" (Pherwani, Unit Trust of India), and seven others. The juxtaposition between success and result is quite clear here. Success is not result alone!

PROFESSIONALISM-EFFICIENCY-EFFECTIVENESS-SUCCESS

We now turn to the triangle: efficiency-effectiveness-success triangle. Management consultants and experts have attempted to analyse the triangle in terms of professional management. Many of these consultants and experts contend that professional management, through the observance of Mbo principles and application of SWOT (the new name is SCOT) and, many other techniques ensure efficiency and effectiveness and consequent success or results.

But, even in professional parlance, clear distinctions are made between efficiency and effectiveness. And, the distinction is substantive, not purely descriptive. Logically understood, efficiency is input-output relationship—how much has been produced or achieved per unit of input or cost. Even if both inputs and outputs are low, efficiency can be high or even 100 per cent. Therefore, high level of efficiency does not necessarily ensure or guarantee high level of output or results. Effectiveness, on the other hand, is plan-output relationship—how much of the plan has been fulfilled or realised. Effectiveness, therefore, focuses on contribution to the higher level objectives or results.

Reddin[8] contrasts efficiency with effectiveness to bring out the distinction between activities and results.

Efficiency	Effectiveness
Do things right	Do right things
Solve problems	Produce creative alternatives
Safeguard resources	Optimise resource utilisation
Discharge duties	Obtain results

Some have re-told the famous stonecutter story to demonstrate the difference in philosophy between efficiency, effectiveness, and success or results (we know that success is not result alone). We repeat the story here, may be as a refresher for many.

Three different stonecutters were asked the same question: "What are you doing?" The first stonecutter replied: "I am cutting stone." The second stonecutter replied "I am earning my livelihood." The third stonecutter replied: "I am building a castle." In the re-told version of the story, the first stonecutter has been described as efficient, the second stonecutter has been depicted as effective, and, the third stone cutter has been epitomised as success.

Reddin's contrasts and stories notwithstanding, the problem still remains, because, in many real-life situations, a clear cut and rather straightforward management system does not work. Drucker, while trying to describe the "effective executive" observed: "There seems to be little correlation between a man's effectiveness and his intelligence, his imagination or his knowledge (professional qualities). Brilliant men are often strikingly ineffectual;...conversely, in every organisation, there are some highly effective plodders. While others rush around in the frenzy and business which very bright people so often confuse with 'creativity,' the plodder puts one foot in front of the other and gets there faster...." Drucker observes, again, while talking of achievement of results: "There are a good many successful business and effective executives—as there are many with at best mediocre results. One searches in vain, however, for an analysis that identifies what the successful are doing to give them results."[9]

According to Professor Argyris of Yale University, the "successful" executive (as he calls him) has ten characteristics, "high frustration tolerance," understanding of the "laws of competitive warfare," or, that he "identifies with groups" being among them. Drucker confounds the syndrome by stating "there are not too many people around with such personality traits, and, no one has known a way of acquiring them. Fortunately, I know many highly effective—and successful—executives who lack most, if not all, of Argyris's characteristics. I also know quite a few who, though they answer Argyris' description, are singularly ineffectual."[10]

I once heard the chairman of a very large corporation telling one of his senior managers: "You are efficient, but, not effective." This observation by the chief executive clearly demonstrates that he had distinguished notions of efficiency and effectiveness with reference to a particular task or situation he was referring to.

It would be quite interesting to know what other practising senior executives think about the relationship between professional management, efficiency, effectiveness, and success. An opinion poll was conducted among 60 senior executives (general managers and above upto Board level) to ascertain their views on the professional manager, the efficient manager, the effective manager, and the successful manager. Almost half of the senior executives surveyed belong to the public sector and another half to the private sector including multinationals and Indian public limited companies.

It is quite interesting to know that to the question, "Is a professional manager necessarily an efficient manager?", as many as 16 managers preferred to remain silent, 24 replied in the affirmative, and, 20 in the negative. On the question, "Is a professional manager necessarily effective manager?", executives were quite clear in their views. 45 responded in the affirmative, 13 in the negative, and, two did not respond. On the question, "Is a professional manager necessarily a successful manager?", as many as 14 preferred not to give an opinion, only 19 answered in the affirmative, and 27 in the negative.

The opinion poll shows the realities of management thinking; or, rather, the contrast between what we postulate in theory and what we perceive in reality. According to the opinion poll, the respondents considered themselves as professional managers—many of them would be efficient, many effective, and many successful. But, 20 (34 per cent) of such managers thought that there is no one-to-one relationship between professionalism and efficiency, and 16 (about 25 per cent) were not sure about the relationship, and, therefore, preferred not to give a clear opinion. It is also quite revealing that as many as 27 (about 45 per cent) professional managers perceived that professionalism and success are negatively correlated.

One important feature of the opinion pattern was that there were no discernible differences in the nature of responses by the executives in the private sector and in the public sector. The response pattern was almost unanimous among the two sectors. There was also no differences in the perception of managers with management qualifications and without management qualifications. This proves that irrespective of whether the manager is professionally qualified or not, the thinking process of the senior management on relationship between professionalism and efficiency, effectiveness, and success shows a good degree of homogeneity.

The response pattern is shown below in a tabular form.

	Private	Public	Total	Percentage
Is a professional manager necessarily an efficient manager?				
Yes	14	10	24	40.7
No	10	10	20	33.9
Necessarily an effective manager?				
Yes	24	20	44	74.7
No	6	7	13	22.0
Necessarily a successful manager?				
Yes	9	10	19	32.2
No	15	12	27	45.8

Note: "Don't knows" account for the difference between totals in the Table and 100.00

So, as the table shows, professionalism is not a complete answer to successful management.

EFFICIENT MANAGER, EFFECTIVE MANAGER AND SUCCESSFUL MANAGER

From the above analysis, we can distill the relationship between efficiency, effectiveness and success. In all practical situations, both efficiency and effectiveness contribute to success. A successful manager has to be both an efficient manager and an effective manager. Efficiency and effectiveness may be interactive to lead to success. The relationship between efficient manager, effective manager and successful manager may be depicted as below:

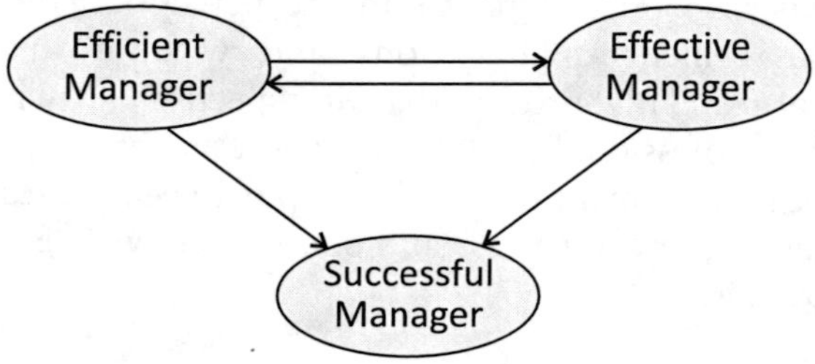

ESSENTIAL TRAITS OF A SUCCESSFUL MANAGER

A successful manager must possess, or develop, certain essential traits. Tarafder has identified forty-three such traits.[11] Forty-three may be too large a number to be practicable even if desirable. The number has been pruned to fifteen to include the essential traits: adapted and suitably modified. This is based on my long experience as a manager and observing other managers who have been successful. Fifteen essential traits are:

1. Building confidence
2. Patience or endurance
3. Learning habit
4. Knowing the difference between "effort" and "result"
5. Improving working relations
6. Maintaining confidentiality
7. Pursuing self-development
8. Avoiding confrontation
9. Creating impact on others
10. Learning from mistakes
11. Managing the boss
12. Availing allocated annual leave
13. Managing time
14. Using situational intelligence
15. Participating in leisure activities/sports

Following ABC analysis, the fifteen traits can be categorised as:

A : Most important traits
B : More important traits
C : Important traits

A : Most Important Traits

1. Building confidence
2. Knowing the difference between "effort" and "result"
3. Maintaining confidentiality
4. Avoiding confrontation
5. Pursuing self-development
6. Using situational intelligence
7. Learning from mistakes
8. Managing the boss

Building Confidence

To be successful, you need to build confidence in yourself. You also have to develop confidence in the organisational system and the surroundings (environment) because these affect or influence or can contribute to your performance. *If there is no self-confidence, there is no performance, let alone success.*

Knowing the Difference between "Effort" and "Result"

"Effort" is not same as "result". Effort produces result. Effort is like an input; result is the output. Effort is not visible; result is visible. Result is rewarded. Organisations want result. Smart managers know this; they know the difference between effort and result. Smart managers become successful managers.

Maintaining Confidentiality

Maintaining confidentiality of office matters is another name for expressing integrity of managers. Your boss or senior managers may sometimes take you into confidence and share some official secrets. You have to show your integrity by maintaining confidentiality. Integrity leads to trust. Trust makes you reliable.

Avoiding Confrontation

Confrontation with anybody is like declaring war. You have not left any room for amicable settlement of issues. If it happens with your peers or anybody in management, it can have serious, sometimes dangerous, implications. Confrontation is a lose-lose situation. Every manager, aspiring to be successful, should work towards win-win situation or outcome. This also shows positive attitude.

Pursuing Self-Development

Self-development helps in this. Self-development is essential for career development.

For self-development, a manager can pursue self-development methods or practices like.

(a) Undertaking short tailor-made courses on knowledge and skill development;

(b) Working with a senior colleague or trainer on developmental programmes;

(c) Looking for and seizing opportunity to officiate for higher level job when some senior is on leave or vacation.[12]

Self-development should be concomitant with career progression.

Using Situational Intelligence

No two situations are hardly same in management. New situations keep developing. Many of these may be unforeseen or unpredictable. Most of these are operational situations—some are contingencies. A manager, to be successful, has to use/develop skills to handle situations as those develop. Some innovativeness or improvisations may be required. A manager may have to use his(her) sixth sense, as they say. If you have a seventh sense, you may use that also. These are required more in a senior manager.

Learning from Mistakes

For producing result, a manager may often have to take initiative, and, also be innovative. If you take initiative and try to innovate, you may sometimes make mistakes. Even great managers and CEOs have made mistakes. So, mistakes should not deter you. You must learn from the mistakes and move forward. That should be the gamesmanship of a successful manager.

Managing the Boss

Your boss is the first person to know about your success; or, if you are not successful or not doing the right thing or in the right way. He(she) can advise or guide you about making corrections or how to improve your performance. You should always keep him(her) on your side. You should regularly seek his guidance so that you always remain on course. This is very important, if not the most important.

B : More Important Traits

9. Patience or Endurance
10. Learning habit
11. Managing time
12. Creating impact on others

Patience or Endurance

Being impulsive hardly pays in life much less in business and management. A manager may be saddled with load of work. Patience or endurance, along with planning, is vital to manage the state of work. A manager can prioritise his(her) tasks. Most of the successful managers do that. But, endurance remains a key factor.

Learning Habit

Learning is a continuous process. Learning helps building new thoughts, innovativeness and improving results. An aspiring manager should never get mentally or intellectually or professionally chocked. He(she) should have a free-flowing mindset and the propensity to learn.

Managing Time

Everyone of us has some 365 days a year, 24 hours a day and 60 minutes an hour. Managers have much less than 24 hours a day because daily working period is about eight hours unless you stretch it. So, your time in the office has to be planned and managed judiciously. If you do not plan, you will not find time for anything. But, if you really plan, time can be almost eternity. Time management is also a skill.

Creating Impact on Others

Creating impact on others or making impression—be it subordinates, peers or seniors—involves a special skill. This is an extension of man management, or, going one step beyond just managing people. Psychologists and psycho-analysts have suggested methods for creating impact on people. Lessons should be drawn from them. Creating impact involves persuasive skills, ability to convince others, sometimes praising others, etc.

C : Important Traits

13. Improving working relations
14. Availing allocated annual leave
15. Participating in leisure activities/sports

Improving Working Relations

The focus is on managing and improving interpersonal relations with subordinates, peers and seniors. This requires amiable disposition, acceptability by others, eliminating negativity in postures, etc. These create the right environment in the workplace and help to increase managerial productivity as well as organisational productivity.

Availing Allocated Annual Leave

Labour-leisure balance is essential for a manager's physical, mental, intellectual and professional fitness. More so, for a manager who aspires to be successful. Periodic break from work helps a manager to recharge batteries and come back to work with fresh vigour and renewed energy. Even during regular office days, working late, except for contingencies, should always be avoided. Labour-leisure balance is important in daily functioning also.

Participating in Leisure Activities/Sports

One of the best ways to spend/utilise leisure hours is to watch films on entertainment and participate in sports activities—indoor or outdoor. The choice of leisure activities depends on the aptitude and lifestyle of individual managers. Proper planning and pursuit of leisure activities is almost as important as official or business activities.

CONCLUDING POINT

Some of the essential traits just mentioned are common with those suggested for climbing the corporate ladder (discussed in Ch. 6). This is quite logical because those who climb the ladder, particularly those who climb fast, are successful managers. *Faster you climb the ladder, more successful you are as a manager; we can also say, more successful you are, faster you climb the corporate ladder.*

The relationship or bridge between efficiency, effectiveness and success should also be closely analysed. This makes the road map smother or faster for transition from an efficient manager to a successful manager—the ultimate objective.

8
Corporate Culture and Values

Visit any IBM office or branch office; any GE facility; any 3M department; any Sony Centre; a Toyota workshop; a Walmart store; a Tata centre; an Infosys office; any international airlines office. You will notice the differences in environment, ambience and staff posture or behaviour. These reflect cultural differences and, largely mould organisational functioning and performance.

WHAT IS CORPORATE CULTURE

Corporate culture is an extension of "style" in soft Ss of management (three soft Ss are skill, staff, style). Some say that culture is more appropriately the seventh S in Mckinsey's 7-S framework: shared values.

We give below an illustrative definition of corporate culture:

> Organisational culture is the set of assumptions, beliefs, values and norms that are shared by an organisation's members.[1]

As the definition shows, the most important characteristics of corporate culture is *sharing* or *common* values, beliefs, attitudes, feelings, etc. Four components of sharing can be focused:

(a) Shared *things* (e.g., the way people dress)

(b) Shared *saying* (e.g., let's get down to work)

(c) Shared *action* (e.g., service-oriented approach)

(d) Shared *feelings* (e.g., hard work is rewarded)

J.R.D. Tata, the legendary former Chairman of Tata Group, has well-enunciated corporate culture dimensions in Tata Group:

> I would call it a group of individually managed companies united by two factors: First, a feeling that they are part of a large group which carries the name of Tatas, and, public recognition of honesty and reliability—trustworthiness. The other reason is more metaphysical. There is an innate loyalty, a sharing of beliefs. We all feel a certain pride that we are somewhat different from others.[2]

If we take any other business group or house—whether Ambanis, Adanis or Poonawallahs—the statement on the organisation's culture will be same or similar.

Corporate culture is not created by any declaration; it is essentially unwritten or unstated assumptions, values, beliefs, etc. developed over years.

Corporate culture mostly follows from corporate policy and philosophy of a company. Corporate policy and philosophy determine both the organisational structure and corporate culture and values. (See figure below):

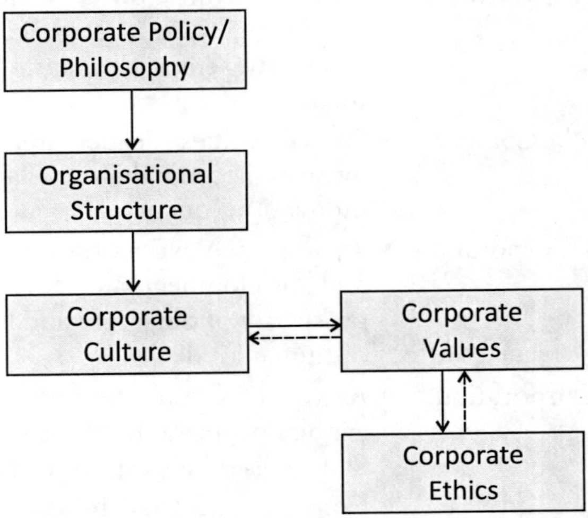

Corporate philosophy of ten global companies are mentioned below. These will show the diversities of missions or visions, philosophy and values of these companies.

Company	Corporate Philosophy/Values
Dell Technologies	• Customer satisfaction; team satisfaction; community satisfaction
Procter & Gamble	• P&G is its people and the values by 'which we live'
Toyota Motors	• Foster a corporate culture that honours individuality while promoting teamwork
Unilever Ltd.	• Overall robustness that is proof against hostile or adverse forces; and attitude towards risk taking that encourages initiatives
Microsoft Inc.	• Values are enshrined in customers, innovation, partners, integrity, people, entrepreneurial culture, diversity, community
Samsung Electronics	• Values: continuous innovation, challenge, speed, strategic focus, simplicity, empowerment, customer focus
Coca-Cola Company	• Shared values: leadership, passion, integrity, accountability, collaboration, innovation, quality
Cannon Corporation	• Kyosei: achieve corporate growth and development and contribute to prosperity of the world and happiness of humankind
Nokia Corporation	• A world of connected societies that enables people to fulfill their potential and realise their aspirations
Electrolux Ltd.	• Commitment to drive performance throughout the entire organisation

The diversities of corporate philosophies of these companies explain diversities of their cultures, and, operational systems.

DIFFERENT KINDS OF CULTURE

Some attempts have been made to explain or classify diversity of corporate culture into more observable categories. Four categories commonly seen are:

1. Power culture
2. Role culture
3. Achievement culture
4. Support culture

Power Culture

Corporate culture in any organisation is set by the CEO. In power culture, the CEO is authoritarian, and, he drives the organisation. The power culture can also be hierarchical, but, the CEO often undermines the hierarchy. Power culture may exist in some entrepreneurial companies, but, this is not common in professionally managed companies.

Role Culture

This is also known as bureaucratic culture. This may also be hierarchical, but, power or authority is exercised through rules, systems and procedures. In this culture, people or employees are induced or motivated by financial and non-financial rewards and, also sometimes, driven by penalty for non-performance. Many companies consider this culture as too formal, and, not professional or progressive. Therefore, not many companies adopt this culture. Public sector companies may implement such culture.

Achievement Culture

Achievement culture is concerned to "make a difference in the world"; it provides opportunities for its members to use their talents in ways that are intrinsically satisfying, and which advance a goal or purpose to which the individual is deeply committed. An achievement culture emphasises action, autonomy, innovation and the shaping of environment. There are many elements of this way of thinking in the corporate cultures of many companies. While working in such a culture can be deeply satisfying, it often makes high demands on its members' time and energy and can lead to "burn out".

Support Culture

The support culture works through close relationship. People learn to trust and care for one another, and they trust the organisation to take care of them—to be responsive to their needs. As in the achievement culture, people are motivated by needs that they feel within themselves, but the rewards are different. Here, the rewards are the sense of belonging, the activity of cooperation and mutual responsiveness. A support culture also has the added advantage that its members are highly responsive not just to each other but to the company's customers as well.[3]

In practice, many companies combine achievement culture and support culture for creating better organisational environment. But, the ingredients of both achievement culture and support culture are their own and can be distinctly different from those of other companies. This enable them to create and promote a culture unique to their organisations. Companies mentioned in the table above and others like GE, 3M and McDonald's exemplify this.

MACRO-LEVEL CULTURAL DIFFERENCES

Corporate culture is a micro-level phenomenon, i.e., it is company specific. But, we can also conceive business culture at macro or country level. In some sense, macro-level culture is built from micro-level cultures. However, while doing so, certain standardisation or commonality is forged.

Some speak of European culture, American or Western culture, Eastern or Japanese culture, and, also Indian culture.

We give below the comparative culture profile of US, Japan and India:[4]

US Culture	Indian Culture	Japanese Culture
Individuals can influence future	Life is preplanned, human action is predetermined	Groupism
I can change work to achieve objective commitment to organisations	I need to adjust, human action is predetermined	Homogeneity

US Culture	Indian Culture	Japanese Culture
Data-based decision, and they are healthy	Decisions flow from the experience and wisdom of authorities	Confucian ethics
I can disagree with out being disagreeable	Deference to age and seniority, suppression of negative feelings	Influence of educational levels
Protestant ethic	Authoritarian values	Respect age/ seniority
Authentic collaboration	Self-realisation	

A close look at three cultural patterns reveals that the US culture is more aligned to hard Ss (structure, systems, strategy) and Indian and Japanese cultures highlight soft Ss.

WORK CULTURE

Work culture of an organisation reflects its corporate culture. We can also say that work culture is a form of manifestation of corporate culture.

In an average organisation, there are usually three kinds of managers in terms of commitment, work and output: performers, workables and passengers.

The *performers* are self-starters. They are self-motivated and highly committed to organisational cause and culture. They perform in whatever position they are posted or put in—easy or difficult jobs. They also show enough initiative.

The *workables* are not self-motivated, but, they are willing to work. The *passengers* are managers who do not like to work. They work for money. These expect adequate compensation for their work. Pay them more: they will work more. You may call them materialistic. They are content if they are paid without much work or with minimum work. They will be happy if they can get their pay packet without working. They can be called idlers.

The relative proportions of these three categories of managers vary from organisation to organisation. High performing and progressive companies will have higher percentage of performers, then workables and minimum passengers. Less performing companies will have different proportions. The existing work culture in the organisation is also responsible or play a role in this.

The Computer Story

Here is a story to explain this.

A large organisation bought a computer (this was quite sometimes back). The Factory Accounts Manager was made the Computer Manager and he was to report directly to MD. The computer manager wanted to recruit some computer professionals for operating the computer.

His peers approached the MD and made a suggestion. "Each one of us will offer a couple of people without replacement so that the computer manager will have about 40 people available—he can choose out of them." The MD thought it was a good idea. He called the computer manager and told him about this.

The computer manager knew what kind of people were available without replacement—they were considered "worse than useless" by their own bosses. But, the computer manager did not want to appear negative to the MD. He replied: "I propose a solution. First, I would like to hire five people from outside who are already working on computers. Second, I shall take fifteen people internally. These fifteen people should not be selected by the managers of the company. I would like IBM to select them because IBM can choose the right people." The MD agreed to the objective approach.

Fifteen selected employees met the computer manager. He told them: "I have two reports about you. Your previous bosses say you are worse than useless so they have spared you without replacement. I have another report from IBM who has selected you and says you are very good. I have an open mind. I have it to you to prove who is right—your previous bosses or IBM." They said: "We will show the rescals who is right."[5]

During next few months, they worked very hard and proved their worth. Now, they had the right motivation, they felt important and they delivered.

Developing Work Culture

The computer story has a lesson. In many companies, proper work culture does not exist or has not been developed at all levels. The organisation in question is an example.

Many of the 40 people offered without replacement were definitely not "passengers." They were "workables." But, they were not managed or utilised properly. The requisite work culture was missing. We can say that this is a case of work culture or corporate culture mismatch at different hierarchical levels.

This shows that many organisations should ensure that work culture permeates to all levels of organisational functioning. Otherwise, the culture development process will be incomplete.

CORPORATE COMMUNICATION

An integral aspect of corporate culture is the internal communication process or system in the company.

A common problem in most organisations is that every employee feels that he is communicating well, but, the other side or parties are not communicating properly. To put it in a more positive perspective, a manager should think: "If I am saying something, does the other party understand it the same light, i.e., does he understand the words with the same meaning?" This is the coding-decoding problem in corporate communication. This should be properly addressed to make communication effective.

Another missing link in effective communication is that many companies do not recognise the need for and practice of two-way communication. In these companies, communication is one-way, i.e., top-down—sending decisions, orders or instructions from the top management or CEO and receiving reports and explanations from the lower levels. But, communication should be two-way, i.e., also bottom-up—receiving ideas, suggestions and solutions from operating managers. This opens up proper communication corridors.

Another important factor is dilution of communication or information. In every company, communication flows from the CEO, sometimes even from the Board, down to the plant level. If the chain or channel of communication is not correctly established, dilutions—we can also call this leakage—of communication or information takes place at different levels, and, this disturbs or disrupts the communication process.

A survey was conducted to ascertain the extent of dilution of communication. The dilution was found to be as high as 70 percent.[6] The survey results are summarised below:

100 per cent board	63 per cent Vice President	56 per cent General Supervisor	40 per cent Plant Manager	30 per cent General Foreman
⟶	⟶	⟶	⟶	
		= 70 percent dilution of information		

The survey was conducted quite sometimes back. But, the survey results are valid even today with some modifications. Even if the dilution is 50 per cent, it is a matter of great concern.

British companies focus on the importance of corporate communication, but, this is said to be more formal communication. This, however, does not mean that internal communication in these companies is not good. A British executive has well summarised the British corporate communication system:

Communication is a key part of our culture in which there is an emphasis on informing people at all levels of company objectives, how the company is doing and what are the problems facing the organisation. The communication is facilitated by workshops, briefing groups and notice boards which display up-to-date information about news within the company.

French and Scandinavian companies are more known for their emphasis on informal communication. In fact, informal communication in these companies increases the efficacy of corporate communication right through the company—up, down and across the organisation.

Transparency and Openness

Communication becomes much easier and effective if there is a natural spirit of transparency and openness which many companies aim for. Managers in many French companies have their regular "open tables" at which managers and staff meet to discuss any issues that are of concern to them. The atmosphere is open and informal.

A number of Indian companies also believe in openness. Russi Mody, Chairman of TISCO for over a decade, was known to discuss matters with workers during his informal lunch with them in the canteen. Narayana Murthy, as Executive Chairman of Infosys, used to have lunch in Infosys canteen to promote informality and openness. Adi Godrej was also known to have lunch often in Godrej canteen.[7]

TRUST AND CONCERN

The policy and practice of open communication really depends on mutual trust. A manager at Electrolux, explains this: We believe that people are honest until they prove that they are dishonest; our approach is that people are honest and want to do a good job. The company's chief executive said that in review: "people are much wiser than you think. It comes down to trust."

That the manager must have some disciplinary control goes without saying. The approach to discipline must reflect the personnel policy and the conditions of employment of the organisation. More broad minded these are, more stable and easier is discipline likely to be, and, so more flexible can the code of conduct be.

The standards of discipline should objectively be the same for everyone; where variations may be required for special categories of managers owing to peculiarities of circumstances, these are to be accepted as based on objective grounds, and, should not be construed to give rise to a position of privilege.

Ethical decisions require three qualities which can be identified and developed in individuals. The first is the competence to recognise ethical issues and analyse the consequences of alternative resolutions. The second is self-confidence to seek different points of view and then to decide what is right at a given time and place, in a particular set of relationships and circumstances. The third is "tough-mindedness" which is the willingness to make decisions when all that needs to be known cannot be known.

Because management should be creative, it must set clearly defined objectives: Only if it sets such objectives, it can rule out frequent and pernicious business malpractice or panic management or management by crisis or management by drives. To quote Peter Drucker: "In an organisation which manages by drives, people either neglect their job to get on with the current drive, or silently organise for collective sabotage of the drive-in order to get their work done. In either event, they become deaf to the cry of the 'wolf', and, when the real crisis comes...they treat this as just another case of management created hysteria."

The more successfully a manager does his work, the greater may be the integrity required of him (value ethics). The impact of his decisions on business, their time span and their risks may be so serious sometimes as to require that he puts the common good of the enterprise above his self-interest. Their impact on the people in the enterprise may be so decisive as to demand that the manager puts genuine principles above expediency.

The manager of tomorrow should base his every action and decision on the principles that he has cultured not only through knowledge, competence and skill but through vision, courage, responsibility and integrity. No matter what a manager's general education or management education is, the central education should be the integrity of character.

EROSION OF TRUST

This, however, is not to minimise the role of corporate trust. There is emerging feeling in corporate corridors about erosion of trust. Erosion of trust may ultimately lead to higher rate of attrition. Some management analysts and consultants observe that many organisations—startups to mature setups—are facing the problem of attrition resulting from erosion of trust. Erosion of trust has a wider perspective: quality of work culture, transparency, motivation, etc.

There can be many signs of erosion of trust. These can be seen in the organisational environment and functioning. Companies should read the signals and act in time if they want to prevent erosion of employee trust.

Five signals, some or all of them, may be noticed:

(a) **Open Communication Slows Down:** Open communication and conversations among managers are not as good as before. Managers have started avoiding discussions, and, tend to say things which are convenient rather than what is true.

(b) **Tendency for Passing the Buck Increases:** For setbacks and failures, excuses and shifting the blame to others are becoming more visible. Transparency and fairness are disappearing.

(c) **Political Camps are Showing Up:** Political alignments and polarisations have started dominating peer behaviour. Employees start sensing politics in management decisions and actions.

(d) **Social Media Support Slows down:** Cultures of high-trust companies are reflected in the posts of various social media platforms. If such posts are declining, this is also a signal of receding corporate trust.

(e) **Inspiring Leaders are Departing:** If inspiring leaders have started deserting the company, this is a clear sign of environmental pollution in the company. These leaders are either not able to motivate themselves any more or they are losing interest in inspiring others.[8] Both are equally detrimental to the company.

CORPORATE ETHICS

Corporate or organisational ethics has three dimensions: development of the manager as a moral person; the influence of the company as a moral environment; and, actions and regulations required to ensure a high level of ethical performance.

Managerial ethics are generally of two kinds: (a) professional ethics or ethics in terms of observance of rules, procedures, systems, etc. (b) value ethics or ethics in the personal integrity sense. *Managerial ethics is usually a shadow of corporate ethics.*

All these are what textbooks say.

Let us turn to the reality of corporate ethics and managerial ethics.

State of Business Ethics

100 years after Harvard Business School introduced its first course on "Social Factors in Business Enterprise," there are over 500 courses on business ethics on offer at America's business schools. A recent survey by the Ethics Resource Center in Washington, DC, found that three-fifths of American firms now have codes of ethics; so do about half of Europe's biggest companies. Such codes encourage managers to do more than just follow the letter of the law; they demand that entire company should be open, trustworthy and green. Altruism, say the ethicists, is good business.

They are up against some entrenched opposition. While business schools are encouraging fledging managers to do the right thing, firms seem to be doing their utmost to discourage them.

Even the best-managed firms can stray. Take Johnson & Johnson, a company renowned for its niceness. Its "credo" urges managers to be "just and ethical" and "is" say Ralph Larsen, the firm's chairman, "the most important thing we have in this company." But that did not stop wayward employees from shredding papers to hinder a federal probe into the firms' marketing of an ache cream. "There was no excuse," says Mr. Larsen. "But, it is a huge undertaking to spread our values around the world."

Arun Manappa in his study on *Ethical Attitudes of Indian Managers*[9] has indicated that the majority of business managers believe in good ethics, but various circumstances often prevent them from putting their beliefs into practice. The managers surveyed constantly reiterated the importance of company policy in influencing ethical action. A man's personal code of conduct was given only second place.

This has also been confirmed by a survey conducted by the All India Management Association among more than three hundred managers at top management, senior management, middle management and junior management levels. The result of the survey is summarised as:

	Agree	Disagree
Managers resort to practice which are considered shady but appear necessary for survival in today's rat race.	83%	17%

These studies/surveys were conducted quite sometimes ago, but, results are not significantly different even today.

Ethical Dilemma?

In most of the organisations today, the manager is left to make a conscious choice. He can either master the rules of the career game (with a high pay-off for ethics) and, start climbing towards the top of the power pyramid or he can join the multitude of competent but anonymous office non-politicians who support the corporate structures on their backs. This has almost become a global syndrome.

We all know it too well that swimming with the tide is much easier and wiser than against it. Under pressure to get ahead, therefore, the individual manager (whose native integrity is not doubtful) is prompted to pursue advancement at the expense of others, to cut corners, to seek to win at all cost, to make things seem better than they are—in short, to take advantage of a myopic evaluation of performance. This is bound to be so because the quantified results or immediate gains are much more visible than the quality factors and future consequences of present actions.

There is, therefore, a policy prescription: Once a company has decided that its ethical intentions and performance will be managed the way it has stipulated, they should accordingly formulate their corporate policy and make it explicit. Codes of corporate ethics should also be decided accordingly.

Let us try to set right the corporate ethics dilemma or debate with an example with which I was involved. This happened during my stint as Head, Non-ferrous Metals Division, MMTC.

Government of India mints (Calcutta, Mumbai, Hyderabad) were big buyers of copper and nickel for minting coins for the country. Calcutta Mint was the nodal point for these purchases.

MMTC wanted to enter this business. The business was already very competitive.

CMD, MMTC, called me and asked me to go to Calcutta, and, discuss with GM, Calcutta Mint, how MMTC could get into this business.

Discussion was held in the privacy of a five-star hotel room about stakes of both sides. The objective was to get GM, Calcutta Mint on MMTC side.

The mint business finally came to MMTC.

I shall not reveal what all transpired between me and GM, Calcutta Mint because that is trade secret. I can only mention that during the whole process of execution of the business, my personal integrity was not questioned.

Here is a lesson: for securing a business, you may follow the company's ethical prescriptions, but, you need not necessarily trade-off your personal integrity or ethics.

MOONLIGHTING AND CORPORATE ETHICS

Moonlighting (an employee or manager taking up another job or assignment while working full time in a company) is a phenomenon or practice which is doing the rounds in corporate corridors these days mostly in IT companies.

The IT services industry is almost waging a war against moonlighting. Wipro has sacked 300 staffers for moonlighting—working for direct competitors. Says Rishad Premji, Chairman, WIPRO: 'Employees can have a transparent dialogue with the organisation about their second or weekend work, but, we discovered 300 employees who were working for direct competitors. "Hence there is no place for them" (TOI, September 22, 2022).

Sandip Patel, MD, IBM, India, says: "Everyone who is hired signs a contract that they would be working full time for IBM, and notwithstanding what they can do with the rest of their time, moonlighting is not ethical." Ganapathy, COO, TCS, feels that moonlighting is an ethical issue and the IT sector would lose from such practice in the long-term.

The most important factor which explains moonlighting is big, some say "massive," shortage of IT professionals combined with the privacy of work from home (WFH). So, this is more an environmental factor or demand-supply balance issue.

At present, moonlighting is confined to the ITES sector. This is not perceived in other sectors much less in manufacturing. Only when moonlighting gets visible in more sectors, this may become a real corporate issue or matter of ethics.

WHO VITIATES CORPORATE CULTURE

We now return to corporate culture. The above example does not mean that the company culture was vitiated or broken. This is only an illustration of how business may sometimes have to be procured in today's corrosive environment for corporate survival and growth. The balance sheet must look healthy.

Vitiating the culture means going against the tide or existing norms, work environment or culture and mutual trust.

OFFICE POLITICS

Office politics may be a major vitiator of corporate culture.

Usually, those who are not fully or highly committed to work resort to office politics as a means of going up. Some may feel that "work alone is not enough" (may be true in many situations). Some managers take to office politicking to keep the peers in check or to get some favour from the boss.

In some companies or certain situations, informal group formation takes place to show displeasure to organisational decision affecting particular group. Sometimes you are dragged into office politics because you are never alone in the office environment.

Highly dissatisfied or frustrated managers and staff who have nothing much to lose vitiate office culture by indulging into office politics in some form or the other because they may not have better way to spend their time. They feel office politicking may help them to turn their future. Whether the reasons are justified or not is not very relevant here.

Sometimes, office politics may start or stop with the CEO or CMD. Here are two contrasting examples.

In the first example in MMTC, I was involved. The CMD was holding my promotion, although I was reporting directly to him. No reason was given for holding my promotion. One day, he called me and said: "If you give a formal complaint against Mr. X (a DGM), I shall promote you." I could not imagine that a CMD could stoop to such a low level. You have to see it to believe it. I obviously did not give anything in writing. The reason was simple: what is the guarantee that a person, who has absolutely no ethics, will keep his words. In such organisations, office politics can be rampant.

The other example relates to STC. The government (Commerce Ministry) had appointed P.L. Tandon, the first Indian Chairman of HUL, as CMD of STC. A GM came to meet Tandon with a file. He started talking about the previous CMD. Tandon stopped him promptly and said: "If you have come to discuss a case, do it. But, don't talk about personalities. If I encourage you, you will do the same thing with my successor when I leave." Needless to say, there was no office politics in STC during Tandon's tenure. But, Tandons are not many.

Some amount of office politics may exist almost in every organisation. This can be in different forms and reasons may also vary. It may even be group gossip or lobbying and spreading rumours. This may vitiate the organisational atmosphere. Up to a certain extent, most companies live with this. We may call this "cultural leakage". So long as these are kept under control the organisation sustains its philosophy and values. The top management or CEO has a big role in upholding this.

BUILDING A SOUND CORPORATE CULTURE

A company may develop an ambitious corporate plan or strategic plan; the organisation may have the necessary competence or resource base; the management or leadership may be keen on fast and efficient implementation. But, the managers and staff should be willing and prepared to take on the challenge, i.e., the organisation should be culturally geared up; in other words, the company should have a sound corporate culture.

Sumantra Ghoshal observes:

> Worldwide, managers an recognising that while process re-engineering, financial restructuring and strategic repositioning are important means to corporate renewal, the bedrock of competitiveness ultimately lies in the behaviour of people. To stimulate initiative, trust, commitment and cooperation within the organisation, and, in its external relationships, top level managers are increasingly recognising that the shaping and embedding of organisational values are perhaps their most important challenges.[10]

Building sound organisational culture is the aim of most progressive companies. GE is one of the foremost among them. GE story follows later. Corporate researchers and management consultants have been trying to evolve ways or methods for developing a sound organisational culture—a culture which is positive, proactive and supports, rather strengthens, successful strategy formulation and implementations.

Based on such empirical research and findings, eight important methods or guidelines may be suggested:

(a) Preserve core ideologies and values of the company;
(b) Stimulate growth and development through challenging objectives;
(c) Allow change to take place;
(d) Encourage new ideas, thoughts and some experimentations;
(e) Allow diverse thinking and initiative;
(f) Accept mistakes as lessons for the future;
(g) Grow more talented managers internally through promotion and career growth;
(h) Create new alignments by translating core values into organisational goals, strategies and practices.

Companies seeking to build a sound corporate culture should generally follow these guidelines. Individual companies may make some changes in their approach based on corporate philosophy, resource base, people policy and staffing pattern.

SHOULD CORPORATE CULTURE CHANGE

Corporate culture is built over years of operation. Should it change ever or after sometime? What does business dynamics say? Eight guidelines prescribed above clearly indicate that corporate culture is not a static phenomenon.

If corporate culture may change, then when should it change and who should change it? The obvious answer is that the change has to be engineered by the CEO. The CEO may initiate culture change because he brings with him a new vision, business philosophy, systems and values for giving new direction to the company—its revenue, profitability and growth. This is best illustrated by the GE story.

Cultural Revolution at GE

The General Electric Company (GE) was incorporated in 1978 as The Edison Electric Light Company. Over the long period of its history, its leadership has changed many times during the process of its evolution and growth. In 1972, when Reginald Jones took over as Chairman and CEO, its culture was well established.

Jones described GE as a family: "We enjoy each other. We don't lose many in the family of GE.... We are so supportive of each other. We try desperately to save an individual who has failed by placing him in a job that better matches his capacities.... We save many people."

Jones did not make any attempt to revolutionise GE's culture. He worked "with the grain." He managed to turn around a financially troubled company into a financially sound enterprise. Nine years later, he handed over the company to a very different kind of CEO, legendary Jack Welch.

Welch was also a product of GE culture. But, unlike Jones, Welch decided to go against the grain. His business philosophy was that GE's business units should be in the first, or, at least, second position in their respective categories. He started developing new rules, systems and procedures. In other words, he undertook the challenging job of changing GE's culture.

Welch described communicating his vision across the organisation as "without question, the toughest job". Welch had more tough job to do in implementation. He shed unsuccessful business units and unneeded people so much so that he earned the nickname "Neutron Jack." More important, he started shaking up the huge GE organisation. He used many methodologies for this.

By 1992, Welch began to shed his "Neutron Jack" image by publicly announcing, in GE's Annual Report, his commitment to human values. He said that trust and respect between managers and workers were essential. He added that the managers should have "the self-confidence to empower others and behave in a boundaryless fashion."[12]

During Welch's tenure, GE's business grew significantly.

The GE story demonstrates that corporate culture can be changed or reoriented, even if not revolutioned, for achieving newer organisational objectives and goals. But, for this, the company must have the most apt CEO.

A WORD FOR MANAGERS

Jack Welch was one of his kind. If you want to change, let alone revolutionise, the culture of your company, first become a Jack Welch.

What this means for vast majority of managers is that do not try to change the culture of your company. Become part of it and help the process of building a sound organisational culture.

If you strongly feel that some aspect of the culture requires redefinition or refinement for better achievement of organisational objectives, be part of the redevelopment process from within the culture, and, not as an external agent, i.e., do not try to impose change. This may misfire. This is a risk no "rational" manager should take. The trade-off may be very high.

Pater Drucker reminds us that "culture—no matter how defined—is singularly persistent." He feels that changing culture may not necessarily change people's behaviour much less produce the desired results. So, self-discipline yourself and move with caution.

Remember: *You are not a jungle fighter; you are only a manager—one in the stream*. You are governed by the flow of the stream.

9

Man Management

Man management is almost an everyday issue in business management. It exists at all levels—induction-level, middle-level, senior level and CEO or top management level. It helps or hinders productivity depending on how it is handled.

Good man management should follow from the corporate culture of the company particularly in those companies which give high priority to people behaviour and values like P&G, Microsoft, Nokia, Wipro, Biocon. Such companies are constantly focusing on man management principles for grooming and developing people.

Man management is a broad or inclusive term. Correctly interpreted, complete man management has three components: reading people, managing people daily and developing people (See figure).

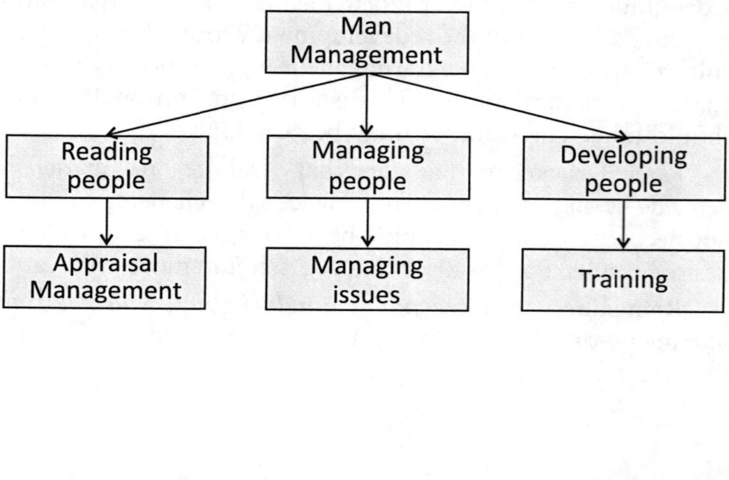

MAN MANAGEMENT: THREE COMPONENTS

Logically or sequentially, the man management process should work like this:

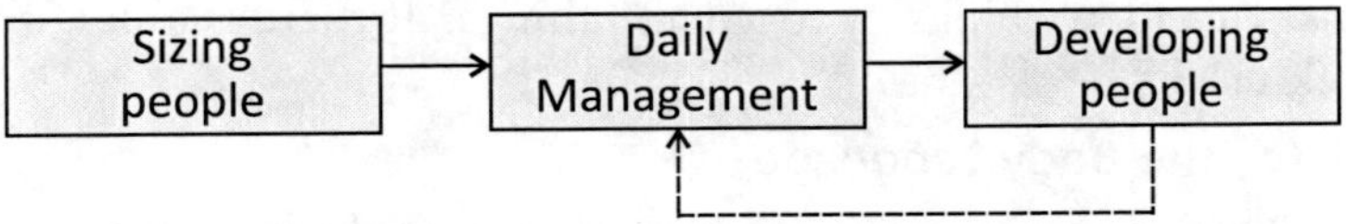

READING PEOPLE

Mark McCromack, chairman IMG, has rightly said: "Business situations always come down to people situations. And, the more—and, the sooner—I know about the person I am dealing with, the more effective I am going to be." So, knowing or reading or sizing up people—be the juniors, peers, seniors or the boss—should be the starting point for proper man management.

Reading people is one of the toughest things be it in life or business and management. If there were prescribed rules or methods, those might have been taught in classrooms or business schools. However, if we are in business, we have to deal with people, and, have to read or know their behavioural pattern.

Some leads can certainly be thought of which can be followed to understand workplace people.

Ten leads can be used:

1. Observe patiently
2. Listen carefully
3. Watch the body language
4. Talk less
5. Use your insight
6. Shake your ego
7. Assess the situation
8. Be discreet
9. Be dispassionate
10. Complete the reading

Observe Patiently

Observe the person you are trying to read or understand—the way he(she) is dressed up, his(her) personality, postures, the way he(she) delivers. All these speak a lot about him(her).

Listen Carefully

Listen to the person carefully—what he is saying and what he is not saying. Seek meaning in what he is saying. Is he trying to say too few things or too many things? If there is ambiguity, seek clarity.

Watch the Body Language

Is the person hesitating or wavering? Does he look nervous or confident? The body language of the person reveals much more than his spoken words. So, the body language is a good pointer.

Talk Less

One of the best ways to read or size up a person is to allow him(her) to talk. More he(she) talks, more he(she) reveals himself(herself). You may try to keep him(her) on the track; but, otherwise, talk as less as you can and listen more.

Use Your Insight

Use your insight more than you talk. "*Insight*" *essentially implies the power of observation.* Insight and shrewdness sometimes go together.

Sharp or shrewd insight into people can be effected through strong power of observation. In most business or management situations, there is "usually more to see than meets the eye."—various people factors operating "below the surface." These can be seen only with insight or hindsight.

Shake Your Ego

Each one of us has some ego. Ego means bias; it narrows down the scope of free expression or communication. Ego also has a positive side—the urge or determination to fulfill or achieve something.

If one is trying to read people, it is good to shake ego and be unbiased and receptive. This may also help to read the ego of the other person.

Many feel that it is easier to read people better with strong ego because that reveals the person faster. Persons with weaker ego may be difficult to read because they may be more self-concealing. In either case, you can read the person better without your ego.

Assess the Situation

The situation or environment or surrounding is an important factor. The person may be influenced by the situation.

So, assess the situation to read him(her) better, i.e., how much his(her) behaviour is influenced by the situation. Psychoanalysts have found that people more often reveal their innermost selves in the most innocent of situations, that is, without any external influence.

Therefore, assess the situation well to read the person well.

Do not Use Discretion

Remember that you have to pose as a passive member or partner in the game of reading people. So, do not use your discretion or try to influence with your belief or thinking. This provides the ideal environment for the person to reveal himself(herself).

Be Dispassionate

This is an extension of not using your discretion. Be dispassionate and keep yourself calm.

Sometimes, the other person may appear emotional or excited prompted by the present situation or immediate past development. If you keep your calmness, you can also help him(her) to come to his(her) usual self and express himself(herself) more dispassionately or objectively.

Complete the Reading

You should now be in a position or ready to read the person you are trying to know or assess. It is a mental process—putting different leads together to complete reading of people.

Appraisal Management

A more structured way of sizing up or assessing people or managers is through appraisal management.

Various forms of appraisal systems are in vogue in various organisations. But, all these forms may broadly fall into three categories in descending order of objectivity; first, rating or ranking in numerical terms by giving marks or scores to various traits of personality and performance; second, gradation in terms of "poor," "good" (or "very good"), "excellent" or "outstanding" through analytical performance review; and, third, purely narrative or descriptive evaluation by the evaluating officer(s).

Efforts by the consultants (this is an area which is a green pasture for the consultants) and the concerned managements to make the appraisal system totally objective and fool-proof have not produced desired results principally because of two reasons. First, is the inescapable human bias or the element of subjectivity (all evaluators are human beings). Second, dilution of the prescribed evaluation criteria like qualifications, merit, seniority, etc., by superimposition of factors (not directly connected with appraisal) on these criteria. These factors are certain "expedients" which exist in almost all organisations in some forms and in different degrees. And, the actual appraisal system in practice in the organisation is the outcome of interplay of the formal evaluation criteria and the expedients. Some become beneficiaries of the system; some become victims; some remain in the neutral zone.[1]

In professional and progressive companies, the expedients are few. In fact, more professional and progressive a company is, less are the expedients. In such companies, appraisals of managers are discussed with them and areas of improvement identified or suggested. This is an important step towards good man management and developing people. Companies like GE, HUL, Infosys, ITC are good examples of this.

MANAGING PEOPLE

Reading people makes the way for managing people. If you have correctly understood a person, you have half managed him(her).

Managing people has three aspects or dimensions: The objective, art of managing people and the outcome.

The Objective

We start with Stephen Covey's outlines of approaches or strategies which individuals/managers adopt to manage and get something from another person. Covey categorises five approaches or methods: Win/Win, Win/Lose, Lose/Win, Lose/Lose, and Win:

1. **Win/Win:** This approach states that a mutually beneficial solution is the best solution because both parties feel that they are winners and win or success of one person is not achieved at the expense of the other;
2. **Win/Lose:** This method means that one party has to lose for the other party to win as in football, cricket and lawsuits;
3. **Lose/Win:** This approach represents people who are quite willing to please or appease others and deriving satisfaction from acceptance or popularity;
4. **Lose/Lose:** This results when two win/lose parties become "stubborn, vindictive" and blind to situations with the only objective that the other party must lose;
5. **Win:** does not matter whether the other party wins or loses so long as you get what you want, i.e., win.[2]

Win/win outcomes are easier when both the parties are positive and proactive and adopt ways to show that the other party can benefit by cooperating with each other. In other words, this is a cooperative or collaborative result. Win is also a good approach because it does not require that the other person has necessarily to lose. There may also be some element of positiveness. Because you work with the same colleagues (peers or seniors) everyday, both win/win and win may be welcome. But, in today's competitive business situations and the race for survival and growth, win/lose may often be a reality.

The objective in corporate man management is to keep 'win' common—be it win/win or win/lose.

Art of Managing People

The art of managing people should be guided by the objectives.

In trying to manage people, we must remember some natural attitudinal human factors. Six important behavioural factors or characteristics are:

(a) **People are Creatures of Habit:** So, change in behaviour or attitude should be slow or gradual;
(b) **People will always Complain**; take it easy or dispassionately;
(c) **We Tend to deflate Others**, i.e., criticise others;
(d) **We make mistakes**—that should be accepted;
(e) **People Seek Attention and Recognition**—this should be kept in mind;
(f) **We all need Motivation to Perform:** there are many ways to motivate.[3]

If you recognise and take account of these factors, you are in a more strategic position to manage other people. The situations or diversities can, however, be many.

Managing Difficult People

On random basis, colleagues we deal with can be classified into three types or categories: cooperative or friendly, amenable and difficult. Cooperative and amenable colleagues can be managed easily. Management problem arises with difficult people.

Difficult people may be your juniors, peers, seniors or boss. Let us keep the boss apart. Managing the boss, including a difficult boss, has been discussed in Ch. 5. That may be referred.

Vis-à-vis your junior, you are the boss and you have to get or extract work from him(her). If your junior is difficult, you may counter by being difficult with him(her). But, this may not serve your purpose. *Difficult vs. difficult = deadlock*. The work is not done. You may write him(her) off. Then for all practical purposes, you lose a person. You may surrender him(her). This is an extreme step. This also creates HR problem.

Remember, not all bosses use an iron hand. This is almost out of fashion today. Instead, you may work on your junior. Try to understand the reason for his(her) being difficult. You may be able to mend him(her) to "less difficult" or "not difficult." You do not lose anything. Instead, the junior, you and the organisation gain out of it.

Sailing with a difficult peer or senior is always tricky or delicate. This may sometimes mean tight rope walking.

Today's peer can be tomorrow's senior and today's senior can be tomorrow's boss. You are not the only person in the corporate power-play. So, remember this and avoid lose/lose situation or outcome as far as you can.

Sometimes, you and your peer may be temperamentally different, but, this need not always carry to or reflect in office matters. I, as GM, Bombay, MMTC, had a Finance Associate (DGM) who was temperamentally different from me, but, this did not block us from agreeing on official issues or decisions because professionally we had almost the same wave length. So, personality difference need not result in decision difference. This should be remembered to carry forward.

Inter-personal Relations

Man management often boils down to inter-personal relations. It is built over a period of time—sometimes short period, sometimes longer period. But, such relation can swing with circumstances.

Here is a good illustration of this from my stint as GM, MMTC, Bombay. During this period, we also had a CGM, MMTC, Bombay (Mehra). We were colleagues earlier and had good personal relations. But, problem started in Bombay. In Dir. (RG's perception, Mehra was a slow mover. He had more confidence in me. So he was directly involving me for disposal of all business work. Mehra was slowly turning against me.

We used to have monthly business review meeting in CO (Delhi). I used to regularly attend this meeting. During one of the meetings, Mehra wanted to visit Delhi. He asked me not to go. I stayed back. In the review meeting, Bombay's presentation/ performance was lacking Dir. (RG) openly expressed his displeasure. It was embarrassing for Mehra. He turned more against me for no fault of mine.

Some changes took place in CO. Dir (RG)'s term was over and he left. Chairman (SVS) also left. Dir (SKA) became the Acting CMD and later became the regular CMD. Mehra started aligning with SKA, and, for some unknown reason (not the Mehra factor alone), SKA never liked me. So, I started being at the receiving end.

The lesson from the story is: to survive or tide over deteriorating inter-personal relation with your immediate senior, you need corporate continuity. This is most often lacking in the public sector. If this was private sector, things would have been different.

Building Cooperative Relationship

Building cooperative colleague relationship is mostly a textbook wish or slogan. It seldom happens in reality. Even if it happens, it is at a price. More realistic is workable relationship. We may also call it corporate relationship. The show must go on. This is important.

Corporate or office relationship can often change with slightest provocation. A transfer or a foreign posting comes and cooperative relationship suddenly turns into competitive relationship. Who will get the posting? Irrespective of who gets the posting, the relationship becomes sour because one person has not got it.

All this, however, does not mean that cooperative relationship does not have any place in corporate man management. It certainly has. We can always work towards building positive relationship with colleagues. We may follow some tips or steps for relationship building or furthering relationship. Six important tips are:

(a) Take continuing interest in the other person as an official colleague;

(b) Attend to all small things concerning him(her) like taking or returning a call or wishing on birthday;

(c) Always keep the lines of communication and dialogue open with him(her) even if there are disagreements;

(d) Deliver anything and everything you have promised;

(e) Volunteer assistance if he(she) is in some problem or difficulty;

(f) Demonstrate your integrity in whatever you do vis-a-vis him(her).[4]

The Outcome

As mentioned earlier, win/win, as in all successful business negotiations, is the ideal outcome. But, a manager may be driven to win/lose because of survival of the fittest. Lose/lose is the road to sink or perish.

For a manager, if the objective and outcome match, he(she) is successful in his(her) man management programme. If there is mismatch, he(she) should review it periodically, ideally weekly, to ascertain the reasons or shortfalls, and, take necessary corrective course. This is essential both for his(her) stress management and productivity.

The organisation or top management also has a role to play in this. They should create and maintain a people environment in the company and encourage managers to manage people the right way. This also implies the need for developing people.

MANAGING STRESS FOR MANAGERS

Every manager has 'stress' as his companion—not a welcome or desirable, but, unavoidable companion. Every individual has to live with some stress in both personal and professional life. Some stress can be foreseen and planned for.

But, some stress cannot be anticipated and, therefore, cannot be prepared for. Here is an example. It is 5.30 pm and you are winding up and planning to leave for home. Your boss calls you and says: "Something urgent. Can you please do this in half-an-hour and give me?" Your stress begins and tension starts developing.

Is Some Stress Good?

According to many including practising managers, some stress is good. It keeps you alert and maintains pressure on you to perform. Without some stress and pressure, life could be too much of a routine, if not becoming full of boredom. That is why some have said: *Stress is 60% necessary evil, 40% unnecessary evil.*

Stress upto a certain point or level may be good for two reasons: First, stress does not allow you to sit idle. It drives you to perform and be productive. It helps you to keep up certain level of productivity and output. If you have no pressure building on you, your productivity will fail. Second, if you are turned or accustomed to a certain level of stress driving you performance, you tend to become uncomfortable with a level of stress above or below your asking or optimum level.

Managing Stress

If, however, stress exceeds your 'comfort level,' it has to be managed. Stress should not overtake you.

As responsibilities increase, stress level also increases. Usually, there is a direct correlation between the two. So, a manager should prepare himself(herself) accordingly.

The first step is to identify the sources of stress. Three common sources are:

(a) *Job ambiguity*: Lack of job clarity can lead to avoidable stress;

(b) *Relationship stress*: Lack of clearly defined working relationship with boss, peers, seniors can result in unnecessary stress;

(c) *Personal problems*: Problems created mostly by the manager himself at home or office can create stress.

Every manager should try to identify the major sources of stress, and, take steps for controlling or managing stress. For sources 'a' and 'b', he(she) should seek intervention or guidance from the boss or management for resolving issues.

Proper labour-leisure balancing (sports, pleasure, entertainment) considerably helps controlling stress. There are also other ways (counselling) for relieving stress. Every manager should seek ways best suited to his(her) personal characteristics and professional life.

DEVELOPING PEOPLE

Proper man management requires development of people. People development, in turn, helps to improve the quality of man management.

One of the essential jobs of a manager and CEO is to develop his(her) people. This helps him(her) to have a well-developed team for performance of tasks and producing results.

Good Training

Training is one of the most important methods for developing people resource.

All of us require training for improving our management skills. Managers at all levels go for training for upgrading themselves. While in MMTC, I was sent for advanced management training (AMP) organised by Government of India (in India and Germany). One of MMTC's Chairmen attended top management programme in Harvard Business School. HUL has a policy of imparting training—mostly on-the-job—to its newly recruited executives/managers.

Training helps people to learn and remember things better. Scholz has mentioned different ways people remember things with different degrees of remembrance. These are mentioned in the table below.

Different Ways People Remember Things

Way to remember	How much is remembered
By reading	10%
By hearing	20%
By seeing	30%
By hearing and seeing	50%
By what they say	70%
By what they say as they do	90%

Training helps both "hearing" and "seeing", and sometimes also "doing" (on-the-job training) for people in addition to "reading."[5]

Most of the companies organise or participate in training programmes for three reasons: first, for development of management skills of managers/staff; second, for spending funds from budget allocations for training; and, third, request by management institutes for nominating managers in their management development programmes (MDPs). Skill development should be the primary factor.

Unfortunately in many companies, both in the public and private sectors, second and third reasons dominate with less focus on real skill development. We shall state here the story of the course attender narrated by a HRD professional.[6]

A chief executive was being introduced to the executives of the company:

"I am Chatterjee, the plant manager," said the first one.

"I am Bhatnagar, the finance manager," said the second.

"I am Murthy, the marketing manager," said the third.

"I am Das, the audit manager," said the fourth.

The fifth kept silent for some time. When the chief executive looked at him, he said, "Sir, I am the course attender" (like the meeting attenders in public sector and the government). He explained to the bewildered chief that different managers were nominated for different training programmes. Because of exigencies of work, some were unable to attend. He had to substitute for such executives. This resulted in his attending one programme or the other nine months a year.

This story may be an exaggeration, but, it is symbolic or typical of what happens in many organisations today. In the Annual Report, such companies state that they have budgeted and spend so much funds for training and development. This is cosmetic.

Training at Hitachi

Hitachi has a multi-level training module for complete development of human resources.[7]

It starts with induction training. All management trainees undergo induction programme for two months. The company circulates its basic philosophy document: "The Guiding spirit of Hitachi." This highlights three principles: sincerity, spirit of forward looking optimism and harmony. The principle of harmony focuses on collective or participative decision making and management.

The complete Hitachi training model is depicted below:

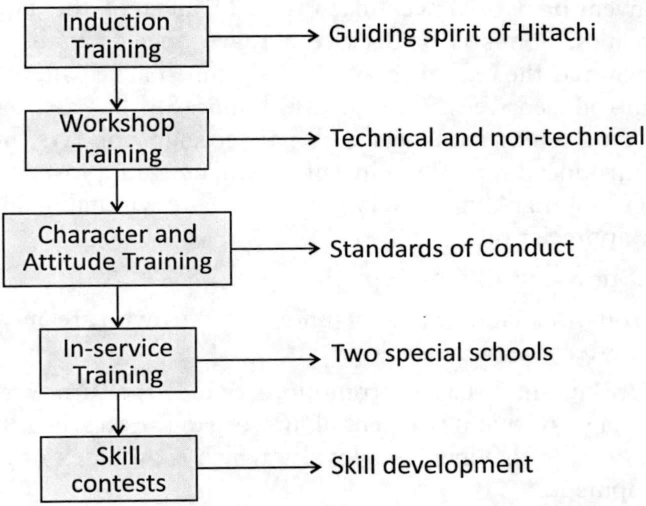

Firestone has developed a successful participative model of training. Other people-centric companies have developed their own models.

More Ways to Develop People

Some feel that structured programmes—training or mentorship—are not always as effective as informal mentoring. This is the experience of some managers.[8] I, however, feel that structured programmes and informal mentoring have their own merits. This is what my experience tells me.

Two methods which are used by almost all companies for developing people are:

1. Incentive system
2. Promotion/career growth

Incentive System

Training motivates people indirectly; incentives motivate people directly.

Paid holidays (domestic) and annual bonus are common in many companies. These are like conventional incentives.

More progressive companies have introduced some unconventional or newer incentives. In most of the Japanese companies, bonus is paid twice a year—once at mid-summer and again at the end of the year. Long time back, Bata in India had introduced weekly production bonus. SBI has a scheme of rewarding senior managers with paid foreign holidays. Infosys had introduced its unique incentive scheme—Employees' stock option (ESOP). Almost every manager made windfall gain from stock appreciation.

Promotion and Career Growth

Promotion and career planning and growth are measures for long-term people development.

Periodic merit-based promotions reduce the turnover ratio of managers which is essential for organisation's health and stability. This also increases loyalty which is an index of people development.

Long-term career planning and growth can create life-long loyalty which is the best index of people development. Here are some examples. Dr. Ashoke Ganguly of HUL joined at induction level and grew to the position of chairman. This is a classic example. Y.C. Daveshwar, ex-chairman, ITC, is another very good example. Jack Welch, legendary ex-chairman, GE, also rose from the ranks.

People Development in Japanese Companies

Japanese companies like Sony, Honda, Matsushita—all symbolise the people development approach.

Most of us are aware that Japan does not have any usable natural resources. They consider people as their natural resource. A senior Japanese executive puts it like this: "... our only natural resource is the hard work of our people."

This explains the people commitment of Japanese companies. Some call it obsession. The Japanese people approach or obsession may be summarised as below:

	for one year	is to plant seed
To plan	for ten years	is to plant tree
	for a lifetime	is to develop a MAN

Man Management, HRM an HRD

In conclusion, one issue may be raised: Is human resource management (HRM) more important or human resource development (HRD) is more important? Both are intrinsically related, but, which should be more important for a company—managing people (HRM) or developing people (HRD)? Our analysis so far has shown that, to manage people in the right way, people should be developed well. In other words, focus on HRM and HRD should be balanced or commensurate with each other.

In reality, in most companies, *managers are less managed; they are more driven*—driven to perform their tasks. This approach must change for every company which has long-term planning or perspective in view.

Man Management and Managerial SWOT

SWOT analysis is conventionally done for companies for policy making and strategy formulation. But, this can be usefully extended to analysis of managers for man management and development.

SWOT analysis of managers should start with annual appraisal reports (ARs). This should be the basis for SWOT analysis. Strengths of the manager should be highlighted to him(her). Weaknesses should be identified, explained to the manager and those should be worked on by both the manager and the management. Opportunities open to him(her) should be mentioned in terms of likely incentives, promotion and career growth. Threats should also be indicated primarily in the form competition from peers. This completes the SWOT analysis.

Highly professional companies (HUL) are already doing SWOT analysis of their managers in their own designated ways. These are not explicitly called SWOT analysis, but, these are so in form or substance.

Many more companies can adopt the same approach or method and proudly announce in their Annual Reports that they are carrying out man management and development in more innovative ways.

PEOPLE-FIRST AND BUSINESS OUTCOME

If we can activate everyone in the organisation to deliver to their strengths, we can harness "the sum of collective individuality to co-create the shift to prosperity for all." This is a bold move. But, it can work.

This requires that the organisation builds a culture that seeks to understand employees beyond their superficial personae and personalises employee expectations, experiences and ambitions. This implies, in other words, a strong people-centric organisational culture.

This will lead us to conclude that "organisations are as good as the people they have." If this really happens, this may be the best way for transformative growth.[9]

10

Managing Time

Time is like a river; you cannot touch the same water twice, because the flow that has passed will never pass again...

—A.P.J. Abdul Kalam

Work expands to fill time available for its completion....

—Parkinson's Law

"Go, Sir, gallop, and don't forget that the world was made in six days," wrote Napoleon to one of his aides. "You can ask me for anything you like except time," he said. Management experts and practitioners only echo this. But, the issue persists.

HOW IMPORTANT IS TIME MANAGEMENT?

Every one of us—no matter how rich or poor, young or old, intelligent or ignorant, successful or struggling—has the same 365 days a year, 24 hours a day, 60 minutes an hour and 60 seconds a minute.

With 365 days a year, let us see what it means if you are asking for a day off:

- There are 365 days per year available for work.
- There are 52 weeks per year in which you have two days off per week, leaving 261 days available for work.
- Since you spend 16 hours each day away from work, you have used up 170 days leaving only 91 days available.
- With 1/2 hour's lunch break each day, you have used up another 23 days leaving only 68 days available.

- A gracious holiday of 31 days by way of Earned Leave is allowed to you. This leaves you with only 37 days available.
- You are off for 16 closed holidays per year. So your available working time is down to 21 days.
- You enjoy very casually 14 holidays per year as Casual Leave, thus leaving 7 days available.
- You are generously allowed 15 minutes grace period every day thus you have used easily another seven days a year.

And, still you want to take a day off!

(If sick leaves are added, you will be clearly running a debit account!)

This may seem to be an exaggeration of time scheduling or time counting, but, it signals to a lot of truth about time management or time rationing.

Time is inelastic and not elastic; you cannot stretch or expand time. You cannot store time; it is perishable. Time lost is lost for ever.

According to many, of all the resources of production, time is the most precious resource.

The success of a manager or executive, depends, to a large extent, on how well he(she) manages his(her) time. This applies to managers at all levels. But, this becomes more important for a manager as he(she) moves up the ladder, because, there is more demand on his(her) time. Do the managers realise this and practise proper time management?

HOW TIME IS MANAGED

In Sweden, a study was conducted to find out what managers or executives were doing and how they were spending their time. The study was done among twelve Sweden chief executives. The study revealed that working of these executives consisted of hundreds of "small blocks of time." None of these executives had more than twenty uninterrupted minutes during the day.[1]

Another study looked into how managers manage including time management. The study analysed the observations and findings in Europe and North America. The analysis or the study results threw light on number of myths about the job of the manager and time management. The study found the work pace of both the CEOs and shop-floor managers as "unrelenting." The chief executives met a steady stream of callers, with appointment or without it, and received mails from the moment they arrived in the morning until they left in the evening. Coffee breaks and lunches were inevitably work related, and ever-present subordinates seem to usurp any free moment".[2] Half of the activities of the CEOs lasted less than 9 minutes and only 10 per cent lasted more than an hour.

J.P. Robinson of University of Maryland directs "Americans' Use of Time" project. According to his study, "a large segment of Americans say they feel a significant crunch—and, the more time-needy they feel, the stronger their desire to take time off." In his survey, Robinson found that 50 per cent of more than 1000 managers surveyed, told that they would be willing to trade a full day's pay for an extra day off each week.[3] Time pressures are making managers re-think about labour (work)-leisure parity.

We give here a different perspective to how managers at senior level plan their time spending or time management—an Indian perspective. The example is of how a Board level executive allocates or spends his time between policy or strategy and operations or routine. When I was Economic Advisor in MMTC, I asked one of the directors (Director A.C. Bose) how he allocates or spends his time between policy/strategy and operations/routines. Ideally or professionally a Board level executive (director) should spend 80 per cent of his(her) time on policy/strategy matters and 20 per cent on operations/routine issues. But, Director (Bose) told me: "I spend 80 per cent of my time on routines and 20 per cent on policy and strategy matters." This is inappropriate. This is misallocation or misuse of time.

In MMTC, many CEOs or CMDs had many ways of spending or managing time. One case is of CMD S.K. Agarwal. He almost routinely used to sit late. Obviously, either he did not plan his time properly or his productivity was low wasting time on "file culture." In the same MMTC, CMD SVS Raghavan had exactly the opposite way of spending or managing time. I shall talk about Raghavan's time management later.

Sometimes, executives, senior executives and even CEOs/CMDs, particularly in the public sector, sit late because of other interests or reasons. I do not want to elaborate on this. May be you can guess.

Is such late sitting necessary? If you ask me—as one who has worked in senior positions in both public and private sectors—I would say "No." It actually depends more on the management style or functioning of individual manager/senior manager. This includes time wasting.

COMMON TIME WASTERS

There are many time wasters. We should know them.

Where Time Goes

Alec Mackenzie has studied time management for over a decade. He has interviewed managers at hundreds of companies around the world. He concludes that reason for times scarcity and waste "are remarkably similar across management levels, industries and national borders."

Five biggest time wasters, according to his study, are:

1. Telephone interruptions
2. Inadequate planning
3. Trying to do too much
4. Drop-in (unscheduled) visitors
5. Crisis management[4]

Telephone interruptions are very common—faced by almost every manager. They are a necessary evil—they are required. But, every manager should know when and how to close a telephone call on time, otherwise, it becomes a time-waster. He(she) should also do screening of unimportant calls which can be availed. It is a tricky management job and a test of your telephonic skill.

Managers often suffer from *inadequate planning* of their day and work. This includes deciding which work is more important, and, which is less important, that is prioritise the day's work schedule. Otherwise, work becomes clueless or directionless.

Trying to do too much often results from inadequate planning of work. As a manager moves up the ladder, demand for his(her) time increases, and, there is a tendency to do too much work in too less time. This leads to or results in time leakage.

Drop-in or unscheduled visitors often upset work schedules of managers. They may not always refuse meeting such visitors, but, they should screen them and also know how to handle them. One good way is to spend few minutes with a visitor, thank him(her) for the visit, and, stand up and say "Excuse me, I have a meeting to attend."

Crisis management is not a daily or routine disruption but, it should be recognised. Crisis management, as commonly happens, means dealing with a crisis after it occurs, that is, reactive management, and, not proactive preventive management. Crisis in business is often man-made or "self-inflicted" (except the pure unpredictable or accidental ones), and, once it occurs, time management goes out of the window. When, in the 1980s, Johnson & Johnson's Tylenol packages were injected with cyanide, time schedules of most of its senior managers and CEO/Chairman Burke's went completely disarray. In 1984, the gas leakage in Union Carbide's Bhopal plant in India (was it man-made, that is because of lack of disaster planning by the management?) completely disrupted time management of the company's top management for months.

Personal Time Wasters

Managers often blame external factors like meetings, drop-in visitors and telephone calls to be time wasters. But, studies have shown that the "man within" or the internal factors are the major time wasters. Here is a list of ten such wasters:

1. Lack of self-discipline
2. Indecisiveness
3. Insecurity
4. Personal habits
5. Excesses
6. Going round a point
7. Overcautious approach
8. Unnecessary paperwork
9. Procrastination
10. Obsession with routines

TIME MISMANAGEMENT

Time mismanagement is an extension of time wasting. We can even say that time mismanagement is worse than time wasting because it is more deliberate.

There are managers, and, even senior managers, who mismanage time. To exemplify this, let me mention about Birla Copper (now Hindalco Industries) where I had worked as a full time advisor.

How was time management in Birla Copper? If you ask me frankly, time management in Birla Copper was not much different from that in MMTC, a public sector enterprise. In fact, management systems, including time management, in large private sector companies and performing public sector companies are not very different. You don't see much of time planning or consciousness as you see in very professional companies, like as I saw in HUL. However, in Birla Copper, time was managed generally well except in one segment.

This was the segment or section headed by D.D. Jalan, VP. In this section, time was badly mismanaged; and, it was all because of him. He had a tendency to sit late everyday—usually till 8 PM. People who sit late like this remain occupied (posing busy) with mostly unproductive work, or, rather, with no 'work' at all. Jalan would keep managers reporting to him waiting indefinitely in a city like Bombay (Mumbai). You can imagine the plight of people who have to sit/wait upto 8 clock in the evening, and, travel long distances to reach home. They must be cursing him, and, very justifiably so.

Once I was involved in a late sitting/meeting incident with him. I should tell you about his request for meeting him late, and, my reaction/response to it. He was in Delhi. He called me and suggested that we meet at 9 pm at the Birla guest house. He had the whole day to meet and talk to me. Anyway, it could not have been serious official matter. Then, he would not have waited till 9 at might. But, that was his style of time management.

Anyway, I reached the guest house at 8.45 pm. I should tell you that I am very particular about time planning or time management. I usually reach 15 minutes earlier for meetings.

I waited till 9.30 pm. Neither he came nor there was any call/message from him. At 9.30 pm, I wrote a small note: "Dear Jalanji, I feel we should have better time management." I wrote the note and left. I hope he got the message. But, such people don't easily learn or change. *It is a genes problem.*

Jalan is only one example, and, of course, a glaring one. There are Jalans in many companies. Through their time mismanagement, they spoil the work culture and vitiate the organisational environment. *More senior the manager, more is the adverse effect of his(her) time mismanagement on the organisation.*

TIME PLANNING

If there are time mismanagers or time wasters, there are also time planners. We should learn from them.

According to many, Peter Drucker is "the most accomplished time manager." In his illuminating book *The Effective Executive*, he explains the principle of good time management.

Let us see how Drucker manages his time. He works as a professor, consultant and author. His time planning or time budgeting is like this: About 50 days in a year for teaching, 50 days in a year on consultancy and rest of the time on his authorship or study. He works without any staff to assist him. He notes down demands on his time on pointed mail-back cards. These contain meticulous planning and managing of his time slots.[5]

Mark McCormack is a "legendarily successful entrepreneur" and an accomplished time manager. Let us see his method of time management in his own words: "The one thing people know me best attribute to me the most is an ability to manage my time efficiently."[6]

"I begin by viewing a week as 168 hours, and, I schedule time for relaxation and rest as well as work. I force myself to have time to relax whether it be to play tennis, read the morning paper, take a nap in the office, or simply to do nothing—to free my mind from any sort of work-oriented thoughts or decisions. To make sure I have this time, I programme these non-work activities into my schedule. If I know, for instance, that my first time commitment is at 7 a.m., I would rather get up at 5 a.m. and spend an hour reading, relaxing and exercising than get up at 6 a.m. and have to rush to my first appointment without having time to myself. My schedule that day would therefore begin at 5 a.m."[7]

"I always perceive my business activity or commitment as a function of the time I have allotted for it.... If a meeting is starting in one hour and I have decided there are ten things I want to accomplish before that meeting begins, I will do whatever is necessary to fit all ten things into that hour. It may mean making a phone call a lot shorter than I would have liked, or, dashing off a note rather than a letter, but, by challenging myself this way, by fitting activities into smaller and smaller segments. I have over the years developed an almost minute-by-minute awareness of how I am spending my time."[8]

Jack Welch, Chairman and CEO of General Electric, is a successful, and, a model, time planner. He has one of the most demanding jobs in the world. But, he says, "If someone tells me, 'I am working 90 hours a week,' I would say, 'you are doing something terribly wrong. I go skiing on the weekend. I go out with my buddies on Friday and party. You have got to do the same or you've got a bad deal. Put down a list of things you are doing that make you work 90 hours, and, ten of them have to be nonsense, or else somebody else has got to do them for you.'"[9] So, his advice is: cut out the nonsense; and, take *time* to *make* time for yourself. If you try, you can do it.

Let me now give some examples of Indian CEOs/chairmen/CMDs. One good example is P.L. Tandon, first Indian chairman of Hindustan Lever Limited (HUL). Tandon would arrive at office five to fifteen minutes before 9.30 AM (office starting time) and leave by 6 PM (office hour ends at 5.30 PM). He had set the culture or precedent and others were following. His time management philosophy was: If you cannot complete your day's work during the stipulated hours, you should review or check your productivity level.

Another good example is SVS Raghavan, CMD of MMTC. Raghavan would come to office at 9 AM (office starts at 9.30

AM). By 9.30 AM, his desk is clear. He has disposed off all papers/files on his desk, and, he is free to meet people and ready for official meeting. He would leave office by 6 PM (office closes at 5.30 PM), and, would expect every manager and staff to have by that time. *It saves both energy and electricity.*

Bhupinder Singh was another good time planner and time manager. He was Director, MMTC and later CMD, STC. He had also set his time schedule properly and managed his time so well that it would appear that he always had free time for managers and visitors.

MANAGE YOUR TIME

The time planners show that you can manage your time if you plan.

In life and work, there is always need to find or take time to manage many things. Let us look at these:

Take time to *think*	: It is the way to know *what is possible*
Take time to *plan*	: It is important for *effectiveness*
Take time to *build*	: It leads to improved *ideas*
Take time to *perform*	: It increases *productivity*
Take time to *delegate*	: It develops *others*
Take time to *excel*	: It improves *efficiency*
Take time to *relax*	: It reduces *stress*
Take time to *play*	: It helps to become *creative*
Take time to *read*	: It keeps you *update*
Take time to *train*	: It allows to *delegate*
Take time to *trust*	: It builds good *relation*
Take time to *recognise*	: It is a great *motivator*
Take time to *encourage*	: It boosts *morale*

All these have priorities; some have higher priorities. Some of these make conflicting demands on time sharing. You have to find ways to resolve these conflicts and strike optimal time sharing or allocation.

In corporate life, there is conflicting demand for time between 'labour' (work) and leisure. There is a constant search for labour-leisure parity. The crux of this is proper time management. If the optimal level of parity between labour and leisure can be achieved, it improves your productivity, and, also increases your life expectancy or life span.

HOW WELL ARE YOU MANAGING YOUR TIME

Are you satisfied with the way you manage your time? Or, does your time keep running out on you? Are you a time-waster, time-sensitive or a time-planner? Use the time quiz to find out:

TIME QUIZ

Time use	*True*	*False*
I always apportion my day so that I can do everything I want to	☐	☐
I usually build in extra time in my schedule to cover unforeseen eventualities	☐	☐
I find it easy to refuse to participate in unimportant activities	☐	☐
I know my best times for concentration and always make good use of them	☐	☐
I do not rush through tasks in hand, but work steadily it my own pace	☐	☐
I always tend to work according to well-set schedules	☐	☐
I have an accurate and clear idea of how best to use my time	☐	☐
I work at my best when I am under pressure and have to meet a deadline	☐	☐
I almost always finish most of my task well on time	☐	☐
I meet self-imposed deadlines by sticking to specific time-slots	☐	☐
Total Trues:	☐	

0-4 trues: Time waster
4-7 trues: Time sensitive
7-10 trues: Time planner

SOME TIME SAVERS

If you are a 'time waster' or 'time sensitive,' here are some time savers for you. This will help you to manage your time better.

Thomas Horton, who worked with IBM for many years and was CEO, American Management Association (AMA), has identified, from his experience, seven time savers which work.[3] The seven time savers are:

1. Use common sense
2. Learn to listen
3. Handle routines as they come
4. Master delegation
5. Schedule your time
6. Maintain calendar integrity
7. Take charge

Use common sense: Plan and decide or determine the relative importance of your daily activities. Prioritise your activities. Deal with the more important ones during the time of the day when you are likely to be relatively free. Make unscheduled meetings brief. One practical way to do this is to walk over to the desk or office (the person) you want to talk to. This helps you to leave as soon as you are through with your meeting and avoid wastage of time.

Learn to Listen: Focus on one topic or subject at a time and concentrate fully without distractions. Then you present your point. He(she) will receive it well. This can help you to shorten the duration of meetings. The general guiding principle is: *Talk less, listen more.*

Handle routines as They Come: Routine matters should be disposed of and/or routine decisions should be taken quickly. Don't keep them pending. This will make/keep your mind free for unscheduled or unforeseen things.

Schedule Your Time: Schedule your daily and weekly activities as precisely as you can. All successful time planners and time managers like Drucker, McCormack, Welch, Tandon, Raghavan made their time schedules and followed them. So, you also make your time schedule and follow it. *Let not interruptions interrupt you.* Tackle them in your own way.

Maintain Calendar Integrity: If you make an appointment or commitment, keep it on time, think before you make the appointment or commitment. But, once you have made it, honour it. This is calendar integrity. This saves time in the long-run and helps to build trust.

Take Charge: Be proactive and objective and focus on results. Determine the means or method accordingly and implement it. Keep the hurdles away. This is the way you can best spend or manage your time. According to Horton: "This is the greatest time-saver of all."

PUT PAPERWORK ON A DIET

According to many, a desk covered with papers/files looks productive—at least to the eye. But, according to Lee Grossman, author of *Fat Paper*, people 'overpaper' for the same reasons they overeat—insecurity, fear and the feeling that something is lacking. This is a bad habit or practice. The truth is: *unnecessary paperwork is an evil.* Shun it.

Here are some ways to cut paperwork:

1. **Encourage Face Contact:** Avoid a slip or memo if the points can be made in persons;
2. **Instruct People to Report Exceptions:** Not to report routine on paper or file;
3. **Explain to the Secretary What should be Kept:** Many secretaries have been taught to keep everything unless told otherwise;
4. **Encourage Staff to Search out Unnecessary/outdated forms and reports:** Destroy them;
5. **Give incentives for Cutting Paperwork:** There are ways to do it;
6. **Control the Photocopier:** Many feel that the paperwork explosion began with the invention/introduction of dry, plain paper copier; so control it.

TIME CAN BE ETERNITY

If you can really plan, you will have time under your control. "Time" for any person whether in office or at home, is how one looks at work and life:

Time is

Too fast for those
who wait,

Too slow for those
who fear,

Too long for those
who idle,

Too short for those
who work,

But for those
who plan,

Time is eternity...

So, try to plan and, make time 'eternity,' i.e., in your planning horizon. You will be able to manage time better.

11 Leadership: Ins and Outs

"Leadership" is being invisible when things are working well, but, being visible when things are going awry...

One of the tests of leadership is the ability to recognize a problem before it becomes an insurgency

—*Arnold Henry Glasow*

Situation demands a Napolean but not a Hitler—this pronounces a lot about leadership. As in war, administration and politics, so also in business and management. Corporate management depends on managers—professional managers, efficient managers and manager-leaders. The professional manager manages professionally, the efficient manager manages efficiently and, the manager-leader leads. But, what is leadership? What are the various leadership styles? Is leadership concurrent with a situation? Does leadership thrive only during contingencies? We delve into answers to some of these old but always newly posed questions (not old wine in new bottle).

WHAT IS LEADERSHIP?

There are almost as many definitions of leadership as there are scholars and writers, including management writers, who have attempted to define this. Frank Goble, in one of his bestsellers on leadership, says: "The attempt to define leadership should be a continuing effort, and, although publishers might wish that I didn't say so, this Book will already be a little obsolete before the ink is dry on the first printing. Nor will this book, nor any other book for that matter, complete the job."[1] This shows not only that the concept of leadership should be ever changing to keep pace with the dynamics of business environment, but, also that there is considerable diversity in perception by the writers about what attributes or traits constitute leadership. And rightly so. Leadership pattern cannot be fitted into a straight jacket; it can never be comprehensively defined. "Leadership," writes historian James MacGregor Burns, "is one of the most observed and least understood phenomena on earth." Indeed, if there are many told volumes on leadership, there are many more untold volumes on this.

We all, however, agree with Chambers' Dictionary that a leader is one who leads. The basic function of a leader is to lead. And, he must be seen to lead. Not like the morning walker where you do not know whether the morning walker has brought his dog for a walk or the dog has brought his master for a walk. You do not know who is leading whom. Not a very elitist illustration, but, it makes sense.

A leader should be seen not only to lead; he should also be seen to possess many other concomitant characteristics—characteristics which emerge from a synthesis of various definitions or conceptualisations. Leadership is many things in one. It is an art of inducing compliance; it is the exercise of influence; it is a differentiated role; it is goal achievement; it is a personality and its effects; it is building a loyal team at the top that speaks with one voice; it is giving directions; it is sometimes listening carefully, sometimes speaking with encouragement, and it is being tough when necessary; it is reinforcing words with commendable action; and, finally, it is being invisible when things are working well but being visible when things are going awry.

MANAGER AND LEADER

An important distinction is to be made between a manager and a leader not only in their functions, but also in their perception of organisational goals, conception of work and relations with others. Let us see an attempted comparison:

The Manager	The Leader
Goals	
• Arise out of necessities	Arise out of desires
• Deeply embedded in history & culture of organisation	Focus of goals is on the need to change
• Strategy assumes more importance than the goal	Strategy is the means to a goal
• Focusses on strategy, structure & systems	Focusses on style, staff, skills & shared goals
Conception of Work	
• Values tradition	Seeks change & new ideas
• Instinct for survival dominates need for risk	Accepts risk where opportunities & rewards are high
• Delegates cautiously	Delegates freely (has faith in people)
• Analytical methodical	Intuitive
• Maintains control over people and ideas	Encourages autonomy
• Reactive	Proactive
• Identifies totally with the organisation	Works in the organisation but can stand outside it
Relations with Others	
• Relates according to their role	Relates in a more intuitive & empathic way
• Prefers high probability of winning & low possibility of losing	Willing to risk losing if rewards for wining are high
• Communicates to subordinates indirectly through the system	Communicates directly
• Perceived by others as detached (&at times manipulative)	Attracts strong feelings of identity
• Conserves what is traditional & current	Exerts influence for change

The difference between managing and leading was highlighted in one of the issues of the *Wall Street Journal*:

People don't want to be managed;
They want to be led.
Whosoever heard of a World Manager?
World Leader, yes.
Educational leader, political leader, religious leader,
Social leader, community leader, labour leader, business leader,
They lead; they don't manage.
The carrot always wins over the stick,
Ask your horse,
You can always lead your horse to the water,
But, you can't manage him to drink.
If you want to manage somebody,
Manage yourself. Do that well.
And you will be ready to stop managing,
And, start leading.

LEADER: A DREAMER WHO DOES

There may be many definitions or approaches to leadership. But, one trait or characteristic of leadership which is common in almost all definitions—explicit or implicit—is that a leader is a dreamer who also does. This is true of leadership at MD or CEO level, director or COO level, Sr. VP/VP level and also further down the order.

Depending on the level, relative role of a leader changes—more of a dreamer at the highest level and more of a doer at the lowest level. The shift takes place between 'corporate level' and 'business level' activities. This is more clearly shown in the table below;

Leader: Dreamer and Doer

Level	1 Dreamer (%)	2 Doer (%)
MD/CEO	80	20
COO/Director	60	40
Sr. VP/VP/CGM/GM	50	50
DGM/Sr. Manager	40	60
Manager	20	80

1. Focus on Corporate Level 2. Focus on Business Level

The functions of manager and leader are both essential in any successful organisation, but there may be lack of balancing between the two. American business is today thought to be "dangerously over managed and underled." Management-leadership mismatch can be found in companies in other countries also, and, in the same companies, during different time periods and situations.

LEADERS ARE BORN?

We now tum to the age-old debate on whether leaders are born or they are made, like whether a genius is born or become so only if given the proper setting or environment. King Ptolemy I, once asked his teacher, Euclid, whether he could learn geometry without learning the basics. Euclid replied: "No, Your Majesty, there is no royal road to geometry."

Many think that there is no royal road to leadership—they are made the hard way. We have heard of born political leaders like Hitler, Napoleon, Roosevelt, Churchill and others. We have also heard of successful business leaders like Rockefeller, Ford, Matsushita, Morita (Sony Corporation), J.R.D. Tata, G.D. Birla, and many others. They were also born to be leaders; and, they judiciously nurtured their leadership alchemies to achieve astounding successes. Many of them have also had faced very hostile environment. The less known luminaries of business leadership are also "gifted"—they are endowed with leadership calibres. May be they needed a more friendly environment (destiny included?) to rise to the top of the ladder.

LEADERSHIP STYLES

As there may be more diversity than commonality in the definitions of leadership, there can also be various manifestations of management systems of leaders which can be described as leadership styles.

Authors who have done extensive work on leadership feel that we have several options if we want to understand or analyse leadership styles. One is to classify it, as do most research studies on leadership; we can do that by using labels: autocratic, democratic, laissez-faire; or, characterisations: the craftsman, the jungle fighter, the company man, the gamesman; or, by placing the leadership style on axes: person-oriented versus production-oriented; or, by differentiating the achievement-oriented from the power-oriented or the affiliation-oriented; or we can characterise their temperaments: intuitive versus analytical. Another way is to study leadership style after defining the traits, qualities/skills or behaviours that characterise it: we may speak of McGregor's Theory X and Theory Y, Likert's System 4 or Argyris' Model II. Finally, we can analyse style through outcome: what did the leader achieve—profitability, innovation, human resource development, growth of the organisation, etc.[2]

The various ways or options mentioned above are not all mutually exclusive; many of them co-exist and may even be complementary. For example, the intuitive, achievement-oriented or power-oriented, the gamesman and autocratic or laissez-faire can all be in one.

Our option to analyse leadership styles is like this: we start with some basic or traditional leadership behaviours; and, then proceed to study corporate leadership in action, and, our search in this is for the commonalities rather than the diversities in leadership styles. We finally open up the leadership frontiers, that is, highlight leadership—the real leadership cult.

Four Basic Styles

We start with four basic leadership styles, viz., directing, coaching, supporting and delegating. *Directing* means that the leader provides specific instructions and closely monitors task accomplishment. In *coaching*, the leader continues to direct and closely monitor task accomplishment, but, also explains decisions, solicits suggestions and accepts recommendations. *Supporting* implies that the leader facilitates and supports subordinates' efforts towards task accomplishment and shares responsibility for decision making with them. In the *delegating* style, the leader delegates many responsibilities for decision making and problem solving to the subordinates.

Likert classified management styles into four systems based on authority which shows close correspondence to the description of the basic or traditional leadership styles.

System 1 in Likert's classification, the least desirable system, is exploitative-authoritative (autocratic directing), which depends on unquestionable authority and coercion and little or no regard for the followers or the subordinates. System 2 is benevolent-authoritative (directing-cum-coaching). Authority is still concentrated at the top but the needs and feelings of the subordinate people are considered in a paternalistic way. System 3, consultative (coaching-cum-supporting) maintains the organisational hierarchy and authority but involves subordinate employees in the decision making process. System 4, participative group (supporting-cum-delegating) is Likert's ideal model. System 4 seems to minimise authority and maximise participatory problem solving based on competence rather than organisational rank?[3]

The general leadership strategy is to change the style over time from directing to coaching, from coaching to supporting and from supporting to delegating as organisational performance improves. At an advanced stage of delegating style, almost everybody in the organisation is seen to perform. Mao Tse-Tung has put it well: "When the best leader's work is done, the people say, we did it ourselves."

The above means, in other words, that a particular leadership style which is appropriate at one point of organisational development may be inappropriate at some other stage of growth and vice versa. We are, in fact, saying that *leadership is not static; it is management dynamics*.

Leadership Styles in Action

Leadership styles seen in action in various organisations are generally either extensions, modifications or combinations of the four basic styles and their detailed manifestations show a particular characterisation, label, etc., as enumerated above. There have been a plethora of studies or analyses of leadership styles. Some are theories and focus on normative behaviours; some are general surveys; there are not many which highlight the behavioural specifics of leaders. A recent survey of theory and research on leadership lists 5,000 references in nearly 900 pages. For all of that, Editor Bernard M. Bass concludes, "It would be instructive to gather behavioural data on an identified current group of charismatic business ... leaders" rather than do a leather hunt for generalisations.

"Levinson and Rosenthal's study" of six selected CEOs of big American Corporations (General Electric, Citicorp, AMAX, Monsanto, IBM and New York Times) is one among such surveys. The penetrative study makes quite comprehensive analysis of the various commonalities in leadership styles. The six leaders studied are Jones (General Electric), Wriston (Citicorp), MacGregor (AMAX) Hanley (Monsanto), Watson, Jr. (IBM), and Sulzberger (New York Times). These leaders, as all successful leaders should be, are goal-obsessed. The goal may not be altogether clear, but, the leader is constantly thinking about what should be done and how it can be done both in terms of personal attainment and organisational achievement. Because of their goal-obsession, the leaders are also sometimes described as "ego-ideals."

Secondly, the leaders have a personal strategy, often vague, but, nevertheless, a blueprint which guides them in accomplishing their goals. Leaders understand that *big plans start small*. Priorities and timing are of essence. Step by step they build their "Moghul" structures. They have a sense of what they want and a realistic, if not always conscious, understanding of how to get it.

Thirdly, the leaders are able to use their power base and implement their strategies because they are thinkers as well as doers. Leaders enjoy conceptualising, projecting, fantasising, succeeding and even failing. When a programme, product, or strategy is not working, they don't throw up their hands; they find in this a new challenge. They take failures in their stride. In fact, what we call failure, they would like to call a mistake.

Bennis, in his survey[5] of 90 successful leaders, including many in the *Fortune 500*, finds that most of the leaders, in their "management of self," look upon a mistake as nothing more than a way of doing things. One CEO, in Bennis' target group, said that if she had a knack for leadership, it was the capacity to make as many mistakes as she could, as soon as possible, and then to get them out of the way. Some leaders viewed a mistake as the next step; some others felt that a mistake was a foundation for something new.

Fourthly, in their search for something new, the leaders work at getting support—from above, below and from the environment, internal as well as external. Early in their careers, they sense who likes them, trusts them, and appreciates them, and they find ways for these people to support their efforts. Leaders get support because they give support. Leaders understand that without supporters, they simply won't have the power to pursue their ideals or goals.

Fifthly, most people would assume that all successful leaders can be characterised as "warriors" since they are all engaged in a highly competitive business warfare. The leaders were indeed warriors. They warred by building not a pastiche called conglomerate, but, solid, integrated and effective organisations.

Finally, a surprising revelation is that the self-management of the leaders was so styled that five out of the six men very willingly handed over the reins to their successors although each one of them could have manoeuvred to hold on longer. This shows that they had really institutionalised their leadership in the sense that they were more concerned with organisational continuity than personal continuity.

So far for commonalities in leadership styles. But, diversities are more characteristic of leader—diversities sometimes demanded by situations, some other times caused by situations and many times dictated by situations. And, therefore, the demand for situational leadership.

EXCELLENCE IN LEADERSHIP

Before we turn to situational leadership, let us spend some time understanding excellence in leadership. Leadership itself in an excellent thing; excellence in leadership is really like double crowning. Let us search the ways to this double crowning.

Sears, Roebuck and Company in the US had conducted extensive (also intensive) research into leadership characteristics for over two decades. Their studies had measured the characteristics and traced the careers of thousands of executives over a period of years. The research results were recently summarised by Professor Guyton. Professor Guyton concludes that the Sears study "lends strong support to the hypothesis ... that there are differences in personal characteristics of more and less successful executives, that the differences can be identified ... and measured."[6]

Frank Goble, in his best-seller, *Excellence in Leadership*, identifies and ebulliently analyses ten major excellence factors which contribute to excellence in leadership. These are:

1. Ambition
2. Persistence
3. Courage
4. Faith
5. Integrity
6. Creativity
7. Objectivity
8. Flexibility
9. Self-discipline
10. Decisiveness

Many successful leaders believe that a man can succeed at almost anything for which he has *unlimited enthusiasm*. Whether we call it energy, enthusiasm, ambition, motivation or need for achievement, it is a driving force. Almost by definition, a leader is a self-starter. People who are unable to motivate themselves through ambition must be content to be followers. Of course, excessive ambition, like anything in excess, can be self-defeating both in achievement of organisational objectives and personal goals. This has also been demonstrated by highly ambitious leaders like Hitler. There are examples in business too.

Napoleon Hill studied more than 500 of the most successful men in America and got to know many of them personally. He found that one indispensable ingredient, the common element in the success stories of them all, was *persistence*. These men kept trying even after repeated failures. He found that great success was achieved only by people who overcame many discouragements, obstacles and hurdles. Hill states, "I had the happy privilege of analysing both Mr. Edison and Mr. Ford, year by year, over a long period of years, and, therefore the opportunity to study them at close range; so I speak from actual knowledge when I say that I found no quality save persistence, in either one of them, that even remotely suggested the major source of their stupendous achievements."

Closely related to the virtue of persistence is *courage*. Courage is the forerunner of persistence. Courage is the willingness to start and persistence is the determination to continue and finish. To achieve something extraordinary, one must have the boldness to take risks and the courage to execute under uncertainties. Therefore, Roosevelt, speaking from personal experience, said, "Far better it is to dare mighty things, to win glorious triumphs, even though checkered with failure than to take rank with those poor spirits who neither enjoy much nor suffer much because they live in the great twilight that knows neither victory nor defeat."

Along with ambition, courage and persistence, *faith* is also essential for outstanding leadership. These are all concommitant virtues. Andrew Carnegie said the secret of his success was "Faith in myself, faith in others and faith in my business." Faith is the key to sustained effort whether the original inspiration is self-confidence or belief in an idea or belief in the laws of success, or nature or something else.

The prevalent concept for many Americans, including many executives, is "Be successful or be honest." In today's value system, this may almost be a global truth. But, Joe Balten, the advocate of tough-minded management, believes that we must "blast the fallacy that you must compromise integrity to run a truly profitable business or house." The study of excellent leadership reveals that *integrity* is an essential quality. It is exceedingly difficult to achieve success in handling people, over the long span, without it. Norman Jaspan, head of a firm specialising in detection and prevention of white-collar crime, says, "Dishonesty starts from the top and works downwards. Show me a half-dozen key supervisors who know their business, and, I will show you a thousand honest employees."[8] Like charity begins at home, honesty begins with the self, particularly for a leader who has many followers.

Creativity suggests the names and ideas of such great men as Newton, Bell, Marconi, Edison and the Wright brothers, among others. Mention industrial creativity to a group of executives and they will immediately name IBM, Xerox, Polaroid, and similar companies. No one can argue with these examples of creativity; they are notable examples of the great American success story.

Creativity, however, is much more than the big breakthrough or the expensive R&D units. Creativity is something the successful people use everyday. Edison's definition of creativity was: "There is a way to do it better-find it." Excellent leadership is a creative process. Lloyd Marquis, when President of the American Institute of Management, analysed the behaviour of thousands of excellent managers. He concluded that one of the most important characteristics was what he called "creative dissatisfaction." In other words, it was more than creativity—it was the constant desire to do better.

Excellent leaders have the ability to view things realistically or *objectively*. Although certain element of subjectivity cannot be ruled out in leadership and decision making, objectivity always dominates their perception. They do not practice self-deception, do not deceive others and are not easily deceived by others. Maslow found this as one of the most important characteristics of psychological health of leaders: "One of the most striking superiorities reported of self-actualising people is their exceptional perceptiveness. They can perceive truth and reality far more efficiently than the average run of people ...."[9]

Objectivity is the ability to perceive things as they are. *Flexibility* is the ability to make changes as required. It is also a measure of good leadership health. In extended form, flexibility implies the freedom to learn through experience, the freedom to change with changing internal and external environments, to be influenced by logical arguments, "admonitions, exhortations, and appeal to emotions" the freedom to respond to the stimulus of reward and punishment, and, "especially the freedom to cease when staled."

Many centuries ago the great Chinese sage Confucius pointed out that followers seldom display virtues not first present in their leaders. To be exemplary, therefore, self-management of leaders should begin with *self-discipline*. "The man who cannot control himself," says Napoleon Hill, "can never control others. Self-control sets a mighty example for one's followers which the more intelligent will emulate."

It is almost obvious, if not axiomatic, that a man who vacillates and procrastinates is a poor decision-maker and a poor decision-maker cannot be a good leader. For successful *leadership, decisiveness* is an indispensable virtue. Decisiveness also presupposes clearly defined objectives. Only individuals with established goals, programmes and policies can lead others decisively. Top executives often complain that their subordinates do not respond. "Such executives," says Batten, "have not taken an objective and penetrating inventory of their own personal goals, desires ...; and, it is fundamental in attempting to motivate subordinates that the superior must at all times know what he, himself, actually wants."

THE SITUATIONAL CULT

Many feel that to search for generalised excellence factors is an exercise in futility. They think that no fixed norms or criteria can be laid down for excellence either in business leadership or in any other field. Characteristics, like those analysed above, may best be described as attainable traits. Some of them may contribute to excellence during particular situations; some others may explain excellent leadership during some other situations; sometimes a totally non-programmed factor may contribute to successful leadership. In succinct, every different situation may demand different characteristics for success or excellence. Gandhiji said during the freedom movement, "every one of us should be his own leader" (so demanding was the situation).

The situational theory of leadership evolved primarily as a reaction to the failure of the traitist approach. Over the past 70 years, hundreds of studies have been conducted but no universal set of traits has been established. In one summary of over a hundred studies, only 5 per cent of the traits were found in four or more studies. Certain traits that seem to be primary ingredients of success in some situations were of limited importance in others. Therefore, the conclusion was reached that it is the demands of the situation that dominate, and, leaders are successful only when their particular traits happen to fit those demands or situations.

Of all the sub-fields of management, situational theory has been associated with leadership styles and concepts for the longest time. Before World War II, Parker Follett, Kurt Lewin, Ronald Lippitt, and Chester Barnard, among others, and, following

World War II many of the best-known experts on leadership such as Douglas McGregor, Fred Fiedler and Rensis Likert have all advocated that leadership is situational and no best style of leadership exists. The genesis of situational leadership may be best expressed in the words of Carlisle, one of the foremost champions of situational management, "... different managers in different organisations face different situations that require different solutions."[10]

Some situations call for leaders who are visionaries; some call for leaders who are outstanding planners and decision-makers; some for leaders who are expert organisers; some for leaders who are best as human resource developers; some for leaders who are specialists in implementation, monitoring and control.

We have many stories of successful situational leaders—leaders who have seized situations, exploited situations and thrived during particular situations.

LEADERSHIP AND CORPORATE TURNAROUND

If situation demands a leader, the real test of leadership is during crisis. That is why we hear about crisis leadership. When a company is in crisis or is sinking, only a leader who fits into the metabolism of the situation can pull it out of the mud by using a strategy tailor-made to the situation. For corporate regeneration, however, it is not always necessary to have bloodshed or bloodbath (that is, to effect very sweeping changes like firing, wholesale reshuffling of portfolios, closing down of operations, etc.); this can be achieved through peaceful means also that is, revamping or reorganising the corporate system through meetings, discussions, pursuasions etc.

In fact, there are generally two ways to corporate turnaround. One is the surgical way more widely practised in the West especially in the US; the other is the humane way more used in the East. There would be many variants of these two general ways depending on the situational contingencies.

The operations in surgical turnaround are like this: The first step is to replace the chief executive of the ailing corporation by a new "iron" chief. The new chief loses no time in asserting his authority: He issues pre-emptory orders, centralises certain functions and spears some convenient scapegoats. Then he goes about firing employees in masses and auctioning whole plants and divisions "until the fat is satisfactorily cut to the bone." The bloodbath over, the product mix is revamped, obsolete machinery is replaced, marketing is strengthened, controls are toughened, accountability for performance is highlighted and so on. How "bloody" this sort of turnaround can be may be seen from the examples of companies like the US video games manufacturer Atari, which cut its labour force by two-thirds to 3,500 to turn itself around. At British Leyland, 40 per cent of the employees (84, 000) were axed to complete the surgery.

Turnaround management of the humane type may involve negotiated and humane layoffs and divestiture, but not bloodbaths. This turnaround too is generally brought about by the new helmsman. But, he spends a great deal of time trying to understand the problems and deliberating on them, takes all the stakeholders including unions, into confidence, gets groups within the organisation to brainstorm together on what needs to be done to get over the crisis, tries to create a new work culture and generally infuses a strong sense of participation among the employees. There are many examples of successful turnarounds of the humane variety.

We give here the example of SAIL, the Indian public sector giant. SAIL's losses were about ₹ 100 crores during 1982-83 and ₹ 200 crores in 1983-84. A price rise during 1984-85 saw SAIL break even in that year. But, rapid increases in coal prices and freight rates threatened a loss again in 1985-86. The steel ministry and SAIL management then called for another price hike.

V. Krishnamurthy entered the scene as Chairman in mid-1985 and promptly lobbied against a price rise on the ground that efficiency had to be improved. Indian steel was already the costliest in the world and any further rise in steel prices would have ruinous effects on the economy, he said. Krishnamutthy spent the next several months talking to small groups of executives, officials, staff and workers in SAIL. He estimates that he talked with over 25,000 persons to identify operating problems, get perceptions of how the company was doing and what people thought could be done to improve performance. The turnaround strategy eventually emerged from such discussions at all levels.

Whether it is surgical turnaround or humane turnaround, it is the leader who is pivotal. He moulds and executes the turnaround. Depending on the contingency style of the leader triggered by his personal characterisations, he decides on the strategy, revolutionary or evolutionary. This is the story of successful turnaround leaders like Krishnamurthy (SAIL), Luther (DVC) and Gujral (Coal India) or the leaders of IRI of Italy (world's largest public enterprise) Atari or British Leyland, and many others.

ONLY BAD GENERALS, NO BAD SOLDIERS

If some leaders know how to fight a crisis and herald a turnaround, there are some others whose leadership miscarriage digs the ground for corporate degeneration or downturn. In both the cases, other managers play a second fiddle. For fall of Berlin, history holds Hitler, and, not the German army as responsible, or, as Drucker puts it: "If an enterprise fails to perform, we rightly hire, not different workers, but, a new president."

In the field of management, there are many cases of leadership change, sometimes for the better sometimes for the worse. And, there can be many ways of corporate devolution. We have one such case here. One electronics corporation in the US had grown for ten years with sales reaching higher levels and profits increasing steadily. But, suddenly the run of success was halted, sales dropped and the company went into reds. A consulting firm was engaged by the Board of Directors to analyse the situation and they concluded that the organisation had outgrown its leadership. At the recommendations of the consultants, the directors brought in a new chief and profits reappeared.

In India, Hindustan Photo Films, Burn and Standard, Sylvania Laxman all illustrate leadership outgrowth. HPF was making heavy losses in the late sixties. With the appointment of a part-time chairman, there was change in leadership and the company clawed its way back to break even levels by mid-seventies and decent profits thereafter. Burn and Standard was loosing on sales for a number of years (loss in sales during 1978-79 was over 25 per cent) because of lack of market competitiveness. With change of leadership (the new CMD took over in 1978), the company managed to raise real employee productivity by 300 per cent over a period of seven years. At Sylvania Laxman (now Laxman Sylvania), top management was reorganised at the instance of the financial institutions in 1977. The company turned profitable the very next year.

Leadership Outgrowth

There are many ways the leadership can outgrow itself-size management, labour-relations management, environment management, etc. When small business grows large through expansion or diversification, the "small" leadership may or may not be able to cope with all the problems of management size brings with it. Nirma, the small-size wonder, successfully displaced the multinational giant, Hindustan Lever in the detergent market; but, with fast and not too organised growth, size seems to have started telling on Nirma leadership.

DVC leadership was marching under the reins of a recalcitrant union without being able to increase power generation till the leadership gave way to P.C. Luther who spearheaded the way to tame the union and make it more amenable, gear up productivity and accelerate power generation. In UTI, Pherwani's predecessor could not induce the vast multitude of the investing public and exploit the people investment environment. With investor-friendly Pherwani taking over and unveiling a host of new schemes, the investment environment was fully exploited and, during a period of only four years (1984-88), UTI increased its investible funds more than eight-folds.

Some leaders do well during stability; some others thrive during a crisis. Luther was highly successful during a crisis in DVC but his later stint in STC, a generally stable organisation, was rather controversial. There are many examples 'the other way round.' So long as the organisation is cruising along, leadership is stable and successful, but, as soon as a crisis develops, the leadership outmanoeuvres itself.

In the highly imperfect world of today, there are also many cases of leadership misplacements. Some manage to get to top positions by manipulative skill only to be found wanting in the job. It has been said that Churchill's words coming from Chamberlain would hardly have had the same effect. What, then, would misplaced leaders perform! Like incompetent doctors, incompetent leaders can make organisations worse. Some leaders give themselves heart attacks and nervous breakdowns; incompetent leaders are worse, they are "carriers"—they give them to their subordinates and employees. That is why George Doriot, erstwhile President of the American Research and Development Company, a firm which specialises in investing in very young companies, said: "I'd rather have a grade A man and grade B idea than a grade B man and a grade A idea."

LEADERSHIP: LESSONS FROM CRICKET

In benchmarking and best practices, we have learnt that a company or a manager can benchmark performance not only on the basis of best practices in the same industry, but also based on performance in some other industry, field of management or even public life. This is true of leadership practices also.

Narayana Murthy, Founder and Chairman Emeritus of Infosys, observes: "...Performance leads to recognition, recognition leads to respect and respect leads to power... Mahendra Singh Dhoni, the most successful cricket captain of India, demonstrated this well in cricket. Perform, he did. He led the Indian team to win in all major international (ICC) competitions—World T20 in 2007, ICC World ODI championship in 2011, Championship Trophy in 2013 and many more."[13]

Dhoni was a quintessential leader. There are many things corporate India and corporate leaders can learn from watching his cricket matches and leadership practices.

Five major lessons highlighted by Naryana Murthy are:

1. *The first responsibility of a leader is to craft a grand vision, articulate* it and raise the aspiration, confidence, pride, hope and enthusiasm of his people Dhoni did this to perfection.
2. *A confident leader is generous to share glory with his team.* Dhoni was a generous leader. Who can forget

Dhoni sharing his day of glory with Sachin Tendulkar and Gary Kirsten when on the victory lap after winning the World Cup in 2011? *Generosity is the hallmark of a great leader.*

3. *A competent leader remains calm during crisis and plans* his moves correctly. Dhoni is a good example of this. He aptly demonstrated this during 2007 T20 world cup final.
4. *A successful leader should be a good strategist.* Dhoni demonstrated this also during T20 World Cup final in 2007. In the last over, Misbah-ul-Huq (of Pakistan) hit a six off the second ball. Everybody was tense. Dhoni went and spoke to Joginder Sharma. He told him his strategy. The next ball was a tricky one from Joginder. It was scooped up by Misbah for well judged catch. India had won. The move turned out to be a very well thought out strategy by Dhoni—almost a master stroke by him.
5. *A good leader should react with equal equanimity to wins and losses* for the country, the company, in the marketplace or the cricket field. During Dhoni's captaincy or leadership, India also lost matches. This also happens in the corporate game. But, a leader has to take a defeat or failure in his stride and move forward; and, prepare, with stronger force, for the next win. This is what Dhoni did. He lost battles, but, won the wars. This is the real test of leadership.

May be, Dhoni always remembered the old adage that a failure is a pillar of success. So, should all good leaders do.

These are great leadership lessons from cricket. Corporate leaders can also learn similar lessons from other captain-leaders in cricket like Kapil Dev, Clive Lloyd, Gary Sobers, Steve Waugh and some others who had always lead from the front and exemplified great leadership qualities.

LEADERSHIP LESSONS: WHAT A LEADER SHOULD NOT DO

All leadership theories, advices and practices mostly focus on what a good leader should do. But, there are also things a leader should not do. These are almost as important as what leaders should do. The "Dos" and "Do Not's" together make total or complete or model leadership.

Ten "Not-to-Do" lessons for leadership are prescribed below.[14] These are explained with reference to the Congress Party and Indian politics. But, these have more general applicability in corporate management.

Ten "Not-do-Do" lessons are:

1. Don't be gutless
2. Don't be selfish
3. Don't be less committed
4. Don't waste time in useless meetings
5. Don't become a dinosaur
6. Don't have blind spots
7. Don't ignore the customer
8. Don't surround yourself with sycophants
9. Don't blame your subordinates
10. Don't forget your limitations

Don't Be Gutless

You can hire smart or competent people if you don't have the intelligence or lack certain skills. But, *you can't hire guts*. You have to show courage and make the bold moves yourself if you aspire to be leader. This is not on Gandhi's now. CM Modi took on the BJP old guards to become PM Modi. So, as a leader, don't be gutless. Show enough courage to sail through turbulence.

Don't Be Selfish

Showing guts or courage does not mean that a leader should be selfish. Today, the Congress Party is in terrible shape. This is very bad for our democracy. A one-sided concentration of power will undermine national institutions. But, the Congress Party cares little about India or its democracy. It cares about the family and, particularly, the son's carrier. If you are running an organisation, think beyond. Think about the organisational good.

Don't Be Less Committed

As an entrepreneur or CEO or team leader, you have to work harder than your subordinates. The present PM's work hours are well known. Elon Musk, Mark Zuckerberg, Tim Cook, Satya Nadela, Sunder Pichai, Adar Poonawalla all work hard and are fully committed to their cause. Is the Congress committed enough to the organisational cause?

Don't Waste Time

Don't waste time in useless meetings and conversations. The recent seven-hours CWC meeting was a drama. Sonia Gandhi offered her resignation, then remained as interim Congress President. She still continues. As a leader, don't waste your or your team's time. But, some leaders do. They forget that time is a very precious resource.

Don't Become a Dinosaur

BJP has evolved dramatically over the last ten years. Also rooted in Indian tradition and history, they are one of the most technologically savvy parties. BJP is like Amazon, growing and opening new frontiers. In contrast, Congress is still like a Lalaji Ki Dukaan where Lalaji scolds his minions for not fanning the flies away from the sweets. Don't be a Lalaji if you want to become a leader.

Don't have Blind Spots

There is privilege, and, then, there is almost "insane, absolute blind spot" inducing privilege like Rahul Gandhi. A lot of privileged people are self-aware. They can also spot talent, respect it and work with them. Such people succeed. But, the epic privileged like Rahul Gandhi view the world differently. Any negative feedback is viewed as stupid or jealous people trying to bring you down. The fact is blind spots always bring you down. As a leader, don't have blind spots. Be self-aware. Be self-conscious.

Don't Ignore the Customer (Voter)

If you are in the business of serving someone, never ignore them. India has been telling congress to change since 2011. People literally came on the streets, but, the party lost two elections very badly. Nothing changed. Congress leadership just won't listen. If you ignore the customer (voter/people), an organisation becomes what congress has become today—a sinking phenomenon or entity.

Don't Blame your Juniors/Subordinates

When several senior congress leaders wrote a letter expressing their concern about the state of the party, the leadership's first reaction was to blame the letter writers. They called them traitors and questioned their loyalty. As a leader, never do that. Don't keep finding fault with your team or juniors and blaming them. This may only hasten your downfall.

Don't Forget your Limitations

Every person and every leader has some limitations. In general, especially when a nation's population is young, a leader needs to inspire. But, Rahul cannot make coherent, unscripted, passionate and powerful speech. Most people/leaders in the world can't. But, the job requires you to do so. A good politician or leader, as per needs, strikes alliances, make certain moves and get the job done.

Good leaders are aware of their weak points and take necessary actions to overcome them. So, as a leader, work on your limitations, and, don't ignore them.

Leaders are human beings. In their enthusiasm to perform or be innovative or aggressive, they may sometimes forget or ignore things they should not do. But, when they fail or face defeat, they realise their mistakes. This comes from self-analysis. *Self-analysis is highly imperative for success in leadership.*

LEADERSHIP IN CHALLENGING TIMES

Challenging times or extraordinary business environment poses new challenges to leadership. Leaders have to go beyond management styles adopted during normal times.

The pandemic has created one of the most extraordinary situations both for national economies and business management. Elements of crisis management are looming large. Several companies have changed management practices, processes and also business models.

Leaders also have to transform themselves. These call for several new capabilities. Six capabilities are more important:

1. Managing stress
2. Self-development
3. Reaching out to teams/managers
4. Handling disruptions
5. Enhancing effectiveness
6. Becoming "new" role model[15]

Managing Stress

All extraordinary business situations like the one created by the pandemic create more stress in life and business and management. Leaders have to manage their own stress (there are different prescribed ways to that) and also show the teams or managers effective ways for stress management.

Self-Development

Stress management helps self-development. It is about remaining fit and steady in adversity. How much you invest in your own development will determine your shelf-life in the hostile environment. Many leaders have identified a suitable personal development plan and worked on it. This also includes developing new skills.

Reaching Out to Teams/Customers

Reaching out and interacting with individual managers or teams during pandemic like situations is a big challenge for leaders. Many companies have adopted WFH method. Some CEOs have evolved a hybrid model. In WFH and also in hybrid arrangement, "virtual" management becomes an important requisite. Leaders have to develop a workable, aiming for the optimal, approach for reaching out to teams/managers.

Handling Disruptions

All extraordinary situations cause disruptions in life styles, daily habits (at home and office) and work methods. A leader needs to sense the unknown and ask himself: "What best will work for me, my team and the company?" He has to search and find answer to this and develop an appropriate methodology for handling disruptions. Disruptions should not overtake you.

Enhancing Effectiveness

How well a leader handles disruptions will determine his(her) effectiveness in management. Sustaining leadership effectiveness is vital. Leaders should possess or develop special abilities to enhance effectiveness during such times. This may require changes in functional systems and management practices and strategies.

Becoming 'New' Role Model

All these can converge in the leader to become a "new" role model for the managers. Managers are followers; they follow the leader or learn from him. So, the leader should become the new role model to emulate. This way he will contribute significantly to organisational success during extraordinary situations like the pandemic.

For developing and implementing a successful pandemic management system or strategies for extraordinary challenges, many leaders may have to reinvent themselves.

The process of reinvention should, in fact, almost be synonymous with successful leadership.

12
Crisis Management

From a tiny spark, comes a great conflagration

—Ben Sirach

Even if you are on the right track, you will get run over if you just sit there

—Will Rogers

A crisis is not an usual phenomenon whether in life or business. It does not happen with any regularity. It cannot be always forecast or is easily predictable. If it is not averted or managed in time with appropriate strategy, it can lead to immense loss or even disaster.

WHAT IS BUSINESS CRISIS

Webster dictionary defines a "crisis" as a 'turning point for better or worse', a "decisive moment" or "crucial time". Webster also defines a crisis as "a situation that has reached a critical phase."

Fink, in his pioneering book *Crisis Management*, has defined or described crisis as follows:

"A crisis is an unstable time or a state of affairs in which a decisive change is impending—either one with the distinct possibility of a highly undesirable outcome or one with the distinct possibility of a highly desirable and extremely positive outcome. It is usually a 50:50 proposition (between the two), but you can improve the odds."[1]

Both Webster's and Fink's definition indicate that a crisis is not a natural disaster. It is man-made and is characterised by risk, uncertainty and criticality. As Webster has put it, a crisis can be a *turning point* for better or worse depending on the intensity of the crisis and the policy or strategy adopted by the affected company or the organisation for dealing with it.

A crisis can occur anytime. Fink puts it like this: "If three Mile Island, Union Carbide's carnage in India (commonly known as Bhopal gas tragedy), The Johnson & Johnson (Tylend poisionings), The Ohio Bank failures, and, the Procter & Gamble/ Rely Tampon controversy—to name but a few recent crises—have taught the world anything, it is that a crisis in business can occur today with little or no warning, anywhere, anytime. And, it can happen to any company, large or small, public or private."[2]

CAN A CRISIS BE FORECAST OR ANTICIPATED?

An important question arises: Is it possible to forecast or anticipate a crisis? The answer is: it depends on the nature or source of crisis.

Let us see the following crisis in McDonald's.

In the summer of 1984, a crisis suddenly occurred at McDonald's restaurant in Sun Ysidro, California. A crazy or derailed individual named James Huberty, entered the restaurant and went on a shooting rampage inside the restaurant. He opened indiscriminate fire on the indiscriminate customers or patrons. As a result of the firings, 21 people died on the spot.

McDonald's did not have an inkling or signal about the firing. But, as a consequence of the crisis, McDonald's national sales declined. The company suffered financially, and, there was a dent in its public image. It took some time for McDonald's to tide over the crisis. Very recently, there was a shooting rampage in a Paris restaurant and many people were killed.

Such crises cannot be forecast or anticipated. But, many feel that the Bhopal gas tragedy could have been anticipated because as *New York Times* reported: "it was the result of operating errors, design-flaws, maintenance failures and training deficiencies".

MMTC's business crisis was of an entirely different nature and, could have been forecast or anticipated. After the announcement of the liberalisation measures for the Indian economy by then Finance Minister Manmohan Singh in July, 1991, more liberalisations or decontrols or decanalisations were almost on the cards. It was only a matter of time. MMTC's and STC's think-tank or the planning group or the strategic management team (if at all they had any) could or should have foreseen the impending crisis.

These examples show that crises for which signals existed in the horizon or internal or external environment like those of MMTC and STC, and, also Bhopal tragedy can, with all probability, be forecast or foreseen. But, those which are "blind occurrences" with no signals, like that of McDonald's, cannot be forecast or anticipated.

NATURE OR FORMS OF BUSINESS CRISIS

Business crises can be of different nature or forms. In the US, a confidential survey was undertaken among the CEOs of Fortune 500 companies on the forms and management of crisis. According to the majority of the CEOs, there are ten forms of crisis to which companies are generally vulnerable. These forms are:

1. Environmental problems
2. Government regulatory measures
3. Industrial accidents
4. Union problems/strikes
5. Financial irregularities/Embezzlement of funds
6. Hostile takeover
7. Product recalls
8. Investor relations
9. Rumours/Media leaks
10. Acts of terrorism[3]

ANATOMY OF A CRISIS

Whatever may be the form of crisis, it is necessary to analyse the anatomy of the crisis for developing a proper crisis management plan and strategy.

A typical crisis has four stages:

Stage 1 : Prodromal crisis or warning stage

Stage 2 : Acute crisis

Stage 3 : Chronic crisis

Stage 4 : Crisis resolution

For "blind occurrences" or crises without any signals, prodromal or warming stage does not exist. Such a crisis abruptly blows into stage 2 (acute crisis). But, for all crises with signals, clear or distant, the warning stage exists. For example, there may be a union threat to the management. The union may warn that, if the management does not negotiate and finalise the new wage agreement within a stipulated period, they would go on strike. In this case, the crisis is looming large and the signal is clear.

If the warning or signal is not properly read or ignored, an acute crisis develops. This means that the damage has already been done. The organisation can measure up the extent or intensity of the crisis in terms of output loss or revenue (turnover) loss or financial loss. The management can also initiate the damage control process. This is what Union Carbide management was doing in Bhopal.

The damage control process actually gathers momentum during the "chronic crisis" stage. The term "chronic crisis" may be misleading because "chronic" gives an impression that the crisis has taken deep roots. It is not so. This is actually the phase of clean-up or healing or recovery.

The "acute crisis" stage and the "chronic crisis" stage are not always clearly identifiable, i.e., where one ends and the other begins may not be very distinct. There may be overlapping activities or operations.

In the "crisis resolution" stage, the recovery or the rehabilitation process is complete, and, the organisation is back on the path of self-sustaining operating stream or growth.

The four stages, in sequential order, make a complete crisis cycle. This is shown in the figure below.

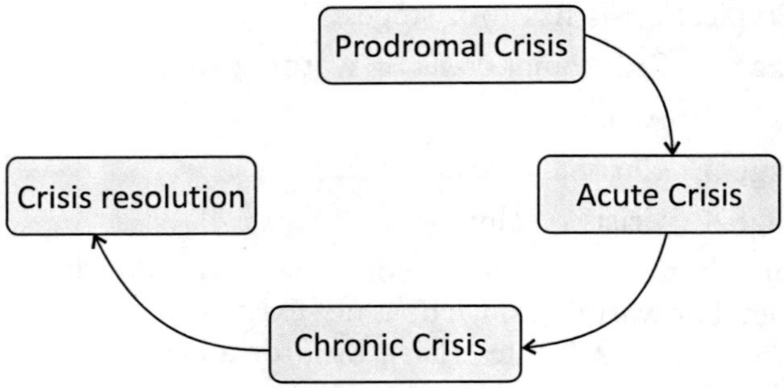

A Complete Crisis Cycle

The duration of the crisis cycle varies from one organisation to another. It depends on the nature and intensity of the crisis and plan, strategy and implementation of the recovery process, that is, the efficacy of the crisis management team.

CRISIS MANAGEMENT PLANNING

Ideally speaking, every business or company, public or private, large or small, should have a crisis management plan. But, how many companies, except Texaco and United Airlines and few others, really plan for crisis?

The critics may, however, argue that it may be an unnecessary or unproductive investment. A crisis may occur once in five years or ten years or may not occur at all during the lifetime of a company. So, why block today's resources for that.

Professionally, and more correctly, speaking, crisis management planning should be an extension of corporate planning. The corporate planning group should be watchful about any signal in the environment—internal or external, for a probable crisis.

If a crisis does occur, crisis management planning should be done in a systematic way in terms of six sequential steps. These six steps are:

Step 1 : Set up the crisis management team—usually interdisciplinary within the corporate planning group or independently.

Step 2 : Analyse the crisis carefully—the reason, the intensity and the possible recovery path.

Step 3 : Work out the crisis management plan in terms of CPM (Critical Path Method).

Step 4 : Based on step 3, correctly estimate the recovery period.

Step 5 : Get the necessary resource allocation done—financial and managerial.

Step 6 : Conduct mid-term review of the implementation process and take necessary corrective actions, if required. Use PERT (Programme Evaluation and Review Technique)

The top management should be continuously involved with the crisis management process either as a member of the team or through review meetings depending on the organisational structure and hierarchies.

CAN A CRISIS BE AVERTED?

This is a million dollar question and a very pertinent one. Prevention is better than cure and averting a crisis is always better than resolving a crisis. Crisis management and resolution involve stress (sometimes panic), uncertainty and significant resources.

Crises may be big or small. It may be difficult to avert a big crisis, but, it may be possible to prevent many small crises. And, often, if a small crisis is not prevented on time, it can blow into a crisis of serious proportions. Fink has given good examples of both.

We first narrate how a crisis was averted, and then, we explain how the same crisis almost developed into a catastrophe, because it was not prevented on time.

In a company, the finance manager is responsible for taking care of the payroll and timely disbursement of salaries of staff/ managers. Only two days are left for the payday. But, the finance manager may not be able to meet the payment deadline because he does not have enough cash on hand. The reason is accounts receivables are running short in the bank. But, salary must be paid on due date. The finance manager takes the warning and uses his crisis management skill. He calls up the bank manager and arranges a short-term loan. The same is repaid as soon as receivable flow in. Salaries are paid on time and the crisis is averted.

In the second situation, consider the same receivables problem, but, the finance manager is not there to manage it because he is out of station. Hardly anybody (except may be the finance manager's immediate boss) knew how the finance manager had managed the situation on the previous occasion. Like earlier months the computer manager generates the pay cheques, and, sends the same to the CEO for signature. The CEO signs the cheques, but, the cheques bounce. Cheque bouncing spreads almost like wild fire. Next morning, the local newspaper carries a story on this and quote the CEO as saying: "While it is true that all of our employees' pay cheques bounced, it really was just a small problem that we took care of. All of our employees have been repaid. We have made good on every cheque. And, these damn rumours that we are going out of business are just not true". This statement by the CEO fuels crisis fire.

Many of the suppliers of the company read the story in the newspaper and start getting worried about their payments. They demand immediate release of all outstanding payments. Not only that, they also refuse to extend additional credit. They also make it a condition that all future shipments/deliveries will be on C.O.D. (Cash on Delivery) or C.A.D. (Cash Against Documents) basis.

As a result of this, the company's cash flow position deteriorates and they have to borrow funds from the bank/market. The bank applies pressure to reduce borrowing/debt. This is a symptom of financial crisis of the company.

Internal rumours grow and employee morale is very low. Some key managers resign and leave the company. Some of them join competitors of the company. Things are going out of control.

Gradually, the company is almost driven to a point of desperation. They start getting involved in law suits—they decide to sue old competitors, new competitors and some former managers for violating Trade Secrets Act. Because of litigation, operating cost of the company increases.

More stories appear in the newspaper/media—about law suits, financial distress of the company, good managers deserting the company etc. The stories are now true.

The company has now reached a point of no return. The possibilities are: it (a) declares bankruptcy; (b) goes out of business; (c) is taken over by the bank; (d) is taken over by a competitor.

This reminds us of the old proverb: *A stitch in time saves nine*. With some skillfull planning/action, if the company could have prevented cheque bouncing, it would not have landed into this catastrophe. This happens in many companies.

Out of Court Settlement

Related to averting a crisis is out of court settlement of legal cases. Private sector companies generally avoid litigation because the cost-benefits often do not justify this but, litigation is quite common in the public sector.

Every public sector company has a big law department (bigger the company, larger the law department and more the number of cases). The management finds it convenient to refer cases to the law department (it is actually abducting responsibility for a decision) irrespective of merit of the case or the cost—benefits of it. The law department is just waiting to grab the cases because these give them work and importance, and, sometimes, they also have financial interest—understanding or arrangement with the lawyers.

The cases may be against suppliers—domestic or foreign, clearing and forwarding agents (C&FA), transporters and buyers. The cases usually go for many years because the law department and the lawyers may not be interested in early settlement, and, in the end, the company usually loses the case. It has been observed that about 75 percent of the cases are lost by the companies. If the amount involved in a particular case is large (including the amount that has already been spent), it becomes a setback and a small crisis. Out of court settlement could have averted many such crises.

I wish to give one such example from MMTC. I was then GM, Bombay. A small buyer had made payment by cheque, but, the cheque bounced. All of us know that cheque bouncing is a criminal offence, but, many do not know what actually happens in such cases. Here is the MMTC case.

After the cheque bounced, MMTC filed a criminal suit against the buyer. The legal proceedings started. Three years had passed. MMTC had already spent about ₹ 2 lakhs and the payment involved was ₹ 3 lakhs. The buyer met me and showed his interest in out-of-court settlement. He was willing to pay ₹ 3 lakhs with applicable interest and resume business with MMTC. If MMTC had pursued the case, at some stage, the buyer might have had to go to jail because he had committed a criminal offence. He might be jailed, but, MMTC would not have received the money. It would still depend on the final judgement. Some judgements can be quite unpredictable. In any case, by the time of judgement, MMTC would have spent more than 3 lakhs.

The buyer's out-of-court settlement proposal appealed to me. We had a progressive finance (DGM, Finance) in Bombay during that time. Majority of the finance managers are conservative, some regressive, because they think that they are the sole guardian of finances of the company. Sorry, finance people! The DGM (Finance), because he was progressive, saw sufficient logic in the out-of-court settlement proposal.

We together (we did not involve many people in this—too many cooks spoil the broth) made out the case, and, sent to Dir (Metals) for his consideration and approval. He also saw enough merit in the case and approved it.

I also got a congratulatory massage from the Director/ Chairman. But, the law department must have been very unhappy because they lost one more case.

I wish public sector companies do more out-of-court settlements of legal cases. There are companies for whom crores are locked. *Out-of-court settlement saves resources. It also shows better management skill.*

CRISIS MANAGEMENT IN A TRADING HOUSE: MMTC[4]

The objective of MMTC's crisis management plan was to re-establish itself as the leader in the Indian non-ferrous metals business in the decanalisation era. During the canalised regime, MMTC had monopoly, not leadership. *Monopoly means automatic leadership*. In the decanalised era, leadership has to be established in the freely competitive market.

With the market environment suddenly becoming hostile in terms of competition, MMTC had to work out its strategy to re-establish its leadership position in the Indian non-ferrous market. We had to work hard to develop our crisis management plan and strategy.

In such situation, the crisis management team is very crucial and Dir (RK) made a good, rather perfect team. And, as is essential during such time, we had the support of the CMD(SNM). Dir (RK) and I formed the nucleus of the strategy team and made other members to follow and implement. The team was almost hand picked—managers—with known capability, motivation and track record of performance. This is very important because the right team is key to implementation and success of plan and strategy. So, we decided not to make any compromise on this.

After months of homework, interaction with the user industry and some experimentations, we worked out our strategy. Some elements of the strategy were organisational which were integral to marketing efficiency and success, but, most of the elements of the strategy were directly in the field of marketing/selling. Major elements of the strategy adopted by MMTC for crisis management were as follows:

1. Profit Centre approach
   → Operational autonomy
2. Combination of planned and emergent strategies
   → Situational management
3. Integrated marketing
   → Backward integration
   → Linking procurement with sale
4. Bonded wareshousing scheme
   → Customer saves sales tax and turnover tax

5. Response time used as a catalyst
6. Pricing strategy
   → Customers can choose their prices
7. Innovative payment mechanism for customer
8. Customer focus

I shall not go into too much of details of these elements because it will be long and you may not be interested.[5] I shall highlight the more important ingredients and steps in the implementation process. In particular, I shall mention response time, innovative payment mechanism and customer focus.

Response Time

In any business of industrial or business products, the response time for sale is very vital factor. There is a common feeling that, in public sector companies, procedures are long, the decision-making process is slow, and, consequently, the response time, whether it is for purchase or sale, is longer than in the private sector. It cannot also be denied that during canalisation, MMTC could have been guilty of slow decision making and response to buyers.

Therefore after decanalisation, it was a major challenge to MMTC to reverse the public image. To do this, we had streamlined systems and procedures, and, had introduced a monitoring system to ensure that decision making did not stand on the way to a sale. Delegation of powers was revised to give manager more freedom and authority to respond to customer matters. This way, not only response time was minimised, but, in many cases, this was used as a catalyst.

I shall give a good example of how response time was used as a catalyst for sale. SAIL wanted to buy some aluminium very urgently for one of their steel plants. They had approached MMTC because it was not possible within their system of functioning, i.e., procedure. The way MMTC responded with the purchase and sale was almost unbelievable to SAIL. MMTC had floated a limited (fax) enquiry/tender in the morning and the purchase and sale were finalised the same day (the terms of sale were discussed earlier). SAIL was also associated with the purchase to make the whole process transparent.

Such a transaction was made possible because of informal management. In fact, informal management played a very important role in MMTC's crisis management strategy. Informal management was discussed in Ch. 3.

Innovative Payment Mechanism

Let me now talk about innovative payment system for customers. Conventional payment instruments are cheque subject to realisation, demand draft or banker's cheque and LC. But, we had introduced two innovative payment modes for customer convenience and to increase competitiveness. Cheque with endorsement 'Good for Payment' by the issuing bank was accepted and treated as a banker's cheque or demand draft and metal would be delivered without waiting for realisation of the cheque/payment. MMTC had introduced another innovative payment mechanism—accepting post—dated cheque (PDC) with standby LC or BG only as a guarantee. This worked out easier and cheaper for the buyer. In addition to these, liberal credit facilities were extended for 60 days, 90 and even up to 180 days to induce customers.

Customer Focus

I now turn to customer focus which was the most important element in the crisis management strategy. "Customer" is the essence or end; all the elements of the strategy should converge to it. We had to quickly understand this fundamental truth or proposition. We had to learn the difference between *allottee* and *customer*.

During canalisation, MMTC used to allot metals to different actual users on the basis of their entitlements decided by the government. MMTC's role was of an equitable distributor or supplier and protector of the interest of the state in terms of quantity delivered and price charged.

After decanalisation, the emphasis or focus immediately shifted to the role of MMTC as a seller trying to protect and serve the interest of the buyer—the customer. *Reversing our role required a drastic attitudinal change*. This was the greatest challenge to us. But, we had to get over the 'allottee mindset' and build a 'customer mindset' into our functioning or operations to survive the onslaught of decanalisation and re-establish our leadership in the Indian non-ferrous metals market.

I wish to give two examples of how we tried to, or rather demonstrated, the change from 'allottee mindset' to 'customer mindset'.

The first example is about my visit. I went to visit one of our regular buyers (during canalisation) in Delhi. We went with appointment. My manager spoke to him and fixed the time. When I sent my visiting card (we now call this 'business card') inside, he was rather surprised. He came out himself and took me in. He told me: "Sir, I am delighted to see you here. Frankly, I did not expect this". I told him, "So far, you have been coming to us. It is now our turn to come to you". He replied: "Don't worry. We will continue to do business with you. We cannot handle import. We are not equipped to do that. Private importers are not reliable. The moment price goes up, they back out from their commitments. Also, I find that MMTC is changing its approach or attitude. This is a very welcome sign".

The second example is about Dir. (RK)'s visit to Bharat Electronics (BEL), Bangalore (now Bangaluru). He went with prior appointment. The appointment was with the concerned Director in BEL Dir. (RK) reached on time. But, he was made to wait for about 45 minutes. When he went inside, BEL Director told him; "Sorry, Mr. Khosla, I kept you waiting. I wanted you to have a taste of waiting." During canalisation, I went to meet your GM (Non-ferrous). I went with appointment. In spite of that, she kept me waiting for 45 minutes. Dir. (RK) replied; "You have done absolutely the right thing. I don't mind it. Now, our roles have reversed. It is now my turn to wait. If necessary, I shall come again. I shall keep coming and waiting for you till I am able to erase the canalisation impression from your mind. I want to show that we are changing and we want to change fast." BEL Director concluded: "I totally agree with you that you are changing. Your visit today is a big step forward."[6]

These are two of many examples or stories of customer management.

To summarise MMTC's crisis management strategy or to conclude, the crux of MMTC's strategy for regaining leadership in the Indian non-ferrous market is; first, response time minimisation essential in competitive industrial business; second, the customer concept or focus; and; third, related to this and the most important, the attitudinal change to treat "yesterday's allottee" as "today's customer". Rest of the elements of the crisis management strategy and their implementation followed from these three basic factors.

All this was not easy within the public sector procedures and accountability systems. But, the non-ferrous team demonstrated that it is possible to find ways to achieve your objective without violating the fundamentals of the system. As a team leader, I attribute our success to dedication of the team and top management support—Director (RK) at the helm and the CMD.

Such successful crisis management can be executed in other public or private sector companies also particularly important in manufacturing companies with high investments. But, this requires the crisis management mindset of the management and innovativeness in business approach or strategy.

LEADERSHIP MISMATCH AND CRISIS MANAGEMENT

Sometimes, surprisingly, the leader, instead of spearheading the crisis resolution process, himself (herself) becomes the source of crisis for the organisation, company or the brand. What should be the crisis resolution process in such eases? Here are some interesting insights.

Leadership Leading to Crisis

On March 6, 2022, Chitra Remakrishna, former MD and CEO, National Stock Exchange (NSE), was arrested by the CBI for misgovernance and several "grave and serious" charges putting the NSE brand into disrepute.

ICICI Bank's former CEO Chanda Kochar had misused her office in a partisan loan sanction to an industrial house (Videocon?). Timely action against Kochar helped the Bank to tide over the crisis and retrieve its reputation to a large extent.

Let us also take the recent war of words between BharatPe Founder Ashneer Grover and the company's Board and the CEO setting of stormy accusations and counter charges, and, controversies. Episodes like this expose fissures in the corporate governance of the company betraying consumer trust and investor confidence.

There are many such cases of leadership involvement in corporate crisis.

Crisis Resolution Process

For restoring organisational image or the brand after questionable or immoral leadership action, experts have suggested a crisis resolution process.

The resolution process should be based on five steps or actions:

1. Remember: the brand is bigger than people
2. Mitigate long-term risk
3. Visualise the challenges and plan in time
4. Design the right strategy
5. Focus on sustainability

The Brand is Bigger than People

One person (the leader) representing a business or a brand can always be a big potential threat to its reputation. But, the potential threat can be averted to a large extent or brand restoration can be easier if it is remembered that the brand is always bigger than one individual.

Mitigate Long-term Risk

A brand's perception may take a short-term hit when the leadership controversy remains in the news cycle. Its long-term ramification or image depends on the steps taken to correct the situation. Sometimes, the exit of the CEO may be the only way to protect the company or the brand. This has happened in NSE and also ICICI bank.

Visualise the Challenges and Plan in Time

Try to assess the nature or magnitude of the leadership controversy or spoil and the challenges involved. "Understand if the person at the helm and the brand expouse the same values, as in the case of Apple, and, not just grandiose visions like the founders of highly funded e-commerce unicorns. Everyone today walks and talks like Elon Musk, but, unless your service or product benefits directly emanate from your aggrandising, you are only filling the brand balloon with hot air."

Design the Right Strategy

This implies an appropriate anticipatory or just-in-time strategy for rehabilitation of the company or the brand. Design of the strategy is vital. The right design landscape should start with defining company's brand's core values or strengths and maintaining them through the brand journey or fulfillment.

Focus on Sustainability

This means, in other words, focus on sustainability. The plan, design of strategy and implementation should render sustainability to the brand. This should be the objective of the conflict resolution process. *Constant search for or focus on sustainability will also minimise, if not eliminate, leadership disruption.*

13
Many Management Styles

Corporate Management seeks harmony in diversity.

Textbooks on management talk of management theories, systems and models. But, in reality, management systems and styles are many and diverse. There are management systems in the public sector. These are almost fundamentally different from those in the private sector. In the private sector, there are Western and Eastern conflicts in management—essentially between the American and Japanese systems. Individual CEOs have their own management styles. Then, companies require different management system during the pandemic and post-pandemic. Most of these are not taught in business schools.

Four different types of management styles are discussed below—existing and emerging:

- **A. Management systems in the public and private sectors: the contrasts**
- **B. Eastern and Western management styles: the conflicts**
- **C. Many CEO styles**
- **D. WFH and Hybrid Model: new styles of management**

A. MANAGEMENT SYSTEMS IN THE PUBLIC AND PRIVATE SECTORS: THE CONTRASTS

India has a very large public sector. It coexists with the private sector in the mixed economy of the country. The management system in the public sector is a big contrast to that in the private sector. These have inevitable implications for business, profit and growth of the two sectors.

"JAGIRDARIS" OF FAMILY AND BUREAUCRACY

Most of the private sector companies (except few multinationals) started and were managed as 'Jaigirdaris' of the families who started the business—the family members holding and manning key positions. You take Tatas, Birlas, Sarabhais (now extinct), Godrej, Ambanis, Adanis, Thapars, Mahindra and Mahindra, Premjis, TVS Group and others. Different management positions were occupied by the family members depending on their pools and pressures with the head of the family mostly occupying the top position (chairman). In such a system or environment, the urge or incentive for productivity was generally low or absent. So also was long-term planning for growth. This is why many cotton textile mills had closed down during the Seventies and, also, Eighties.

Slowly, over time, some professionalism has been introduced in company management. Many family managed companies have transformed themselves with professionally managed companies. Unilever is one of the best examples of this. Tatas also have professionalised to a very large extent. But, many companies have preferred to retain the family management culture. Aditya Birla Group companies are an example of this. So, are Ambanis and Adanis.

During the industrial evolution process in India, a stage came when government entered the industry. The government entered industry in two ways: first, by nationalising some of the existing enterprises in sectors or industries like steel, coal, fuel oil; and, almost simultaneously, setting up greenfield projects in sectors like heavy electricals (BHEL), oil and gas (ONGC, IOC), machine tools (HMT), non-ferrous metals (HZL, NALCO, HCL), electronics (BEL), etc. The public sector was born.

Public sector management was conceived and idealised as a perfect marriage between the 'brain' (entrepreneurship) of the private sector, and, 'beauty' (checks and controls) of the government sector. This form was thought to be the ideological optimum. But, what many countries, including India, have witnessed or experienced is only mismarriage with 'beauty' dominating over the 'brain'. Today, there is no entrepreneurism, there are only checks and controls.

As government entered the industry, *new jagirdars* from the civil service emerged in the industrial field. The family members in individual enterprises were replaced by the clan of civil servants. The management jobs or managerial positions in the public sector industry were decided and valued largely in terms of different grades in civil service.

CONTRASTS IN MANAGEMENT

Extension of civil service or bureaucracy is reflected in the structures and management systems of public sector companies. The most important is separation between 'job' and 'work' or output. In the family managed enterprises or the private sector, an employee/manager gets his salary or emoluments because of work or output, but, in the public sector, a manager's emoluments and perquisites are based on his job or post, and, not on his work or output. This has almost a disastrous effect on productivity of public sector managers. The public sector has not devised its own method for defining and measuring productivity of managers.

In both public and private sectors, there is assessment of managers' performance. This is done through annual performance review. In the private sector, this is usually called 'Performance Appraisal.' In professionally managed companies, appraisals are also discussed with the manager concerned and areas for improvement suggested. The appraisals form the benchmark for increments and promotions.

In the public sector, the performance review is called "Confidential Report (CR)." annual performance rating is done on a 5-point scale: outstanding, very good, good, average, poor. All managers with rating 'Good' and above are eligible for promotion. Managers with 'outstanding' rating should be entitled to out-of-turn or superseding promotion. But, in reality, this does not often happen. One of my colleagues (a GM) in MMTC told me: "I am walking with an 'outstanding' in my pocket." He got his promotion in normal course and seniority. This reflects on the evaluation or review system in the public sector.

The accountability factor in performance should be mentioned. In the public sector, the instrument (I call it fear) of accountability discourages all initiatives to perform. There is accountability in the private sector also. *Wherever there is compensation, there is accountability*. But, this has a different meaning and perspective in the private sector. Managers are allowed or encouraged to take initiative to perform or produce result and accountability is in terms of performance or output or result. In the public sector, accountability is more in terms of fault finding. If there is a lapse, vigilance takes centre-stage, and, a manager may be pushed to the wall to prove his credentials or honesty. A dishonest manager may sometimes know how to get away (if he knows the tricks of the trade), but, the honest manager may be "trapped"; he may have to sweat it out to establish his integrity.

The way public sector management has taken shape or been moulded is due to dominance of the civil service or bureaucracy. It can be said that *the fundamental difference between the private sector and public sector is bureaucracy*. All other differences between the two sectors follow from or are the results of this. Many management experts have said: "Remove bureaucracy and public sector will be efficient."[1]

Late Prime Minister Rajiv Gandhi wanted to eliminate or minimise bureaucratic interference in the management of the public sector. He very clearly analysed that they were not real stakeholders in public sector companies. Senior civil servants (usually at the level of Additional Secretary) would occupy CMD posts in public sector, (many CMD posts in the public sector are always vacant) be there for few years and go back to the cadre. Rajiv Gandhi said: "If you want to serve the public sector, you are welcome. But, you have to resign from the civil service and try to make a career there as other professionals are doing, and, not spend that period as paid holiday." But, unfortunately for the public sector and fortunately for the bureaucracy, Rajiv Gandhi died prematurely.

Efforts have been made to improve the working and performance of the public sector.[2] One important instrument was MOU (Memorandum of Understanding). Holding company solutions have been attempted. Other structural and management reforms like VRS have been suggested and tried.

But, the problems of the public sector remain. The French have a saying: "More things change, more they remain the same." This is so true of the public sector. In contrast, in the private sector, particularly in the professionally managed private sector, *change is almost permanent*.

PRIVATISATION OF PUBLIC SECTOR

Because of non-performance of the public sector companies (except few selected ones), privatisation has been thought of as the viable alternative for survival and growth of the sector. Privatisation has become a global phenomenon. Privatisation, however, is not an unmixed blessing. There is also debate on privatisation. The debate relates to disinvestment choice, timing, issues and modalities.

The privatisation debate has gone through three distinct phases. The first phase was primarily ideological beginning with Reaganomics and Thatcherism. In this phase, most of the literature focussed on "whether" to privatise. In the second or R&D phase, the focus was on modality or "how to privatise." In the third or current phase, the focus is on "when" and "how much" to privatise.

India is presently in the third phase. There were a number of privatisation moves earlier also. But, the current plan is the most comprehensive one. The complete blueprint of the plan is contained in the Strategic Disinvestment Policy (SDP), 2021 of the Government of India.

The SDP proposes privatisation of all central public sector enterprises (CPSE) other than those is four strategic sectors: 1. atomic energy, space and defence; 2. transport and telecommunication; 3. power, petroleum, coal and minerals; and 4. banking, insurance and financial services. Even in these four sectors, SDP 2021 promises to limit the presence of CPSEs to a "bare minimum." Even two banks—Central Bank and IOB—are to be privatised. All these are to be handled by the Department of Investment and Public Asset Management (DIPAM).

This is almost a gigantic task. DIPAM has so far not lived upto the task (DIPAM was established in 2016). It is still to open its account.

Considering the scale and magnitude of the privatisation drive, many feel that a department (DIPAM) is not enough. Some experts have suggested that a separate ministry should be created—the Ministry of Privatisation[3]—to carry out the task. So far, there are no such indications from the government.

Let us hope that something will be done speedily so that the public sector does not continue as a "white elephant," and, management styles of public and private sectors can be rewritten in a new perspective.

B. EASTERN AND WESTERN MANAGEMENT STYLES: THE CONFLICTS

The East and the West never meets—this age-old dichotomy has not remained confined to social and cultural spheres; it has permeated to the field of management also. This is not surprising because, in ultimate analysis, administrative and management patterns—in their detailed manifestations—would only reflect the prevalent social and cultural values. Therefore, the Eastern and Western conflicts.[4] And, as we all know, Japan symbolises the Eastern model of management as America does the West.

THE CONFLICT PREMISE

Takeo Fujisawa, the co-founder of Honda Motor Company, once remarked: "Japanese and American management is 95 per cent the same and differs in all important respects." It is like the difference between a man and a woman. About 90-95 per cent things are common between a man and a woman: only 5-10 per cent is different. But, this makes all the difference in life. So, is the difference between Japanese and American management (on different planes, however).

The genesis of the 5 per cent difference, which, according to Fujisawa, "means differing in all important respects" is the differentiation between the *art* of Japanese management and the *methods* of American management. According to some, the difference is a matter of seven Ss; or, rather, a matter of difference between the American "hard" Ss and the Japanese "soft" Ss.

The American companies, and the Western companies in general, tend to envisage three "hard" Ss: strategy, structure, systems. An American or a Western manager's method of implementing a management decision is to study the structure, work out the strategy and introduce or implement through the already designed control systems. But, the Japanese manager's way of managing things or running an organisation is through highlighting the "soft" Ss: staff, skills, style and super-ordinate goals (goals beyond or above the geometrical ordinates: philosophy, values, guiding concepts or principles which an organisation fosters among its members). The phenomenal success of many Japanese companies results from their meticulous attention to "soft" Ss "which act as a lubricant in the organisational machine to keep the "hard" Ss from grinding one another away."

STRUCTURE OR ORGANISATION CONFLICT

"Organisational structure provides, at best, the skeleton of an organisation. The ... vital organs derive from other sources."[5] There are "hard copy" systems involving reports and computer print-outs containing written numbers, words, and instructions. There are also "soft copy" systems involving meetings, discussions and counselling to take decisions to resolve conflicts. The "hard copy" system represents the American prototype; the "soft copy" system epitomises the Japanese style.

Most of the formal organisational structures had their origin and involvement in America and the Western countries. And, formal structures have been widely used in these countries. Organisational structures are intended to be the binding force for the personnel in various functions and departments. In contrast, most Japanese companies don't even have a reasonable organisation chart. Nobody knows how Honda is organised except that it uses lots of project teams and is quite flexible. When organisational loyalty is more like family loyalty, is there really an impending need for a formal organisational structure? After all, below every successful formal structure, there are undercurrents of an informal understanding or system which holds together the formal organisation and makes possible its smooth functioning.

Chester Barnard, while commenting on organisation-executive relationship, observed: "Organisations are a system of co-operative activities—and, their co-ordination requires something intangible and personal that is largely a matter of relationships." Barnard's observations made more than fifty years ago, sound very much like what we hear today in most of the Japanese companies. Managers spend much of their time in communication, using informal processes with others—peers, superiors and subordinates. The Japanese executive firmly believes in the dictum that it is a manager's *span of relationships* and not his *hierarchical span of control* that determines his effectiveness and success. The American manager rarely thinks so.

We can more clearly see the Japanese and American contrasts in the organisational forms used by the chiefs of two giant corporations—ITT (International Telephone and Telegraph), an American giant, and Matsushita (Matsushita Electric Company) a Japanese giant. Harold Geneen, who managed ITT for nearly two decades, is quite clearly regarded as the arch type of an American boss. Geneen developed in ITT a powerful central management group, created "tension," and produced "intense competitive pressures which drove the executives of his organisation relentlessly." The head of each division was responsible in detail for all aspects of this operation, and, was constantly scrutinised by the top management. To put it in Geneen's words: "There are internal controls, monthly management reviews, constant pressures and samplings to measure progress."[6]

In contrast, Matsushita's conception of an organisation was always fluid. He never took his organisation charts too literally or too seriously, and, had built-in safety valves to make them less formal and more human. For example, his controllers and other headquarters staff were always referred to as "coordinators." There was competition, but, never under relentless pressure and tension. Matsushita always endeavoured to strike a perfect balance between centralisation and decentralisation (in contrast to Geneen's highly centralised system) with appropriate posting of line and staff personnel in the plants and the head office. This paved the way for extraordinary efficiency of his divisionalised system. And, there was always the undercurrent of a humane approach and not a formalist approach. *Professionalism always implies certain amount of formalism.* In America, formal structures and organisational patterns are, in one sense, forerunners of professionalism. The Japanese system, by the same token, is less or least professional, at least in the American sense.

Formalism in the professional approach makes the Americans conscious of methods, techniques and strategies. This consciousness has been often equated with rationalism and professionalism with the rationalist approach. So, professionalism, formalism and rationalism are the American cults; common sense or traditionalism, informalism and shared values are the Japanese styles. To amplify: "Analyse, plan, tell, specify, and check up" are the verbs of the formal or rational American process. "Interact; test, try, fail, stay in touch, learn, adapt, modify, and see" are the verbs of the informal Japanese managing process.

Americans and Western may be shattered to know that there is not a single business school in Japan. Yet, the Japanese succeed more in business than the Americans who boast of the best business schools and management education in their country. So, the source of, or secret to, success lies somewhere else.

We all know about Japan's phenomenal success in cornering the small car market. Talking of this success, Fortune explains:

> The Japanese deserve credit for far more than the circumstantial triumphs of being able to supply efficient cars to a country (the United States) caught short of them. They excel in the quality of fits and finishes, mouldings that match, doors that don't sag, materials that look good and wear well, flawless paint jobs. Most important of all, Japanese cars have earned a reputation for reliability borne out by the generally lower rate of warranty claims they experience. (But), technically, most Japanese cars are fairly ordinary.[7]

What, then, is the secret? What is the Japanese magic? It is the love for the product, among many other things? Frederick Herzberg, an observer of American management practice for forty years concludes: "(American) managers don't love the product. In fact, they are defensive about it." On the other hand, we hear the story (already stated earlier) of a Honda worker who, on his way home each evening, straightens up windshield wiper blades on all the Hondas he passes because he just can't stand to see a flaw in a Honda! The contrast is all too clear.

Chairman of Sony, Akio Morita, was having lunch in New York one day with Professor Peter Drucker and Bill Bernback, the advertising man whose agency designed many fascinating advertising campaigns for Sony. The subject of management came up, and, Drucker said, "When I speak with Japanese managers, they don't seem to me to be rational in their thinking. The strange thing, though, is that they end up coming to the correct conclusions. How is that possible?"

Bernback pondered for a while. "My profession is advertising and I don't know much about business administration," he said. He continued, "But, in order to make rational decisions, you have to know all of the facts and the environment that surrounds the facts." But, it is probably impossible for a human being to know everything. American managers may belief that they are rational, but, they are rational only on the basis of facts that they have come to know. They are bound to be lots of facts and environmental factors that they don't know. If these are missing, it is natural that no matter how rational a conclusion might seem, it is going to be off base. Compared with this, Japanese managers seem to have a kind of oriental "sixth sense." Probably instead of putting one fact together with another, they grasp a general idea as a whole and then use this information together with that "sixth sense" in making decisions. This way they have a better grasp general idea, than one get only through careful reasoning.[8] Call it sixth sense, fourth eye, management by judgement or irrational rationality, but, the Japanese do it.

Morita aptly summarises the contrast between American professionalism and the Japanese art of management: "Americans pride themselves on being rational in their business judgements:

the total logic of American business schools seems to be cold, de-emphasising the human element. We, in Japan, see the bases for success in business and industry differently. We believe that if you want high efficiency and productivity, a close cordial relationship with your employees, which leads to high morale, is necessary."

Sometimes, it is more important to generate a sense of affirmity than anything else, and, sometimes you must make decisions that are technically irrational. You can be totally rational with a machine. But, if you work with people, sometimes logic has to take a back seat to understanding.

MOTIVATION CONFLICT

If "self-consciousness" is the principle of the Americans, "self-motivation" is the principle of the Japanese. The family culture in the Japanese companies creates the ideal environment for motivating people. *Self-motivation leads to group motivation, and, group motivation finally leads to corporate motivation.*

Absence of formal appraisal system in Japan is an effective aid, we may call it an instrument also, to motivation for the maximum number. In a management system dominated by formal appraisal and evaluation, only the few brilliant people (maybe the top 10 per cent) are especially rewarded. The majority of the employees (may be rated "average") generally have a tendency to become apathetic to the interests of the organisation. They are neither fully committed nor disloyal to the organisation. This is a snag in the discriminatory reward system. If, instead, organisational efforts are geared to motivating the general employees, given a proper work, the organisation is likely to win over the dedication of a much larger number of its people than otherwise. 'This is what Japanese companies have shown and achieved. And, because of their people approach and exceedingly good interpersonal relations, creating and sustaining an appropriate work environment has only been too easy.

The recognition of people as the most important (natural) resource, and, concern for the fullest development, including emotional growth of this resource, is the greatest motivating factor in Japan. If the company can generate a feeling among each of its employees that he is not merely an economic resource, that he means much more to the company, that he is an indispensable member of the company family and that it is a life-time bond, motivation becomes almost spontaneous.

The concept of self and self-centredness drives the Americans and Westerners to become independent in their approach in the sociological sphere and in management. The feeling of dependence, interaction and interdependence induce the Japanese to "Work Group" approach (this is different from the committee approach in the West and in America). The "Work Group" is the basic building block in Japanese organisations and a prime motivating factor. Because of the central importance of group efforts in their approach, the Japanese are extremely sensitive to and concerned about group interactions and relationships. They regard group phenomena primarily in terms of morals and emotions rather than role and functions. Their view of groups is said to be closely analogous to the marital relationships in the West—the Japanese recognise the kinds of problems, concerns and subtleties in work relations that the Westerners focus on in marriage concerning trust, sharing and commitment. Like a Western marriage, the Japanese work group imposes tasks and roles which are not always clearly delineated, based on understandings, sometimes need revision and require a "constant investment of emotional capital."

We illustrate the motivational contrast in America and Japan through two stories based on the experience of a top Indian executive. The Indian executive was shopping in a department store in Japan. He wanted to purchase something for his mother-in-law. He found something big and nice but, very inexpensive. So, he purchased it and told the Japanese manager accompanying him that it was a gift for his mother-in-law. The Japanese manager whispered something to the sales girl in Japanese and immediately the Indian found that the sales girl was collecting a plastic box, wrapping paper, ribbon, etc. He told the Japanese manager, "Look here! I don't want to spend any more on this fancy packing material:" The manager said, "I did not tell the sales girl to get any special packing material. All I told her was, "This gentleman has purchased this item to present it to his mother-in-law." She herself decided to pack it well. Probably, she thinks that this present is not only from you but it is also from this department store!"

In the same trip, the Indian executive proceeded to America.

In those days (1961), digital wrist watches had just come into the market. He saw a board: "Sale: Digital wrist watches-$9.99." He went and saw the wrist watches. They looked very attractive. Instructions regarding how to use them were in a small booklet in very small print. So, he called the standing sales girl and asked her if she could explain to him how the wrist watch worked. The sales girl said, "Sorry, Sir, for 9 dollars and 99 cents we can't give this service."

See the difference in styles of the two sales girls—difference in their service attitudes. This is the motivation conflict between the East and West. This can also be called cultural difference or conflict.

The difference between the US and Japanese companies or management styles go much beyond this. We put this in the words of Akio Morita: "If you ask a Japanese executive, 'What is your most important responsibility?', he will invariably say that continued employment and improving the livelihood of the workers is at or near the top of the list. In order to do that, the company must make a profit. Making of profit will never be at the top of the list. Most of the American executives I know put the highest priority on return to the investors or this year's profit. They have the responsibility because the investors gave it to them, and, to stay in their jobs, they have to continue to keep the investors happy. The board of directors represents the investors, and, if top management fails to give the return the investors feel they need, he will be fired. For that reason, he is entitled to use the factory and the machinery of the company, and, also the workers, as tools to accomplish his aim."[8]

This summarises the Eastern and Western conflicts:

C. MANY CEO STYLES

Every company has its own management system and style of functioning. So, have CEOs. Company systems and styles are mostly derived from CEO styles.

Every CEO is distinct or unique—has his(her) own management style—be it managing business or people or customers. If there are hundred CEOs, there are hundred styles; if there are thousand CEOs, there may be thousand styles; globally, there may be million CEOs with million styles. They defy all theories and models. It is fascinating to know the diversity of CEO styles.

Because, we cannot capture so many CEO styles in a space like this (a separate book can be written on the subject), we present here in brief, distinctive styles of ten CEOs in different businesses or industries—both Indian and global. The CEOs are: Jack Welch (GE), Michael Dell (Dell computer, now Dell Technologies), Akio Morita (Sony), Konosuke Matsushita (Matsushita Electricals), Verghese Kurien (Amul), Azim Premji (Wipro), Kiran Mazumdar Shaw (Biocon), N.R. Narayana Murthy, (Infosys), Sanjib Mehta (HUL) and Suresh Narayanan (Nestle India).

JACK WELCH

Jack Welch was the legendary CEO of GE, the world's most valuable company. Jack Welch was named CEO of the Millennium.

Jack Welch conceived and moulded GE as a flat organisation. The concept of the command and control (hierarchical) structure is gone. The CEO will increasingly be the orchestra leader of very bright people doing their things, and, sort of cheering them and coaching them.[9] The CEO will not be the all-knowing power base any longer. He has to have lot of communication and lot of energy. He has to be everywhere, be focussed and visible.

According to Welch, the Internet is the biggest revolution in business history since the industrial revolution. Today, if a company has an idea and a unique product, it can go to the internet. In a day, the company can become global. It has only to offer the product with a well designed site. GE implements this truthfully.

Brick-and-mortar companies may have to reinvent themselves. There has to be fusion between conventional methods and new technologies. Infrastructure building companies, network companies which provide opportunities for brick-and-mortar companies will succeed. The trend has already set in.

Welch gave high focus on people, man management and career growth. People must have opportunity to move up the management chain. "If we don't provide growth path for them. If we don't provide careers for them, they will go tomorrow." "We have to provide the opportunity, the environment, dignity and growth to every employee in GE," said Welch. GE is proud that it has achieved this. This is the key to GE's success.

MICHAEL DELL

Michael Dell is the founder, chairman and CEO of Dell Technologies, formerly known as Dell Computer Corporation. Michael Dell is an extraordinary entrepreneur CEO unlike many professional CEOs.

Dell Technologies has one of the leanest corporate organisations in the world, arguably the leanest. The company employed "few people as order takers, a few more to fill the orders," and, as Michael Dell recalls, a manufacturing staff consisting of "three guys with screwdrivers sitting at six-foot tables." With such an almost staffless organisation, Dell almost performed miracles. In 1992, at 27 years of age, Dell became the youngest CEO of the company ranked in the *Fortune* 500 companies.

Michael Dell is a champion of the direct marketing model. Dell had the conviction that cost saving in selling PCs directly (it also saves time) is enormous, with its impact on profitability, compared to indirect selling though distributors or channels. In 1996, Dell Technologies started selling PCs on the Web. In 2001, Dell had achieved a global market share of 12.8 percent surpassing Compaq to become the world's largest PC maker and marketer.

Michael Dell is also a champion of recessions. *He used recession as opportunity*. During 1991, the peak of 1990-92 global recession, Dell decided to launch its most aggressive marketing campaign and taken on the established computer giants. The campaign coincided with the introduction of its first notebook computer. In 1991, advertising in the entire computer hardware industry was down by almost 18 per cent. IBM, Apple, Digital and Tandy—industry's leading spenders—all made large cuts in promotional spending ranging between 25 per cent and 40 per cent.

But Dell broke away completely from the industry pattern or trend. The company increased its marketing spend by about 350 per cent to $6 million from just half a million in 1989 and $1.4 million in 1990. This paid large dividends. By 1993, the company was one of the top five computer system makers in the world culminating in its becoming the market leader in 2001. It is the company's recession marketing strategy which made this possible.

Michael Dell believes in big business expansion through acquisition. He executed this though Dell Inc. During 2015, Dell Inc. decided to acquire the enterprise software and storage company EMC Corporation. The acquisition was finalised in September, 2016 at $ 67 billion. This has been labelled as the "highest-valued tech acquisition in history."

AKIO MORITA

Akio Morita was the co-founder, CEO and Chairman of Sony Corporation (popularly known as 'Sony'—it is also the umbrella brand). Morita is renowned for his exceptional vision and intuitive ability to execute.

Akio Morita was an entrepreneur par excellence—more an entrepreneur than a CEO or chairman. Morita personified Japan's rise from post-war rubble to industrial richness and became the unofficial ambassador of its business community to the world.

Akio Morita's management style or strategy is built on people or staff, market, competition and innovation.[10]

Morita was a team-man or people-man. Morita realised that Japan has no natural resource "except our people's energy." So, this must be utilised fully. He rightly visualised that employees should form the core of Sony's organisational success.

He observes: "There is no secret ingredient or hidden formula responsible for the success of the best Japanese companies. No theory or plan or government policy will make a business a success; that can only be done by the people .... Those companies that are most successful in Japan are those that have managed to create a shared sense of fate among all employees, what Americans call labour and management, and, the shareholders."

Morita strongly emphasised, and, implemented participative management. He says: "A company will get nowhere if all of the thinking is left to management. Everybody in the company must contribute, and, for the lower-level employees, their contribution must be more than just manual labour. We insist that all our employees contribute their minds." He made participative management the corporate philosophy of Sony.

Morita foresaw that if Sony is to grow really big which he had envisioned, it cannot be limited by the size of the market. It cannot be confined only to the domestic market. This means, in other words, that Sony must look to export.

Earlier Japanese goods were known to be of poor quality. Morita decided to change the image of Sony products. He concentrated on improving quality and started making high quality products. High quality products have higher cost and high price. So, Sony started exploring "affluent sophisticated" markets like Europe and the US, and, established its reputation as a maker of high quality consumer electronic goods. Soon, Sony became a global brand.

The Japanese market is competitive, but, the export market in general, and, the European and American markets in particular, are more competitive. Morita was fully aware of this. But, he was not afraid of competition. In fact, according to him, competition is the "fuel of Japanese enterprise."

Morita realised that competition should begin at home. In the competition in the domestic market, Sony should develop its ability to compete abroad. Winning the competition battle should increase market share of the company.

For Sony, market share in the domestic market, and, also, in the foreign market, is more important than immediate profitability. Market share establishes the product firmly. This has been the guiding principle for Sony's marketing strategy.

Morita was highly innovative. He wanted to thrive through constant or regular innovations.

Sony was/is hailed as a pioneer in many consumer electronics goods. Sony had brought out products which were never marketed before—actually, not made before—like transistorised radios and solid-state personal television sets. Because of their reputation as a pioneer, some called Sony the "guinea pig" of the electronics industry.

One of the greatest innovations of Morita and Sony is the 'Walkman.' This epitomises perfect miniaturisation of personal electronics. This miniature product has literally changed the music-listening habits of millions of people all over the world. And, Walkman is not the result of any R&D or market research. This is the product of Morita's and Sony's innovative zeal. As Morita puts it: "I do not believe that any amount of market research could have told us that the Sony Walkman would be successful, not to say a sensational hit that would spawn many imitators.

KONOSUKE MATSUSHITA

Konosuke Matsushita was the founder, CEO and Chairman of Matsushita Electric company. In terms of strategy and style, Matsushita is a contrast to Akio Morita in many ways.

We start with organisational structure. Matsushita developed a divisionalised structure "as a means of keeping things small and entrepreneurial." Matsushita was one of the first to recognise that centralisation versus decentralisation is an "unresolvable conflict" and great organisations must have both. In Matsushita Electric company, decentralisation and centralisation are seen "revolving in kind of spiral." Matsushita devised his own unique way to deal with line/staff tension in the company.

In terms of strategy, Matsushita consistently violated the strategic rules by which Japanese business was governed. Instead of using the Matsushita name (as was customary in Japan), he introduced the *National* brand name and vigorously promoted it though advertising. He created his own channels of distribution and went directly to the retailers, and, forged a "close and continuing partnership" with them. This was almost considered revolutionary during his time.

Another important element of Matsushita's corporate strategy is "followership." Matsushita did not attempt to pioneer new technology, but, always emphasised quality, cost effectiveness and competitive price. Matsushita rarely invents a product, but, always succeeds in manufacturing it for less cost and marketing it "best." Matsushita's strategy was to "leapfrog competition."

As a matter of strategy, Matsushita focused more on market share than profit as higher production generates cost saving through price reduction to increase sales and market share. This is a sure way to reach market ascendancy

Matsushita had the conviction that profits are linked to business growth. Investments which promote growth will eventually pay off in profit in the long-run. In business, profit is also important because it provides investible funds for growth. It should be mentioned that Matsushita, together with Takahashi, pioneered the world's first profit centre.

Matsushita developed his own unique style of management. The highlight of this was his intensely "hands-on" approach. He established a style of management which was small-business-like and fully consistent with his aim to instil an entrepreneurial spirit among the employees, and, staff or people development. Matsushita firmly believed that "an enterprise as a whole was no better than the people in it."[11] He did everything, including training, to develop his people.

Matsushita's personalised style, strategy and values combined together to make MEC so large and successful in its category alongside GE, Phillips and Siemens.

VERGHESE KURIEN

Verghese Kurien was the founder, Chief Executive and Chairman of Gujarat Cooperative Milk Marketing Federation (GCMMF), popularly known for trade name 'AMUL' (Anand Milk Union Limited)—India's biggest food sector enterprise.

Verghese Kurien's management style and strategy were fundamentally different from those in conventional products or business. His strategy was for fostering the cooperative milk movement in India.

GCMMF was earlier known as Kaira District Cooperative Milk Producers Union. Till Kurien joined, GCMMF was almost like a sleeping organisation. Daily milk collection was only about few thousand litres. Kurien introduced speed, spread and volume in the milk collection and distribution system. He pioneered and engineered far reaching developments. GCMMF was undergoing a revolution.

Today, there are about 200 'Anand's in India handling about 20 million litres of milk everyday. GCMMF has 20 diary plants with total milk handling capacity of more than 7 million litres per day. GCMMF has launched similar and associated movements all over India and also in the neighbouring countries of Sri Lanka and Bangladesh. In Gujarat alone, there are more than 2 million milk producers who are members of the village cooperative. Societies in more than 11,000 villages with 12 District Unions federated with GCMMF.

The revolution in the production of milk or the White Revolution (also called Operation Flood) has reached more than 1,00,000 villages all over India covering more than 200 district unions and 15 State Federations with a total membership of about 12 million milk producers/farmers. They together handle about one-third of India's marketable surplus milk.

The World Bank made an evaluation of the White Revolution or Operation Flood. It said in its report: "The overall expansion of the dairy industry from the early 1970s has been comparable to the more widely recognised Green Revolution crops of wheat and rice. Operation Flood is unusual in that it is a single-commodity integrated development project.[12]

The Anand model is much more than a statement of organisational structures and activities. Kurien's strategy is networking of farmers. This is based on certain ideals and values of milk producers and distributors, including women empowerment. These values and principles are vital for the resurgence of our country, or, for that matter, of poor people anywhere in the world.

Kurien desires that the white revolution must continue. Kurien's dream or hope for the future is: "Let there be 1000 Anands." He humbly adds: "There are a lot of Kuriens." Let these Kuriens bloom. Then, Anands will also bloom.

AZIM PREMJI

Azim Premji has been the MD and Chairman of Wipro, the diversified company. Currently, Premji is only the Chairman.

Premji took over, or rather inherited, Western India Vegetable Products—name later changed to Wipro—from his father at a very young age of just 21. He faced resistance from some of the existing shareholders of the company. But, he was determined. He had confidence in himself. He soon proved his mettle and established his leadership.

Azim Premji is a visionary leader. He foresaw the opportunity in emerging information technology and grabbed it. From vegetable products, Wipro fast diversified into information technology computing with likes of ORG systems, DCM Data Products and Hindustan Computer (HCL). The company later diversified into personal computer (PC). Computer and information technology businesses are Wipro's current focus.

Wipro's business philosophy focusses on human values, customer, integrity, innovativeness and value for money. In the words of Wipro or Premji:

"With utmost respect to *Human Values*,
We promise to serve our *customer with Integrity*,
Through a variety of *Innovative*,
Value for Money products and services,
By *Applying Thought*, day after day."

Given these guiding principles, Premji wishes to run Wipro professionally. He expects all his managers to be professional. He gives his view of professionalism: "In my view, a professional manager is one who delivers results without compromising on the core values, hates bureaucracy and is apolitical."[13]

Professionalism should lead to efficiency in delivering products/results. Premji puts very high focus an efficiency.

Premji believes that, for achieving sustained growth, Wipro should be a "Learning Organisation." The company should continually learn from the environment (includes competition). He says: "No matter how good you are, someone out there knows how to do things a little better." Learning from the environment prepares the company well for success or growth in a competitive world.

In Wipro becoming professional, efficient and successful, Premji emphasises pivotal role of two factors: central leadership and organisational values. The leader takes all key decisions and gives direction to the company.

Premji summarises the role of values in the growth of an organisation like this: "Values help achieve success and also make success enduring and lasting. Values combined with a powerful vision can turbocharge you to scale new heights."

KIRAN MAZUMDAR-SHAW

Kiran Mazumdar-Shaw is the founder, MD and Chairman of Biocon India, the largest biotechnology venture in India. She has been leading a silent revolution in a virgin field more than 30 years.

Kiran is a dreamer, entrepreneur and professional. She is very unconventional and unusual. Her business philosophy is creativity and innovation. As she says: "R&D is the very life force of the Biocon India Group."

In terms of style of management and functioning, Biocon is very unconventional. As Kiran says: "You would not find this style of management in most companies. This is because we really believe in *flat* organisation. We believe very strongly in *networking* throughout the organisation. I do not believe in giving management territories or boundaries to any person in the company. I encourage them to interact very freely and not worry about designations."[14] This, closely approximates *informal management* style.

Kiran runs Biocon as a knowledge company. The way you run your business determines whether you are a knowledge company or not. Kiran says: "All copycat companies are not knowledge companies even if they are into biotch. Because they are not innovative.... You are a knowledge company only if you are innovative and inventing. You are not a knowledge company if you are licensing a technology and manufacturing."

About profitability and success, Kiran has her own view or conviction. She thinks that money or profit is necessary or important, but, "The fast buck and greed element has to go away. One has to work for the joy of creating something." She adds: "I always believe that money comes automatically. Money comes automatically when you succeed." Every company should strive for success. Money will flow.

N.R. NARAYANA MURTHY

Narayana Murthy is the founder, CEO and Chairman of Infosys Technologies. Currently, he is Chairman Emeritus.

Because of Narayana Murthy's vision, entrepreneurship and leadership, Infosys has evolved from offering on site services to project management to business solutions. This has been achieved over a time span capitalising on opportunities in the environment. The global Delivery Model and achieving quality certifications were the initial steps. Establishment of the Domain Competency Group (DCG) and Infosys Business Consulting Services (IBCS) were steps or strategies to understand the needs of customers better and to provide a one-stop shop for the clients.

Three factors have overwhelmingly contributed to the extra ordinary growth and success of Infosys: Leadership, Employee Stock Option Plan (ESOP) and physical infrastructure and environment.

Narayana Murthy strongly feels that "A good leader makes the impossible possible." According to him: "Leadership is about creating a vision, communicating that vision to one's followers and exhorting them to move towards that vision"[15] and accomplishment. Exhortation is not really necessary because Narayana Murthy has created a culture of long-term relationships within the organisation.

Narayana Murthy's most innovative corporate move or instrument for motivating staff is Employee Stock Option Plan (ESOP). Narayana Murthy implemented and popularised ESOP among employees at all levels in Infosys. He offered all of them stock options—option to posses Infosys stocks. It is not just motivation or loyalty; this gives a feeling of "ownership." This infuses commitment and surely helps to increase productivity.

Infosys has created a world class physical infrastructure and environment. Says Narayana Murthy: "Look at the physical infrastructure that we have created here. It is truly world class. We have shown quality and productivity in everything that we do. Look at our Annual Report. It has been voted as the best in India for several years. So, I would say, as Aristotle did, "Excellence is a habit."

Narayana Murthy makes excellence a habit in Infosys.

SANJIV MEHTA

Sanjiv Mehta is the current CEO and CMD of Hindustan Unilever (HUL), the largest FMCG company in India. Sanjiv Mehta is a truly professional CEO/CMD.

As a highly professional company, HUL follows its long-term business model or strategy irrespective of whether it is boom time, downturn or even pandemic. The business model envisages constant interaction with the environment and responding to changing consumer behaviour and preferences through appropriate product-price offerings. This is the core business philosophy of HUL or Mehta.

Mehta observes: "Businesses must become far more adaptable and resilient even as best prediction models fail to assure a non-risk world....Leaders must get comfortable with ambiguity and chaos."[16]

To implement their business model in practice, HUL puts commensurate focus on product—brand management, cost management and supply chain management so vital in FMCG business. In HUL, products and brands are always evolving. The company is tackling cost headwinds. The company ensures supply security through seamless operations at both the back-end supply chain (factory operations) and at the front-end (delivery).

HUL and Mehta are fully aware that these are unprecedented times (the pandemic and the market downswing) and it requires playing different levers of business smartly. "But, Mehta says, we play the game for the long-term, and, three imperatives are: we don't want to lose consumers or market share, we want to keep the price-value equation, and maintain the sanctity of our business model. That's how we are going to play"[17] the game.

HUL is fully committed to sustain its market leadership. Mehta reiterates: "We don't want to lose market share." Armed with a large portfolio of brands straddling the price and pack pyramid, Mehta knows how best to leverage the price-value equation to retain consumers in HUL's franchise. This is the core of his management strategy.

SURESH NARAYANAN

Suresh Narayanan is the CEO and Chairman of Nestle India, the Indian subsidiary of the Swiss food giant, and, India's largest listed food and beverages company. Narayanan is the first Indian MD/Chairman in seventeen years to head Nestle India.

Narayanan, with his own management style, successfully steered the company through one of its biggest crises which began in 2015.

Narayanan has strong conviction about the corporate organisation at Nestle—the way the organisation functions and decision making. According to Narayanan: "The whole purpose of organisations is to recalibrate, to empower, to enable decision making at the appropriate levels." Managers in Nestle—in factories, branches and marketplace—take their own decisions under certain guidelines from the corporate leadership. This is balancing centralisation and decentralisation. Narayanan says: "This is the way organisations grow up and mature into new models of leadership relevant in the new context."

For a company like Nestle, marketing is the focal point of management strategy. To Nestle and Narayanan, marketing is much more than the conventional definition of 4Ps. Narayanan says: "Marketing is a deep dive into all aspects of the value chain and is much bigger than the way we define it. And, I dare say, in many contexts, too important to be left only to marketing managers. The CEO has to be involved.[18]

For business success, Narayanan highlights the 5R Principle: Relevance, Resonance, Reinforcement, Rejuvenation and Rechartering.

Relevance comes from organisational values and brands. Nestle's brands—Nescafe, Milkmaid, Kit Kat and Maggi—are highly relevant to the Indian consumer.

Resonance reflects the way Nestle cultivates its relationship with the consumer over a long period of time.

Reinforcement is the way the company innovates constantly in the marketing mix.

Rejuvenation indicates the company's capability to introduce new categories and new propositions.

Finally, *rechartering* is redefining or reconstructing the growth process from time to time.

Narayanan strongly believes that, if Nestle has to sustain itself as India's largest food and beverages company, "we have to continue to recharter our journey with people, purpose, partnerships and profits." He further adds that, companies which are successful are "those which look at not just their own people, but, also .... all stakeholders."

This is Narayanan's complete management strategy.

D. WFH AND HYBRID MODEL: NEW STYLES OF WORK MANAGEMENT

The pandemic has forced companies into a new style of functioning—work from home (WFH). This is an option without choice.

DIFFERENT VIEWS ON WFH

WFH may be a compulsion during the pandemic, but, companies and CEOs differ on whether WFH can be a more regular mode of corporate functioning or management. It also depends on the type of industry involved.

In the IT industry, WFH may be generally workable. In Infosys, about 98% employees are working from home globally.

The company, however, hopes that soon 28%-30% employees may start working from office. After more than a year of WFH, TCS and Wipro are planning to gradually get most of their staff back to office. One has to wait and see how soon this can happen.

According to some companies and CEOs, the manufacturing sector also can adopt a WFH model. Kirloskar are among them. Vikram Kirloskar, Vice-Chairman, Kirloskar Motor, says: "We have enabled work from home option for all non-production employees. Workforce is being engaged through employee-led CSR activities, skill trainings, regular business updates and clear and transparent internal communication."[19]

HUL, however, has a different view. Sanjiv Mehta, CMD, HUL, views things in another perspective. He focusses on personal interactions. He says: "Innovations need collaboration (and collaboration implies personal interactions). You need people to physically sit around, discuss, debate and brainstorm. The future of work is not going to be either or. There will be a good balance. All people won't need to come to work every day. But, don't write the obituary of the office and physical interactions."

Differential perceptions by companies and CEOs show that WFH may be more than just pandemic compulsion.

Assessing Performance During WFH

Two issues which commonly come up with regard to WFH are: first, getting organised at home, and, second productivity of people in WFH. These lead to a bigger issue of assessing employee performance during WFH.

Organisations may develop their own methods for performance review during WFH. All the same, it may be a tricky job. Some suggestions have been made about how to make such review more realistic.[20] Companies may like to align these suggestions with their own methods to make performance review during WFH more utilitarian and effective.

Six factors or guidelines have been suggested:

1. Before the meeting (virtual)
2. Gather information
3. Begin with empathy

4. Support vs. privacy
5. Closer to in-person, the better
6. End upbeat (optimistic)

Before the Meeting (virtual): The process should start before the review begins. Both the reviewer and the reviewee should prepare their performance reports and exchange them. These will form the base for the review meeting.

Gather Information: Because personal meeting/interaction is not possible, the reviewer should gather as much information as possible about the reviewee from other team members, customers and other stakeholders.

Begin with Empathy: The reviewer should have clear information about where the reviewee has excelled and where he(she) has missed out. Because it is WFH, more personal factors like working in a cramped apartment, dealing with problems or illness at home or managing parents or children should be taken into account.

Support vs. Privacy: The reviewer may have it to the reviewee which or how much personal factors/details he(she) may like to reveal—factors which affect productivity or performance. These will influence the review process/final review. The reviewee seeks the reviewer's support.

Closer to In-person the Better: A video conversation is more closer to in-person than a telephonic talk. This should always be preferred. The timing should be mutually convenient.

End Upbeat (Optimistic): Recognise the reviewee's mood and expectations, and, end upbeat or on a positive or optimistic note. The reviewer may close by saying: "We have got all your points or data. Let us see what best we can do for you now and for the future."

IS 'HYBRID' THE MODEL FOR THE FUTURE?

Many large companies are now showing preference for the hybrid model—a workable combination of WFH and working from office. The model has cost advantage for both the employer (saving on real estate and office overheads) and the employee (saving of travel and transport).

Unilever is quite emphatic about WFH—office combination. Observes Leena Nair, CHRO, Unilever: "For all the sadness the pandemic has brought,... one thing I hope we can take from this is the flexibility it has brought to business and people. It would be dreadful to return to the way so many of us were working—40 hour weeks, long commutes."[21] She adds further: "We're still developing our plan, but, one thing is certain: Things will never go back to the way they were before 2020."

Pepsico recently announced its global shift in workplace policy for corporate associates under "Work that Works." Citing studies, Pepsico said, "employers who offer flexible work see a 10% increase in productivity, 31% less absenteeism and 10% less turnover" of employees.

Pepsico India CHRO Pavitra Singh says: "If we look at this model through an employer's lens, output is being delivered, and, in fact, productivity levels have increased now. I feel that it is here to stay."

Vaidyanathan, COO, KPMG India says: "We will most probably follow a hybrid model once we reopen."

Many other opinions have been expressed—by companies and consultants—justifying the hybrid model in terms of its cost-benefits. The form or operational logistics may vary from company to company depending on organisational peculiarities or uniqueness. We may soon see innovations in the hybrid model to improve its appeal or workability.

4-DAY WEEK: A NEW TREND?

Different countries and companies have experimented with 4-day work week.

In Iceland, the experiment during 2015 and 2019 resulted in workers reporting less stress and burnout and improvement in productivity and work-life balance. A New Zealand company tested the method in 2018. Because of reduced stress and better employee engagement, the company has permanently adopted the policy. During 2019, Microsoft tried 4-day week in Japan. They found that productivity, measured as sale per employee, went up almost 40%; and, more than 90% staff liked the change.

Beroe Inc, procurement intelligence company, was trying to tackle two problems at the same time—attrition and productivity. The company thought of 4-day work week as a solution to both the issues. By the end of the first month, productivity increased by 50%. Inspired by this, Beroe amended work week with Friday off, and, this has led to many improvements in the organisation—attrition has almost disappeared, productivity has increased, and, so also employee satisfaction score.[22]

STARTUPS AND 4-DAY WEEK

Startups are also trying to adopt and adapt to 4-day week.

During the second week of the Pandemic (Summer, 2021), a number of Indian companies and startups temporarily introduced a 4-day week. These include Swiggy, Ad agencies DDB Mudra, MullenLowe Lintas and OYO. Some of these companies introduced mid-week break instead of conventional week-end off.

Another company which has permanently adopted a 4-day week is cyber-security firm TAC security. Says Founder-CEO Arora: "We got an opportunity and decided to take the plunge.... We have adopted by cutting down extra-long meetings. Initially, we took couple of days to adjust, but, we have adapted effortlessly without compromising on timeliness or work." For the company, both productivity and employee morale have been boosted.

We may wait and watch more developments in the 4-day experiment. We will know more about company experiences and plans.

MANAGEMENT SYSTEMS ARE EVOLVING...

Management systems keep evolving because of organisational compulsions and environmental development. The process of evolution may relate to CEO styles, corporate management modes/models or work methods. Technology is also driving the pace and form of evolution.

We can conclude by saying that system evolutions are different forms or manifestations of management dynamics. *Good management is never static; it is neither comparative statics*. Sustainable management, like that of GE, Phillips, Tatas, is characteristically dynamic; also, more evolutionary than revolutionary.

14

Excellence in Management

'Excellence' is a Buzzword...?

Many have talked and written about excellence and excellence in management. But, there is no clear definition or conceptual clarity on excellence and also identification of the ingredients or the driving factors of excellence in management.

Noted authors Parkinson and Rustomji, published their book *Excellence in Management* in 1978. But, the book can, at best, be said to be on good management. There is really no focus on excellence.

WHAT IS EXCELLENCE IN MANAGEMENT

"Excellence" should be defined, because, "excellence" is one word which is often talked about, but, not clearly or precisely understood. Conceptual clarity of "excellence" or understanding "excellence" in right perspective is important before we discuss excellence in management.

According to Oxford Dictionary, "excellence" means "surpassing merit," i.e., it goes beyond merit or good. It is something extraordinary. The meaning, genesis and implications of excellence in management will be more clear as we proceed.

Excellence in management is generally understood in two ways: corporate excellence and managerial excellence. But, conceptually, and, also in reality, these two may actually be called two components or constituents of excellence in management. We can depict this as below:

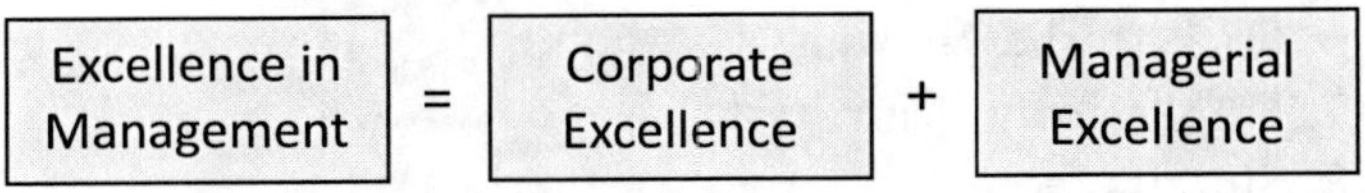

Corporate excellence and managerial excellence are not unrelated or exclusive to each other. These two are actually interactive as shown below:

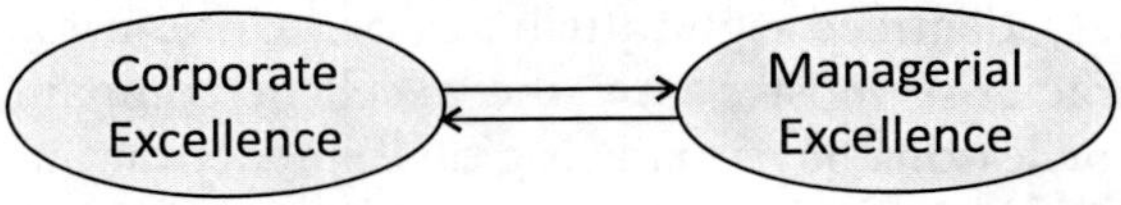

There is *no corporation (company) without manager; there is no manager without corporation (company)*. This shows the nature or level of interactivity.

Two terms or concepts which are sometimes mistaken for excellence are 'efficiency' and 'effectiveness.' Both efficiency and effectiveness contribute to achieving excellence, but, none of these by itself is excellence.

CORPORATE EXCELLENCE

In Search of Excellence by Peters and Waterman[2] is till today the most comprehensive work on corporate excellence.

Peters and Waterman analysed corporate excellence in terms of America's best-run companies. According to their study, America's best-run companies were IBM, 3M, P&G, McDonald's, Delta Airlines, Johnson & Johnson, Digital Equipment Corporation—IBM and McDonald's in particular.

EIGHT STANDARDS OF EXCELLENCE

Study results of Peters and Waterman are summarised in terms of eight distilled findings or standards of excellence. The authors call them "Criteria for Success."

The eight findings on strategy or standards of excellence are:

1. A bias for action
2. Close to the customer
3. Autonomy and entrepreneurship
4. Productivity through people
5. Hands on value driven

6. Stick to the knitting
7. Simple form, lean staff
8. Simultaneous loose-tight properties

In *In Search of Excellence*, the authors decided to have a close look at management excellence itself, and, based on a survey of a sample of a cross-section of successful American companies, identified eight attributes or "Criteria for Success" that characterise most nearly the excellent companies. These findings or lessons have made a global impact on management thinking and particularly on those who aim at management excellence. Every practising manager may like to know these findings. (Many managers may already know because the study is considered to be one of the bestsellers):

A Bias for Action: The excellent companies may be analytical in their approach, but, they are not paralysed by that fact. In many of these companies, the standard operating procedure is, "Do it, fix it; try it." Says the senior executive of a Digital Equipment Corporation "when we have got a big problem here, we grab ten senior guys and stick them in a room for a week. They come up with an answer and implement it." Moreover, the companies are great experimenters. Instead of allowing 250 engineers and marketers to work on a new product in isolation, for fifteen months, they form bands of 5 to 25 and test ideas out on a customer, often with inexpensive prototypes within a matter of weeks. What is striking is the host of practical devices the excellent companies employ to maintain corporate growth and excellence.

Close to the Customer: These companies love to learn from the people they serve. They stand for quality, service and reliability. Many of these companies get their best product ideas from customers. Service is not a motto; it is an obsession with these companies. A car salesman of one of the excellent companies says, "There is one thing I do that a lot of salesmen do not, and, that is believe the sale really begins after the sale—not before." In a meeting of sales managers in one of the excellent companies, the purpose was to discuss some customer problems. On the front table, there were eight or ten piles of papers, identifying the source of problems: manufacturing problems, engineering problems, and, the like. After much discussion, Mr. Watson, a big man (and a senior sales executive) walked slowly to the front of the room, and, with a flash of his hand, swept the table clean and sent papers flying all over the room. He said, "There are not any categories of problems here. There is just one problem. Some of us are not paying enough attention to our customers."

Autonomy and Entrepreneurship: The excellent companies foster many leaders and innovators throughout the organisation. 3M has been described as "so intent on innovation that its essential atmosphere seems not like that of a large corporation, but, rather a loose network of laboratories and cubbyholes populated by feverish inventors and dauntless entrepreneurs who let their imaginations fly in all directions." They encourage practical risk taking and support good moves. They follow Fletcher Byrom's ninth Commandment:

"Make sure you generate a reasonable number of mistakes."

Productivity through People: The excellent companies consider people as the most important resource and the root source of quality and productivity gains. They do not foster "We-They," "labour-management" attitudes. IBM's corporate philosophy is contained in three simple beliefs. The most important of these beliefs is: "Our respect for the individual." This is a simple concept. But, in IBM, it occupies a major portion of management time. Texas Instruments Chairman Mark Shepherd talks about it in terms of every worker being "seen as a source of ideas, not just acting as a pair of hands; each of his 9,000 people involvement program, or PIP teams (TI quality circles) does contribute to the company's sparkling productivity record."

Hands-on Value Driven: These companies believe that the basic philosophy (value system) of an organisation has far more to do with its achievements than do technological or economic resources, organisational structure, innovation, and timing. Values are not "hard" like organisation structures, policies and procedures, strategies or budgets. They are "soft;" but, there is immense solidity in their softness, and, it is this solidity which is the driving force behind the excellent companies. The content of the value system of these companies are few basic beliefs. These have been summarised as: (i) A belief in being the best; (ii) a belief in the importance of the details of execution, the nuts and bolts of doing the job well; (iii) a belief in the importance of people as individuals; (iv) a belief in superior quality and service; (v) a belief that most members of the organisation should be innovators, and, its corollary, the willingness to support failure; (vi) a belief in the importance of informality to enhance communication; and (vii) a belief in and recognition of the importance of economic growth and profits. The chief of one of the excellent companies adds: "Set and demand standards of excellence. Anybody who accepts mediocrity—in school, in job, in life—is a guy who compromises, and, when the leader compromises, the whole damn organisation compromises."

McDonald's Ray Kroc regularly visits stores and assesses them on the factors the company holds dear, Q.S.C. & V (Quality, Service, Cleanliness and Value).

Stick to the Knitting: Robert W. Johnson, former Chairman of Johnson and Johnson, put it this way: "Never acquire a business you don't know how to run." Or, as Edward G. Harness, past chief executive at Procter and Gamble said, "This company has never left its base. We seek to be anything but a conglomerate." While there were few companies, the odds for excellent performance seem strongly to favour those companies that stay reasonably close to businesses they know.

Simple Form, Lean Staff: Along with bigness, comes complexity. And, most big companies respond to complexity by designing complex systems and structures. They then hire more staff to keep track of all this complexity and it is here that mistakes creep in. The excellent companies seem to be fully aware of this. The underlying structural forms and systems in the excellent companies are elegantly simple. Top level staffs are lean; it is not uncommon to find a corporate staff of fewer than 100 people running multi-billion-dollar enterprises.

Simultaneous Loose-Tight Properties: The excellent companies are both centralised and decentralised. On the one hand, as a general corporate policy, they have pushed autonomy down to the shop floor or similar functional areas. On the other hand, they are fanatic centralists around few core values they hold dear. 3M is almost marked by organised chaos surrounding its product champions. At Digital, the chaos is so rampant that one executive noted, "Damn few people know who they work for." Yet, Digital's fetish for reliability is more rigidly adhered to than any outsider could imagine.

MANAGERIAL EXCELLENCE

Ever since the publication of *In Search of Excellence*, the corporate world seems to have been almost mesmerised by the word "excellence" and what goes into its making. Not that there were no good studies or surveys on corporate effectiveness or success earlier; in fact, there were many, but, this was a landmark. And, corporate researchers and management consultants have been excited, may be inspired also, to work on managerial and organisational excellence. S.K. Bhattacharyya's *Achieving Managerial Excellence*[3]—a survey of ten carefully selected organisations including both multinational and family owned enterprises—is one such study and offers qualitative insights into excellence in the Indian environment.

Achieving Managerial Excellence

Bhattacharyya had identified and analysed ten excellent Indian managers. These managers are: C.H. Choksey (Asian Paints), Rahul Bajaj (Bajaj Auto), T. Thomas (Hindustan Lever, later Hindustan Unilever), Ajit Narain Haksar (ITC), Henning HOlck—Larsen (Larsen & Toubro), Dhirubhai Ambani (Reliance Industries), K.M. Mathulla (Hindustan Machines Tools), V. Krishnamurthy (BHEL), H.T. Parekh (ICICI) and V. Kurien (Amul). It is interesting to see that ten excellent Indian managers also include two public sector managers—Krishnamurthy (BHEL) and Mathulla (HMT).

Bhattacharyya has used Mckinsey (US based Mckinsey & Co. Inc.) 7-S model of organisational diagnosis as the prime tool for analysing managerial excellence in Indian organisations.

The 7-Ss in Mckinsey organisational model are strategy, structure, systems, style, staff, skills and superordinate goals (certain guiding principles or a set of corporate values which go beyond the traditional and quantified goals and objectives). The former three are "hard" Ss and the latter four are "soft" Ss. In the 7-S framework, superordinate goals are assigned the role of the central determinant of organisational excellence. Bhattacharyya's analysis of excellence is based on the hypothesis that the interaction of these seven organisational factors and the balancing between them determine managerial and organisational effectiveness (used almost synonymously with excellence). The functioning of the ten organisations under study has been analysed with reference to each of the Ss; in addition, they are also analysed with respect to corporate culture—"that indefinable, but real ingredient of excellence."

Findings or Lessons

According to Bhattacharayya, "The first and foremost lesson learnt" from the study of ten Indian organisations is "that there are no abiding and immutable principles which, if followed rigorously, will guarantee success."[4] Having concluded that there are no immutable principles of managerial excellence, Bhattacharyya, however, adds that "the ability of an organisation to achieve the harmony and balance between the seven elements in the organisational diagnosis model seems to be a fairly reliable criterion for assessing whether the organisation will achieve success and effectiveness in the long run." In fact, the present study indicates that while none of the ten companies have achieved complete harmony in terms of the relationship among the seven elements in the model (or has attained equal level of excellence individually in respect of all these elements), the conclusion can be reached that the extent and degree of such harmony and balance in their cases is of a substantially high order compared to others.

The lessons learnt from the study of excellently managed Indian companies may be summarised as four major findings: (i) the need for periodic organisational health diagnosis in terms of seven elements, (ii) projection of most of the organisations as a long shadow of the leader (iii) the pervasive influence of the organisational climate, and (iv) the indefinable element of energy and organisational ferment common to most of the organisations.

One basic lesson learnt from the study of Indian organisations is that a periodic evaluation of seven elements to assess the harmony and balance between them either internally or along with external factors can lead to identification of problem areas which hinder organisational effectiveness; or, in other words, the model can be used as "a periodic corporate pathological test, so to say" for determining the extent and degree of organisational effectiveness.

If such organisational introspection exercises are periodically conducted, this infuses an openness in the process and provide opportunities to people—particularly managers—to contribute their thoughts, comments and suggestions, the results of which are often very rewarding. Almost all the companies studied have gone through such exercises. In these organisations, the top management has been very perceptive and courageous in subjecting themselves and their organisations to such periodic analysis, and, more importantly, acting in a purposive way on many of the conclusions derived from such analysis. It is interesting to note that several of these changes have encompassed—often in stages—significant changes in the areas of strategy, structure and systems and led to redefinition of the superordinate goals.

In the areas of staff, skills and style, such analyses have led to fresh thinking about the kind of people to be inducted, the opportunities to be provided to them, the training and development needs, redefinition of management values as also which are critical for success.

Managers as Leaders

In each of the ten organisations studied, there was perceptible influence of the leaders concerned who "moulded, shaped and fashioned" the organisational vision, culture and objectives. C.H. Choksey of Asian Paints, Rahul Bajaj of Bajaj Auto, T. Thomas of Hindustan Lever, Ajit Haksar of ITC, Henning Holck-Larsen of Larsen and Toubro, Dhirubhai Ambani of Reliance, K.M. Mathulla of Hindustan Machine Tools, V. Krishnamurthy of

BHEL, H.T. Parekh of ICICI, and V. Kurien of Amul are not viewed in their organisations as managers; they are seen as leaders who founded, or came to the organisation and imbued it with a vision and a purpose distinctly their own, evolved distinctive organisational culture, and most importantly, provided inspiration and motivation for achieving excellence.

In several of the companies studied, it was found that the leader was successful in institutionalising the spirit of excitement, enterprise, and innovation so that the organisation continues to excel even after the leader departs. One can call it "moulding the organisational spirit" or succession planning. Larsen and Toubro provides an excellent example in this regard. It was thought that after the departure of Holck-Larsen, it would crumble, or at least perform at a much lower-level of organisational effectiveness. It is a tribute to Holck-Larsen that the performance of the company after his departure was marked by greater heights of achievement and innovation. Even now it may be subjected to some external pressures and jolts, but it continues to be one of the most resilient and effective management set-ups in the country. The climate of calm confidence and willingness in the organisation to face problems and overcome them by managerial action is perhaps the greatest tribute to the leadership qualities of Holck-Larsen.

In the organisations studied, it was clear that in several instances, the organisational climate was a distinctive factor in the attainment of managerial excellence. The first element in organisational climate is the sense of individual pride in belonging to the organisation and in being part of the collective effort which leads to higher achievement. At least in four of the organisations studied this pride was clearly evident. In Hindustan Lever, the great pride was in belonging to an organisation which was often perceived in the outside world as a managerial model of forward looking values, styles, practices, and systems. In L & T, there is quiet pride in belonging to what is widely seem to be one of the best managed technology-based manufacturing companies in the country.

In contrast, in ICICI the pride is derived from the knowledge that, in the financial marketplace, it is seen to be a development bank which sets the highest standards in appraisal, disbursement, monitoring, and, most importantly, in developing the most forward looking practices. It is seen to be championing (or fostering) and developing new activities and objectives which are well ahead of the rest of the financial community. The managers of Amul have the pride of missionaries in overcoming barriers created by entrenched interests. The pride is constantly reinforced by the recognition that Amul managers receive from dairy farmers and producers who see Amul and its managers as performing a unique social service in their cause.

Another important element in the organisational climate relates to openness of the communication process. While many organisations proclaim that the doors of the senior managers are always open, in reality, there are unwritten ground rules for entry and exit and codes of protocol to be maintained at different levels of management. ICICI represents perhaps the most open culture amongst all the organisations studied. In L&T, on the other hand, the openness is evident from the ability to jointly discuss performance, in the context of goals, in a positive climate and seek and work out steps to overcome shortfalls. The same openness of approach is used to tackle almost all management and organisational problems. And, this is possible because the whole climate emphasises that the superior who reviews has also the professional and managerial obligation to help his subordinate in tackling the problem. This ability to be supportive and collaborative while resolving problems, is a very positive organisational feature in L&T's climate.

One of the most interesting features of several of these managerially excellent companies is the sense of positive restlessless and ferment that permeates their managerial community. There is always an unstated urge to go beyond the current level of individual or organisational achievement even though they may be outstanding compared to others. The whole working environment is marked by continuing urge to excel. This leads to a visible level of organisational energy and enthusiasm in attacking all management problems with a zest, vigour and purpose which is conspicuously absent in some of the average companies which seem to be in perpetual management motion without really accomplishing anything very significant.

EXCELLENCE IN MANAGEMENT: CRITICAL PERSPECTIVES

The eight criteria for success or excellence so well essayed and analysed by Peters and Waterman are lessons from the American companies. Will the criteria be same for the European companies? Or, the Asian companies, particularly the Japanese companies? Or, the Indian companies? And, even for the American companies, will the criteria be same for all times? Or, for all situations or environments? That is, we ask a more fundamental question: Is there any universal set of excellent management principles or criteria for success? The answer: "certainly not."

Not surprisingly, the Peters-Waterman management gospel took its first fall when several of the companies idolised as being excellent produced near-disastrous results after the publication of their book. (IBM is the most recent to take a tumble, if not a fall.) The prescriptive nature of the management principles contributing to managerial excellence became the cause of uneasiness among many serious writers (for example, Daniel T. Carroll's article in *Harvard Business Review*, November-December 1983, "A Disappointing Search for Excellence," and, comments of many original thinkers such as Peter Drucker). Bhattacharyya also agrees that "there are no such management principles which will ensure organisational success at all times in all circumstances for all companies."

Neither Peters and Waterman nor Bhattacharyya have given any clear definition of excellence. Is excellence measurable? It can be a logical question.

Peters and Waterman have said that excellent companies are "product champions." But, there are many other American companies which were product champions in their categories like GE, Xerox, Coca-Cola. Can these also be called excellent companies?

Both Peters and Waterman and Bhattacharyya have equated excellence with success. There are also many more companies which have attained success other than those mentioned by the authors. There are also different degrees of success. Then, what should be the cut-off level to be classified as an excellent company? Or, should there be different grading or categories of excellent companies based on the degrees of success?

We fully agree with Drucker that "very different definitions of excellence can be equally valid as shown by the experience of successful companies."[5] General Motors—for example, prizes excellence in business development and business management. At General Electric, on the other hand, people were, for many years, encouraged, not to concern themselves with business, but, to excel as scientists or engineers. IBM, until recently, rewarded ability to produce, sales and customers, with the district sales manager as the key man.

We again use Drucker's words to say that "there is no test except experience by which to judge a definition of excellence."[6] Experience shows that excellence principles appropriate to "stability" companies are different from those prescribed for "steady growth" companies which are, again, different from those required for "fast growth" or flier companies. All these principles would, again, be different from corporate turn around strategies required to revive or resurrect sick or sinking units. Entirely different sets of excellence principles are called for marshalling men, materials and money for these different corporate systems. To take some Indian examples, the corporate turnaround stories of HMT in the early seventies and of DVC in the early eighties pointedly focus on these management decisions and moves which had transformed these companies as excellent management practices during the periods of turnaround. But, once the companies are brought back on rails, more conventional management behaviour may be excellent behaviour.[7]

This also implies that even for the same company, no excellence definition will remain valid forever; it must change with changes in corporate objectives, size and performance or growth cycles. Both General Electric and IBM have had to add to their excellence definitions during the last fifteen years. Changes in size, and, especially markets, made General Electric add business management to its central excellence areas. The computer led IBM to add stress on excellence as a professional scientist and engineer. Any change in the idea of business, size, products, markets or structure may require change in a company's definition of its specific excellence needs or excellence areas.

Corporate excellence, therefore, requires that, in all companies, there should be built-in flexibility for change. We can also generally say that, for companies striving for excellence, the corporate base should neither be too narrow (like a pigeonhole) nor too open (like a floodgate). A company which defines its excellence in terms of a very narrow speciality—"the polymer chemist"—for example, inflicts anaemia on itself. And, a company with excellence requirements that read like the headlines in the classified telephone book—from "accountancy" to "zipper repair"—is unlikely even to attain mediocrity in any one area.

MORE EXCELLENCE HORIZONS

'Excellence' is almost becoming a catchword. Excellence is treading into newer horizons: excellence in customer experience management, excellence in business continuity and excellence in digital business transformation.

ET Business Impact Awards 2022[8] have rewarded these excellence areas:

1. Excellence in Customer Experience Management: Participating organisations have implemented innovative products/services to create a premium, innovative, personalised harmonised experience across their customer's journey. Kotak Mahindra Bank implemented this best and was the winner.

2. Excellence in Business Continuity: Participating organisations have implemented solutions that have enabled business continuity amongst people, assets and brand equity despite disruptions in the environment. The excellence award went to Centre for e-governance, Karnataka.

3. Excellence in Digital Business Transformation: Participative organisations have implemented inventive solutions that integrate digital technology to fundamentally change the way business operate and deliver value to customers. The award winner was Indian Oil Corporation (IOC).

In all the three categories of excellence, the focus was on sustainability which is now emerging as a key feature of corporate excellence.

CONCLUDING POINT

In what we have stated above, we have tried to provide some boundaries or frontiers to the concept and use of excellence. One may amend or elaborate or improve upon the excellence frontiers. But, our central point is clear: we heavily discount or reject the thesis that there is anything like the greatest management principle in the world. There are great management principles; there are excellent management principles. But, the 'excellent' principles or *excellence* is still to be clearly differentiated and made unique in corporate management analysis and practice.

Section II
Marketing

15

Marketing Myopia

Companies run after short-term profit maximisation, follow short-sighted policies and programmes and become victims of marketing myopia.

Theodore Levitt (1960) coined 'marketing myopia' to explain short-sighted policies and practices of some business firms. Companies afflicted with marketing myopia define their business narrowly and are almost obsessed with their products with complete disregard to changing consumer tastes and preferences and market behaviour. Although global business environment has changed significantly during the decades, one can still see many cases of marketing myopia.

Myopia is not acquired deliberately. It creeps into a firm's vision stealthily because of the pursuit of purely short-term objectives. We look into the major factors behind marketing myopia which characterise many companies even today.

CLASSICAL MARKETING MYOPIA

Levitt had identified five factors which are synonymous with marketing myopia. These are:

1. Narrow definition of business;
2. Preoccupation with a product or technology;
3. Too much faith in mass production;
4. Over-optimism about the expanding market; and
5. Belief that the product is for ever.[1]

These should, more appropriately, be described as the causes of myopia. One more cause which is very relevant in the Indian context is the sellers' market syndrome. We shall discuss these factors below.

Narrow Definition of Business

Corporate history is full of examples of companies losing markets because of narrow definition of business. Definition of business for these companies is based on product types they are manufacturing at a particular point of time. Myopic vision leads these companies to believe that they are in a product-specific business and they ignore the wider generic horizon. This finally results in their decline or demise. For example, some companies making audios may think that they are only in the business of selling radios, cassettes or music systems and not in the entertainment (both audio and video) business which is actually the generic field.

Cinema died in Europe and America because theatre companies felt that they were in the business of screening movies rather than in the entertainment business. Rail companies declined in these countries because they thought that they were only in rail-carrier business and not in the transportation business which could use alternative modes.

In India there are many examples. Top-selling brands of the 70s and 80s, such as Murphy radios, Yezdi motorcycles, Lambretta scooters, Fiat (Padmini) and Ambassador cars, HMV records, HMT mechanical watches, Det detergent powder, Philips Milk of Magnesia and many others, either died out or lost their market shares primarily because they defined their businesses very narrowly. These companies were either unaware of product and market dynamics or had ignored them.

HMT could have survived if they did not continue to stick to the mechanical watch technology at a time when digital and quartz technologies had already become fashionable. And in the process, brands like Titan stole the show. By the time HMT turned to quartz technology, it was too late.

Murphy could have retained its business, and, may be its market-leadership also, by diversifying into TV business. What stopped them was their mistaken belief that they were only in radio manufacturing and not in the entertainment business.

Radio was declining, but entertainment was throwing up new possibilities every day.

Preoccupation with Product or Technology

Many companies tend to view themselves as a purely manufacturing organisation—producing things rather than satisfying consumer needs. Marketing is treated as a residual activity or is assumed to be taken care of automatically. As Ries and Trout put it: "People looking for a Product Horse often make a mistake of falling in love with the hype. When a product concept is widely talked about in the general press and on television, it's usually a false signal." But, top management of the company remains obsessed with success and profit possibilities from technical R&D or the technology.

DuPont (USA) researchers invented a new fibre, Kevlar, in 1972. This fibre had the same strength as steel but was only one-fifth the weight. DuPont dreamt of a billion dollar market. Years later, DuPont was still waiting for the bonanza. Kevlar is a very good fibre for bullet proof vests, but there is no big demand for such vests. In 1987, the Wall Street Journal reported: "After 15 years of work, $ 700 million in capital outlays and $ 200 million in losses, Kevlar has found only fringe uses in widely scattered markets. It looks that Kevlar is turning out to be an overhyped DuPont disaster."

Another classic example of preoccupation with technology is that of Concord supersonic passenger aircraft developed by a consortium of European aerospace companies during the 1980s. The aircraft was developed through years of painstaking research involving an expenditure of billions of dollars. The product is ready for commercialisation since long, but, where are the buyers? Concord is an apt example of the "better mousetrap fallacy".[2]

There are plenty of similar examples in India also. In the 1980s, a well-known television brand came out with a new 'picture-in-picture' (PIP) feature. It was claimed as a technological marvel. But it failed miserably for the simple reason that, at that time, except in few metros, there was only one channel available to viewers all over the country. Some other examples of hi-tech casualties are 3-D TV by Niki Tasha, self-start Sportief mopeds by Chamunda Mopeds, Allwyn Lambretta scooters and Standard 2000 cars.

Too Much Faith in Mass Production

Mass production and mass marketing ignore segmentation and differentiation of consumer choice. The focus is on economies of scale or low cost of production and the assumption is that consumers will buy all that is produced or is available. But as we know, this can happen only in a sellers' market.

Henry Ford pioneered the philosophy of mass production in early 1900 and also practised this for a long time in the production of automobiles. Bajaj Auto continued to produce the same model of scooters at full licensed capacity for about 25 years till competition from 100 cc motorbikes and other scooter manufacturers like Vespa and Kinetic Honda threatened its business. Till late 1980s, manufacturers of Ambassador and Padmini (earlier Fiat) cars, Mahendra Jeeps, Rajdoot motorcycles, Kelvinator single-door fridges, HMT mechanical watches and Topaz blades remained preoccupied with mass production and managed to hang on to the market.

But, time has changed now. In today's competitive environment, obsession with mass production may prove fatal for companies in consumer durables, FMCG and services sector. Companies producing consumer goods such as toiletries, detergents, packaged foods, packaged tea, dress material, garments and shoes, durables such as televisions, domestic appliances, mopeds, cars, bicycles and providing services such as telephones, banking and air travel will have to clearly understand the fallacy of mass production if they wish to survive and grow. Companies are moving from mass markets to segments and to niches. A myopic outlook of sticking on to mass production and mass marketing will only lead to downfall.

Belief that the Product is for Ever

In a competitive environment, no industry can ever remain a sunrise industry and no product can continuously remain on a growth curve. In an article in *Harvard Business Review* in 1960, Prof. Levitt had observed that there is no such thing as a growth industry. There are companies which capitalise on growth opportunities. But, an industry which assumes that it is always on an accelerating path is mistaken and it invariably descends into stagnation. The history of every dead and dying industry shows a self-deceiving cycle of accelerated growth and a slow and quiet retreat to obsolescence. Prof. Levitt's observations, made almost about four decades ago, are very much relevant even today.

History is replete with stories of product obsolescence. In Europe and America, the steam locomotive industry perished with the advent of electric locos; manual typewriters went out of business with the arrival of electronic typewriters; cinema halls closed down with the proliferation of videos and VCRs; transistor technology gave way to chips and integrated circuits; mainframe computers bowed out to mini computers, microprocessors, and PCs; magnetic tapes in audio and video systems are being replaced by compact discs; retail banking is being threatened by ATMs; postal services are being challenged by e-mail; and so on.

In India, many industries and firms have lost their business because of product obsolescence. In big cities, airmail and postal services are already facing the onslaught of courier companies; laundry soaps have already been replaced by detergent powders; tailors are losing ground to ready-made garments; fountain pens are giving way to ball pens; video libraries succumbing to satellite transmission; and so on.

Any complacency that a product is unique and without any substitute is only an expression of marketing myopia.

Over-optimism About the Expanding Market

Markets expand as a result of general economic growth or an increase in population or both. If markets expand, sales should increase and so also profit for all industries and firms. This is the common hypothesis.

But this hypothesis does not stand the test of time and space. It is not true across countries and, even in the same country, it may not hold good during different periods of economic or population growth. If markets are generally expanding, demand for a particular industry or product may not necessarily be expanding. This is the dichotomy of 'macro' and 'micro'—the aggregate or industry and the individual firm or unit. Markets expand commensurate with changing technology, consumer tastes and preferences, product innovations, etc. Therefore, the impact is not the same on all products. If the automobiles market is growing in India, it does not mean increasing sales of all models of cars (some models of Premier Automobiles and Hindustan Motors may even perish); increasing consumption of aerated water does not mean increase in sales of Campa-Cola or some other particular brand; increase in demand for audio music systems does not mean higher sales of HMV records or, even audio cassettes.

Therefore, any belief that, in an expanding market, every industry or company will gain is fallacious or myopic. It would depend on the specific product category or brand and not on the generic names. This is what market reality suggests.

Sellers' Market Syndrome

A sellers' market is one in which demand or consumption is significantly higher than domestic production and, therefore, all producers or sellers can sell their products. There is apparent competition (except in pure monopoly) although competition in the real sense is absent. There is no clamour for market share because everybody is able to sell everything they produce or want to sell. *It is more distribution than marketing*. Therefore, normal laws or principles of marketing do not apply.

This is particularly true in countries like India. In the protected business environment till 1991 and even thereafter, most Indian companies were operating in a sellers' market. Till recently, few Indian companies had really practised marketing. One can say that marketing has been the most neglected function in India so far. Even many multinationals have not paid much attention to it. Had they been sensitive to consumer needs and market dynamics, perhaps Nirma would not have become one of the largest producers and marketer of detergent powder in the country.

The concept of sellers' market itself is myopic. Persistence with the same old product (may be with cosmetic changes), lack of customer orientation and price increases at regular intervals typically characterise a sellers' market. Let us take the automobile sector. Fiat (Padmini) and Ambassador had been in a sellers' market for very long. Maruti 800 has also been enjoying a sellers' market. In a sellers' market, "today" is mistaken for "tomorrow", and there cannot be anything more myopic than this.

The reality is that no market remains a sellers' market for ever. But, when the sellers' market suddenly turns into a competitive warfare or a buyers' market, it becomes too late for the old operators to respond to the market demand or transform themselves. The Indian small-car segment is a very good example. With the onslaught of Indica, Santro and Matiz, Palio and others to follow, Padmini which has already lost enough ground would lose further, Maruti 800 will live with difficulty (even with slashing of prices). Ambassador also would lose ground (but may still be able to survive thanks to the public sector and the government sector). These are all results of myopic vision.

MARKETING MYOPIA TODAY

Philip Kotler observes: "Marketing is in bad shape. Not marketing theory, but, marketing practice."[3] This is more concerning.

Companies are doing market research, concept development, product development and testing, market analysis, customer analysis and all that, and, finally commercial launch. But, inspite of all these, 75 per cent of new products, services and businesses fail.[4] Why? The answer is marketing myopia—short-sightedness of marketing policies and strategies.

Symptoms of Marketing Myopia

Marketing or marketing mix consists of four Ps—product, price, promotion, place (distribution). But, many companies have reduced this to one P.

Here is an example. The VP, Marketing, of a major European airline, was asked certain questions. The questions and VP's answers are:

Q. Do you fix the fares for the airline?

A. "Finance does that."

Q. Do you influence the food served on the airplane?

A. "No, human resources handles that."

Q. What about the cleanliness of the planes?

A. "That's maintenance's job."

Q. Then what do you do?

A. "I manage advertising and selling."[5]

These show that the airline is treating marketing as a one-P function: promotion. This is a clear symptom of marketing myopia. Marketing, obviously, is not done in such isolated or myopic way.

Worldwide, CEOs spend more time discussing matters with the COOs and CFOs and less time talking with CMOs. The reason seems to be that the COO and CFO speak the CEO's language, but, the CMO does not.

It is not that CEOs are not concerned about marketing. They are quite concerned about product differentiation and positioning, price pressure, and customer satisfaction; these are very much in their minds. But, there is a strategic gap. "The importance of marketing as a mindset has gained momentum across the entire organisation, while marketing as a function has lost ground."[6] The problem lies here. This is also a sign of marketing myopia.

How Brands Disappear

Many established brands disappear from the market from time to time. Even a classic brand can fall into the marketing trap of myopia.

'Dalda' (vegetable vanaspati) of HLL (now HUL) was almost a classic brand. It became a generic brand. It was almost a household name for many years—a "cash cow" for the company. But, it had a sad demise. Vegetable vanaspati has not disappeared from the market, but, Dalda has disappeared.

Milkfood yogurt is another example, but of the opposite type. Milkfood Ltd., which had a strong presence in the dairy products and ice cream, decided to launch a flavoured yogurt. Milkfood yogurt was launched in Delhi and Bombay in three flavours: mango, pineapple and strawberry. The promotional punchline was: "Making magic out of curd." The brand attained high visibility. Milkfood yogurt seemed to be a big hit in the first few months.

But, after that, the decline started. The positioning of the product was not clear. The product was perceived more as an ice cream to be consumed only occasionally as a dessert. The product was more expensive than ordinary ice cream. It was a case of myopic positioning. By the time the company realised the positioning mistake, it was too late to save the product. Milkfood yogurt disappeared from the market.

Many iconic brands have fallen on the wayside because of myopic marketing vision. Take the cases of once popular brands—Flying Machine India's home-grown can, Eagleflask, Cuticura talcum powder, Forhans toothpaste, Selsun shampoo, Kissan squashes. The reasons for decline or demise of these brands may be different, but, the common factor is lack of marketing vision.

Even low-involvement low-priced brands have gone to oblivion. Let us take the writing instruments segment. Reynolds was the first brand to establish itself in the Indian market. It established itself so powerfully that it almost became generic. Today it is hardly visible on retail shelves or mass media vehicles. A plethora of other brands have taken over.

In automobiles also, there is no dearth of examples. Maruti-Suzuki had launched Zen in the mid-segment. It became very successful in its category. It had almost created a niche for itself. The company, in its myopic strategy, replaced Zen by Zen Estilo which became a disaster. Both Zen and Zen Estilo have disappeared from the market. Fiat, the Italian car giant, had launched Fiat Uno and Fiat NE in the Indian market. Both failed miserably mostly because of myopic distribution policy and after-sales service. Ford Ikon was launched with lot of funfare. But, the car could not excite the customers. After-sales service was also very poor. The brand disappeared from the market.

PRICE WARS ARE MYOPIC STRATEGIES

Many companies indulge in price wars to save the product, or, more often, to survive in immediate competition. These are myopic strategies. These hardly have any long-term impact on the brand's life or success. This implies, in other words, that the long-term is being mortgaged to the short-term price pressure.

The price war between Coca-Cola and Pepsi is well known. In July, 1994, Pepsi reduced the prices of its entire range of 300 ml soft drinks to ₹ 5 to match the price of coke which had been launched in Delhi and Agra. Coke further reduced its price to ₹ 4.50 in Delhi and Pepsi promptly matched it. For several months, both the companies continued the price war. In this price war of the two multinationals, smaller Indian brand like Campa Cola suffered heavily.[7]

In another price war, the leading newspaper, *The times of India* (Delhi Edition) locked horns with the then market leader *The Hindustan Times* (currently TOI is the market leader). In April, 1994, The Times of India reduced the price of its Delhi edition by ₹ 0.80. Hindustan Times initially refused to toe the line. But, when TOI started eating into its market share, HT was compelled to reduce its price to ₹ 1.50. Other newspapers—The *Indian Express* and *The Pioneer*—were also dragged into the war.[8]

The Indian market had witnessed several other price wars which even led to company casualties. Examples: Cibacca toothpaste, Corona Shoes, Universal luggage, Sudha Soft drink concentrate, among others.

More recently, price wars were among the FMCG giants. P&G has cut prices of Tide and Ariel by 25-50 per cent, Pantene by 40 per cent and Rejoice the company's low-priced shampoo by 30 percent—all within a span of six month. The other FMCG giant HUL responded or retorted with price cuts of its major brands between 15 and 50 per cent. The price war was on.[9]

These and other price cuts show that many companies indulge in price wars with a purely short-term objective.

FACTORS BEHIND MARKETING MYOPIA

Factors or reasons behind marketing myopia relate to policy, planning and strategies of marketing. Both the company and the marketing department—the CEO and the CMO—have to share the spoils. Factors can be many. Ten more probable factors or reasons are given below.

1. The company is not sufficiently market focussed;
2. The company or marketing is not customer-driven; it does not fully understand its customers;
3. The marketing team needs to better define, understand and monitor competitors;
4. The company's marketing policies, planning process and plans are deficient in terms of impact;
5. The company's brand building capabilities are weak;
6. The company's product, brand and service policies are not regularly reviewed;
7. Most FMCG companies are failing to make their products/brands effectively compete with newer emerging categories;
8. Marketing ignores constantly changing market or environmental conditions;
9. The marketing department does not make best use of modern technologies;
10. Most marketing approaches lack the long-term perspective. The focus is only on short-term strategies; the strategies are not futuristic.

STRATEGIES FOR OVERCOMING MARKETING MYOPIA

Companies (or marketing departments) can take some strategic initiatives—all marketing led initiatives—to overcome marketing myopia. These relate to brand rationalisation, segment movement, channel migration etc.

Seven strategic initiatives are recommended:

1. Brand rationalisation
2. Segment movement
3. Selling to solutions
4. Channel migration
5. Market-driven to marketing-driving
6. SBU-centric to corporate marketing
7. Reorganising the organisation[10]

Brand Rationalisation

Brand rationalisation can be done in different ways. One way is to make modification in the brand or introduce brand extension like HUL did for Surf. Another way is "milking" the brand, i.e., keeping the brand, but, not allocating any resources to it till the brand dies a natural death. A third choice may be to "delist", that is, to shut down or withdraw the brand from the market if it has become unviable in terms of cost-benefit. A company may decide its course depending on the brand's position in the market.

Segment Movement

This indicates movement or shift from traditional market segments to new strategic segments. Airlines is a good example. A low-cost airline (like Southwest Airlines) is totally different from the traditional airlines because it "involves a total makeover of operations and purchasing as well as marketing." This is the essence of segment shift. Among the international carriers, Air India Express flying between New Delhi and Dubai has similar segment shift.

Selling to Solutions

Many companies confine their marketing to only selling, that is, exchange of goods and payments. This is a myopic approach. Companies should move from selling products to providing solutions. Companies like IBM have achieved this. As its computers started becoming 'commoditised,' IBM started focusing on services and solutions. This approach can be adopted by most non-FMCG companies for building customer relationship.

Channel Migration

Traditional marketing channels are distributors-wholesalers-retailers. The emerging new channel options are supermarkets, malls and the Internet. In the US, about 50 per cent of the purchases today are through the Internet channel. In India and many other countries, supermarkets, malls and the Internet are all picking up. Channel migration is taking place. Managing channel migration, i.e., managing channel conflicts or maintaining compatibility of the channels—the traditional and the new—is vital for success of this initiative.

Market-Driven to Market-Driving

Companies can transform themselves from being market-driven to market-driving. Instead of the market driving the company and its product(s), the company can drive the market. This can happen essentially through innovations and is largely customer-driven. Innovations are inspired by the customer. Henry Ford had rightly said: "Listening to the customer would have led him to think of creating a faster horse. Listening to the customer can only get you incremental innovation. Really big innovations come from teaching from the customer and that's a big marketing exercise."

Change or transformation from market-driven to market-driving is almost like a paradigm shift in marketing.

SBU-CENTRIC TO CORPORATE MARKETING

This stems from the perception, rightly so, that marketing should not be marketing alone. If the marketing department is treated as a SBU, marketing may not receive enough attention and focus from the CEO or the corporate organisation. Since marketing (and selling) is almost the only revenue generating activity, almost the whole organisation should be concerned about and involved in it with proper role definitions. Every employee should feel that he(she) is a stakeholder in marketing. This makes marketing well-founded, forceful, and effective.

REORGANISING THE ORGANISATION

Reorganisation of the organisation should take place around the market, product or customer. Many multinational companies have been trying to reorganise around products and countries or global markets. Today, 17 per cent of P&G's total sales are to Walmart. Companies like P&G may reorganise themselves around their top ten customers who may account for half of their sales. Other companies may also reorganise around their products and customers.

For this to happen effectively, companies will have to gear up or amend their organisational systems or structures to meet the reorganisation challenge. For example, in the reorganised structure, the manager in-charge of a customer will become very focal. The country manager for global companies may become relatively redundant.

The strategic initiatives just mentioned have been adopted or implemented by some of the world's top companies in more recent times. These can be successfully used as models by many other marketing departments/organisations for long-term marketing solutions.

CONCLUDING POINT

Marketing myopia or business myopia is a more pervading phenomenon than it may appear. Most companies run after "myopic maximisations"—be it in sales or profits or market share or media effects—without really trying to see through the tunnel. And, inevitably, one day the dead end comes, and it becomes a point of no return or no revival.

Hamel and Prahalad in *Competing for the Future* (1994) explain how many organisations failed to come up with new or "future" products. Such companies, in spite of having the best of resources, failed because they could not escape the myopia of present markets, sales and profits.

Talking of "future" products, we should give the example of Centre for Monitoring Indian Economy (CMIE). What is interesting about CMIE is that it introduced a completely new product (information services)—growing a market for it and simultaneously building a brand. This is one way to combat marketing myopia: Stay ahead with a "future" product.

Only those companies, not many in number, which constantly interact with the changing environment are aware that only the 'long-term' is permanent. Such companies are sensitive enough to environmental changes (shifts in demand pattern, changes in consumer behaviour, emerging competition, etc.) as well as the marketplace to make timely changes in marketing and organisational strategies and practices. Such companies do not become myopic. Companies such as GE, Sony, 3M, Unilever or HUL, P&G, ITC are good examples. There are other examples also.

16

Important Marketing Laws

Marketing laws are more like laws of Nature—not legalised or formalised, but they govern the marketplace.

In marketing, as in any other field of management, we make mistakes and learn from those mistakes. But we should also take care to see that we do not make too many mistakes too often. One way to ensure this is to follow some basic principles or laws of marketing. These principles or laws are essentially distilled findings from years of marketing research, marketing programme implementations and successes and failures of companies in the marketplace. Let us have a look at ten such laws.

Ten important marketing laws are presented below:

1. The Law of the Leader
2. The Law of the Big Size
3. The Law of Competition
4. The Law of Product-Price Mix
5. The Law of Time
6. The Law of Subjectivity
7. The Law of the Mind
8. The Law of Position
9. The Law of Marketing Remix
10. The Law of Services

THE LAW OF THE LEADER

If You are No. 2 or No. 3 in the Market, Your Strategy is decided by No. 1 (the Leader)

The leader follows the principle: it is better to be first than to be better. The leading brand in any product group or category is almost always the first brand in the customer's mind: IBM in computers, Coca-Cola in cola, Godrej in almirahs, Hindustan Lever in dalda....

The No. 2, No. 3 and others have either of two options: accept the leader and be content being a follower or be a contender for No. 1 position by adopting a strategy of contrast. If you are in the first category, you emulate the leader and try to improve your market share. In any case, avoid any confrontation with the leader and try to make a niche for yourself in your own way. This is the story of many new detergent brands in the Indian market vis-a-vis Surf. If you are positioning yourself against the leader (usually if you are No. 2), you try to make leader's weaknesses your strengths or convert the leader's strengths into weaknesses by offering opposites or alternatives—Pepsi created the Pepsi Generation (against Coca-Cola), Newsweek introduced its own writing style against Time's more colourful presentation, Savvy's up—market focus against Femina, etc.

In marketing, as in life, offence may often be the best form of defence. Let us take the story of Burger King versus McDonald. Burger King's most successful years as No. 2 came when it was on the attack on McDonald. It opened with "Have it your way" which scored over McDonald's mass manufacturing approach to hamburgers. It reinforced its position through other attacking tactics. At some stage, Burger King changed its approach to almost being a follower to McDonald and sales declined. The message is: in both cases, Burger King's strategies were only "reactive" to McDonald's campaign.

One can also take the case of Hindustan Lever-Colgate-Palmolive duel (Close-Up and Pepsodent versus Colgate) in the dental care market in India. Colgate is the leader and Lever is the challenger. But Lever's outflanking strategy is predominantly a reactive strategy. This is based on exploitation of the weaknesses in the leader brand's public projection through a series of reactions—promotional and brand extensions—targeted at displacing the leader brand.

Your company's strategy, therefore, is derived from that of the leader. Either you strive to be a copy book of the leader, or you provide an alternative. In both cases, the leader drives you. Sometimes it is visible; sometimes it is not.

So, discover (meaning "understand" or "probe") the leader. This would help you to lead later.

THE LAW OF THE BIG SIZE

Marketing Plans of Big Companies Ignore the Emergence of Small Competitors

Big companies, particularly multinationals, concentrate on preparing marketing plans and strategies to combat the existing large competitors who pose immediate threats to their market shares. They tend to ignore the emerging small-size players. The small player(s) make an almost invisible entry, thrive on the economics of small size (low fixed costs), gradually snatch market share and finally get established as dominant players. It becomes rather too late for the big ones to thwart them, and so they have to contend with them.

This actually follows a more universal law of nature. Big animals ignore small animals. But, many small animals have a way of outwitting the big animals. A strong (physical) man ignores a weak man. But the weak man can always outmanoeuvre the strong man with his wits and tactics.

There are many examples in the corporate world. When IBM was the market leader and was planning hooking up all the PCs to its mainframes, they did not reckon with the appearance of Microsoft on the scene who completely destroyed IBM's plans. General Motors failed to foresee the small car trend. Chloride India (Exide) has been sitting in their high pedestals of car batteries while small regional and local players (like "Sahni" in Delhi) have emerged as strong competitors because of cost effectiveness. "T-Series" made a small entry to gradually become big enough to challenge HMV in audio cassettes. "Babool" made a very modest entry to become dominant against the likes of Colgate-Palmolive, Forhans (now extinct) and other toothpaste majors (although of late, we do not see so much of Babool). A classic example is Nirma's outflanking of Surf and annexation of significant market share.

But the big companies do not seem to learn. They have some obsession with size—their avowed professionalism and institutionalisation. From such a position, they only see the threats from the big companies; that too, the more immediate ones. They do not see the small players quietly emerging on the horizon much less considering them as a threat. This is also one kind of marketing myopia.

All small entrepreneurs get encouragement from this. And the "Big" beware! *One more small competitor is appearing on the horizon. He is tomorrow's potential big. So don't ignore him.*

THE LAW OF COMPETITION

To Formulate Long-term Strategy, You must Know the Competitors' Plans

In marketing, as in corporate activity, we need both a short-term strategy and a long-term strategy. Short-term strategy is to maximise today's sales, revenue and profits. The long-term strategy is for survival, growth and diversification. For formulation of long-term strategy, a company must identify the plans of the existing as well as potential competitors. This is essential for knowing about changing product profiles, new substitutes or complementaries, possible invasion by foreign players, brands, etc. Without this knowledge, long-term strategy will be a failure. A company may be planning to increase its market share based on the present competition level and the market structure, but, any move by a competitor, existing or new, may upset all its plans.

IBM developed a massive marketing plan to hook up all PCs to its mainframes-IBM's Office Vision. But, the plan failed because of developments in Sun Micro-systems, Microsoft and other companies. This happened because Office Vision foresaw everything except competition. General Motors was slow to react to the small car trend; this cost the company dearly. Premier Automobiles did not correctly foresee the shape of the automobile revolution in India and we know the result. Failure to forecast competitors' actions or reactions is a major reason for many marketing failures.

All this means forecasting the future, which of course, is not easy. In strategy exercises including forecasting models, it is commonly assumed that the future would be an extrapolation of the past and the present. This may sometimes be a valid assumption and may give good results in statistical forecasts which deal with pure numbers or time-series data which do not deal with behavioural parameters.

But this may not be true of market behaviour in which there are many imponderables, the most unpredictable being the competitors' moves and shifting strategies. Simple extrapolation may not be enough. A company may have to conduct in-depth marketing research and intelligence. They may also have to foresee technical innovations. All this is not easy. But, this may be the only way and long-term success may depend on how well a company does it or masterminds it. Otherwise, the company may lose long-term directions or the competitors may overtake them. This is happening in the computer field quite regularly.

THE LAW OF PRODUCT-PRICE MIX

Not product, not Price, but, the product-Price Combination sells[2]

Is marketing all about product, that is, quality, or, is marketing all about price? Or, is it product and price both? Which is more important—product or price?

The general principle in marketing is: higher the quality of a product, higher is the price, lower the quality, lower is the price. All premium products like Mercedes car, Bose music systems, Ray-Ban sunglass have high price. Cost is not the consideration. Customers pay for high or premium quality. At the other extreme, there are low quality, low cost products like T-series cassettes, Ghari detergents or local brands of detergents, Thermoking (local brand in Delhi) air conditioners, various local brands of electrical and electronic products, and, above all, most or all Chinese products. In all these, price is the most important consideration; there is a clear trade-off with quality.

The pricing strategy of most companies have three major objectives:

1. Choose a price point for your product to attract large volumes.
2. Sacrifice margins from premium pricing in favour of higher revenue.
3. Add more and more customer value to push up sales and profit despite smaller margins.

What is customer value? Or, what is creating value for the customer? Does customer value creation come from quality or price? Does the best quality or the lowest price create maximum value? Most often, it is neither the best quality (which is not affordable) nor the lowest price (the quality may not be acceptable). The norm or basis for optimal or maximum value creation is:

Affordable price plus acceptable quality

Such value creation does not exclude high or premium quality. If a customer can afford a Bentley or Ferrai, then why not? Similarly, a low income group customer may buy a soap or detergent of very low quality. That is his affordability, and, he accepts or compromises on the quality. But, for the vast majority of the buyers—whether in consumer goods, or industrial products or services—it is the golden rule of affordability and acceptability. This is the price-product combination. This can be clearly seen in consumer goods, industrial products and also in services. The conclusion is clear: the notion of high or best quality for maximum customer value or satisfaction is a myth or mistaken hypothesis. Customer value or satisfaction comes from a *particular* product—price combination.

The real strategic task of companies is to identify, establish and exploit the ideal or best product—price combination. This is true of all the three product categories: consumer goods, industrial products and services. This is most typical in services with highest variability followed by consumer goods and industrial products.

So, *companies should constantly search for the ideal or optimal product-price mix to maximise sales, market share and profitability.*

THE LAW OF TIME

Full Marketing Effects Take Place Only Over a Period of Time

The law can also be stated as: Long-term effects of marketing are quite different, often exactly the opposite, of the short-term effects.

In the short-term, it is easy to increase sales and perhaps, profits by sales or marketing gimmicks, price discounting, opening of outlets, product extensions, etc., but in the long-run, sales die out because there is no proper base or sustenance. Coca-Cola clothes were introduced in 1985; two years later sales volume reached $ 250 million; the following year, sales dried up almost overnight saddling the company with millions of dollars of inventory. What happened to Coca-Cola clothes also happened to Donald Trump. Donald Trump branched out and put his money on anything the banks would lend money for—a hotel, three casinos, two condominiums, one airline, one shopping centre. The result: Trump is $ 1.4 billion in debt. What made them successful in the short-term is exactly what caused them to fail in the long-run. This also happened to Philip Brothers (Phibro). Once almost the largest international metal (non-ferrous) trader in the world, the company sparkled, dazzled and rose to unprecedented heights; decline and death also were as fast.

The opposite also happens. Companies, which plan with a long-term perspective usually start modestly or steadily. They may not be the first with the product in the market, but, they develop a base and core competence and diversify and grow around it. IBM was not the first with mainframe computer. Remington Rand was first with UNIVAC. But, because of their massive marketing efforts (backed by evolving technology), IBM won the computer battle early and established themselves firmly in the marketplace. UNIVAC became the short-term success;

IBM the long-term success. Apple got off the computer ground with just $ 91,000. Short-term effects were very modest; but the long-term marketing effects were the opposite. The same applies to Dell Computer (now Dell Technologies). They emerged as the leaders among the personal computer brands which were being launched around the same time. Initial marketing effects of Bata India were not very successful, but we all know about the long-term results.

The short-term and long-term effects of marketing strategies remind one of the effects of alcohol. Is alcohol a stimulant or a depressant? Chemically, alcohol is a strong depressant. That is its long-term effect. But in the short-term, by suppressing a person's inhibitions, alcohol acts like a stimulant. Many marketing moves exhibit the same phenomenon. The long-term effects are often exactly the opposite of the short-term effects.

We have some very good examples in the Indian car market. Contessa from Hindustan Motors was introduced with an apparently big immediate impact on the market. 118 NE (Premier Automobiles) made a bigger impact. Standard 2000 (Standard Motor Co.) was also launched as a premier car. But all these cars lost the long-term battle (Standard 2000 disappeared soon after it was launched). Cielo (Daewoo) also headed towards the same fate. The opposite is happening to Honda City (Honda Motors). The car made a slow sedate start. But its long-term prospects are already clearly visible.

So, short-term success should not give complacency to companies just as a slow or modest start should not discourage them. The long-term effects in both cases can be quite different. The long-term strategy would finally spell success or failure for the company.

THE LAW OF SUBJECTIVITY

The Product is Important, but Perception of the Product is more Important

Many marketing mistakes stem from the assumption that we are fighting a battle of products in the marketplace. It is really the perception or positioning of the product that matters. It is said that *good brands are made by companies, but great brands are made by the market*. Why does the market allow certain brands to flourish infinitely (e.g., Coke abroad, Lifebuoy in India) while it floors some brands even before they take off (e.g., New Coke abroad)?

It is easy to see the power of perception over product. Three largest selling Japanese cars in America are Honda, Toyota and Nissan. Most marketing people think that the battle between the three brands is based on horsepower, designing, quality and price. Not true. It is what people think about a Honda, Toyota or a Nissan. If marketing were a battle of only products, the same market shares should hold good for all the three cars in both the countries, designing, price, etc., being same. But, in Japan, Honda is nowhere near the leader. There, Honda is in third place behind Toyota and Nissan. Toyota sells more than four times than Honda. So what's the difference between Honda in Japan and Honda in the USA? The products are same but the perceptions in customers' minds are different.

It is commonly accepted that Japanese make better quality cars than Americans. So if you had a bad experience with a Japanese car, you have just been unlucky because Japanese are known to make very high quality cars. On the other hand, if you have had a good experience with an American car, you have just been lucky because American cars are perceived to be of low quality. Such perception has more universal applicability: to overlook or ignore the fault or default of a product if it has high positioning in the customer's mind.

Some soft drink marketers believe that marketing is a battle of taste. New Coke is No. 1 in taste in the USA. The Coca-Cola Company conducted 200,000 taste tests which proved that New Coke tastes better than Pepsi-Cola and Pepsi tastes better than their original formula now called Coca-Cola Classic. But, who is winning the marketing battle? The drink that research has proven as the one with the worst taste—Coca-Cola Classic, is in first place. The drink that research has shown to be the best in taste, New Coke, is in third place.

Ries and Trout have put the law in a more forthright way: *marketing is not a battle of products, it is a battle of perceptions*. So true of consumer goods!

In India, Philips bulbs have a great market perception. These are considered to be of higher quality than two comparable brands in the market—GE and Sylvania Laxman. But ask any electrical engineer or an electrician: he would not certify Philips bulbs to be of superior quality. There is no guarantee also that these bulbs would last longer than others. But still, people go to a store and ask for a Philips bulb first. This is the law of perception.

THE LAW OF THE MIND

It is Better Strategy to be First in the Mind, and Then in the Marketplace[3]

What is the best way to establish a product in the market? Launch in the marketplace, do the promotional work and hope for buyer's acceptance? Or, first try to capture the buyer's mind, and then place it in the market? Many stories of marketing successes and failures show that it is better to be in the mind first, and in the marketplace later.

The law of the mind follows the law of perception or subjectivity. If marketing is a battle of perceptions and not product, then the mind logically takes precedence over the marketplace. If a product or brand is established in the mind of consumers, it is almost automatically established in the marketplace because the buyers have already accepted it, but not necessarily the other way round.

The world's first personal computer was MITS Altair 8800, not Apple. But Apple quickly captured buyers' minds (partly helped by its simple name), although it started with a very modest market entry. It finally emerged as the leader among the five personal computer brands which were on the launching pad at the same time. MITS Altair 8800 has been forgotten. IBM was not the first in the marketplace with the mainframe computer; it was Remington Rand with UNIVAC. But because of its unique marketing strategy, IBM got into the mind first and easily won the computer battle. Wang was first in word processors. But the world moved fast to computers. Wang spent millions of dollars on PCs and minicomputers. But Wang is still perceived as a word processor company. The mind does not change so easily once it is made up. It works both ways—for the good as well as for the bad.

Companies which launch their products in the market without proper positioning or winning the minds of consumers always run the risk of failure. Launching of Milkfood Yogurt in the Indian market (Delhi and Mumbai) is a very good example. Yogurt was not positioned as a distinct product. Some compared it with curd; more people compared it with ice cream. The product was finally abandoned.

On the other hand, see the "mind effect" of Ratan Tata's dream car Indica. Even before the car was launched, it was already oversold in the minds of millions of Indians. The other two contenders in the same car segment—Hyundai's Santro and Daewoo's Matiz were lagging behind. Indica's market success was just predictable at that time. Perception about the car, however, was later discounted by its actual performance on the road.

THE LAW OF POSITION

The Strategy to use Depends on which Position a Company Occupies in the Marketplace

All products are not created equal. All brands are not leader brands. Therefore, all strategies are not leader strategies. There are separate strategies to be used by No. 2 or No. 3 or No. 4 brand in the market. Each brand should use a distinct strategy based on its position in the marketplace.

There is generally a relationship between market share and a company's position on the market ladder. *A company tends to have twice the market share of the brand below and, half the market share of the brand above it*. Although this is not to be taken as axiomatic, this is a good thumb rule. Therefore, before launching any marketing programme, a company should carefully ascertain its market share and position on the ladder, and ensure that the programme is fully commensurate with its position in the market. If it does not, the strategy becomes a market mismatch and the brand suffers.

We have an example in Royal Crown Cola in the USA. In 1969, the Royal Crown Company revitalised its franchise system, hired the former President of rival Pet Foods and a veteran of both Coke and Pepsi. The company also retained a high powered advertising agency. "We're out to kill Coke and Pepsi. I hope you'll excuse the word, but we are really out for the jugular," declared the agency head. The result? The only brand that got killed was Royal Crown. When you are a weak No. 3 like Royal Crown, you are not likely to make much headway by attacking the two strong leaders. What Royal Crown should have done was first to carve out a niche for themselves instead of straightaway attacking the, niche of the two giants too openly. This step should have been taken much later, if at all.

We give the opposite example here. 7-Up was occupying the top rung of the lemon-lime soda ladder in the US. In the soft-drink market, however, the cola ladder is much bigger than the lemon-lime ladder—almost two out of three soft-drinks consumed in the US are cola drinks. 7-Up wanted to climb the cola ladder and did it successfully through a marketing campaign labelled "The Uncola". This was the right strategy. 7-Up became the alternative to a cola drink as tea is to coffee.

To create a niche, only a particular strategy may work under particular market conditions. A company should identify that strategy. If a new steel cupboard manufacturer wants to enter the market, it obviously does not adopt a strategy to challenge or displace Godrej Storewel which has become almost a family name. Similarly, a new entrant into the vanaspati market does not straightaway challenge Dalda of HLL.* A new entrant in the toothpaste market or a lower-rung brand does not take on headlong with Colgate. They should first create a position or niche for themselves based on their product, price and marketing outfit. The strategy should embody all this. As they start establishing themselves, they may look for a new strategy and a new niche. This should be a continuous exercise.

---

*. After many years, HLL (HUL) sold its dalda business to Bunge Pvt. Ltd., who relaunched it as Dalda oil, but, we do not hear much about it now.

THE LAW OF MARKETING REMIX

Marketing Remix and not Marketing Mix is the right strategy[4]

All marketing strategies are expressed in terms of 4 Ps or marketing mix. But, the question is: 4 Ps or marketing mix or marketing remix?

Four Ps and marketing mix are usually understood in the same sense and many use the two terms interchangeably. But, they are not same. This would be clear from the definition/observation of James Culliton, the American marketing expert, who coined the expression "Marketing Mix" and described the marketing manager as a "mixer of Ingredients": According to Culliton:

The marketing man is a decider and an artist; a mixer of ingredients who sometimes follows a recipe prepared by others; sometimes adapts a recipe to the ingredients; and sometimes, experiments with ingredients that no one has tried before.

Marketing mix is the initial blending of the 4Ps or the ingredients for formulation of a marketing plan or strategy. In the initial marketing mix, the ingredients are mixed with different weights or priorities or focus. For example, when Nirma was introduced in the Indian detergents market, maximum weight or focus was on price, because, it wanted to compete with Surf on the price factor. The product was accordingly designed and promotion and distribution followed. Later, based on market or customer feedback, some changes were made in the four elements of marketing mix. This is *marketing remix. So, marketing remix is a change in the initial marketing mix based on changing market and environmental conditions*.

This may be better understood by looking at the marketing remix strategy of HUL, Cadbury, and Samsung.

Marketing Remix Strategy of HUL: HUL's Surf was the indisputed leader in the Indian detergents market till the entry of Nirma exploited the price segment of Surf (Surf was a premium brand) and used a flanking strategy. The Indian detergents market in the mid "80s" witnessed the famous strategic war between Surf and Nirma. By 1984, because of intense competition from Nirma, downward movement/declining trend of Surf commenced and continued, and, at one stage, Surf's market share declined drastically.

At this stage, HUL started working seriously on its marketing remix strategy. In fact, HUL was already quietly working on a rejuvenation strategy. The last two years of the "80s" saw HUL turning around its detergent business. The turnaround was brought about by a well designed strategy based on market research on buyer perceptions, expectations, and behaviour. The company's analysis revealed that the price sensitivity of customers varied across different demographic groups. Their research showed that upper middle income and higher income group housewives perceived white and blue coloured detergent powders to be the strongest and best in washing and they were low or moderately price sensitive. The lower income and middle income housewives, on the other hand, perceived yellow and green coloured detergents as the most satisfying and were moderate to high on price sensitivity.

At this stage, HUL started working seriously on its marketing remix strategy. Based on its market research (in which HUL is very strong), HUL developed and positioned three brands of detergent powders, namely, Rin (blue), Wheel (green) and Sunlight (yellow) and continued to upgrade Surf and maintain its position as a global detergent. Through this strategic repositioning of Surf and brand extensions (Rin, Wheel, Sunlight), HUL remerged as the market leader in detergents in the "90s."

The crux of the strategy was marketing remix with primary focus on product and almost equal focus on price. Promotion and distribution followed. The HUL case is almost a classic example of success through marketing remix strategy.

Marketing Remix Strategy of Cadbury: Cadbury's Dairy Milk chocolate (CDM) was the market leader, but sales were hardly moving. For seven long years, CDM suffered stagnancy even as many other consumer products boomed. This is a story of how the company rejuvenated an old brand through marketing remix to create the marketing mega hit of the 1990.

The vital question Cadbury was confronted with was: what should it deploy to rejuvenate CDM in a way that would appeal to child lurking within the adult? Cadbury, and Ogilvy and Mather (O&M), who co-created CDM's campaign, worked together on development of this concept. To translate the concept into a commercial, the O&M team decided to simply portray occasions of childlike, but not childish, behaviour from adults without explicitly identifying adults as the target customer. "We left the connection to be made by the consumer" explains O&M; "Nowhere did we actually say: you're an adult, you can eat it. Because nobody wants to be told." But, the montage of the child in the man—the old man kicking the football; the pregnant woman craving a chocolate; young girls breaking into a sprint; the young man tossing a bar of chocolate at his sweet-heart departing in a bus—was created. That the communication had to be liked, before it could penetrate the cultural resistance to chocolate consumption by the adults, was obvious.

The precedent Cadbury have created by lifting the brand bodily out of one customer segment and planting it in another will continue to be the benchmark or model for brand rejuvenation. In fact, The Real Taste of Life campaign, which served Cadbury's chocolate in general, and CDM in particular, into the consciousness of adults, has already become a classic in the history of advertising and marketing. This was achieved through marketing remix—with predominant focus on advertising and marketing communication.

Marketing Remix Strategy of Samsung: Samsung is currently the market leader in mobile phones in India. In this product category, however, market shares are changing fast. Nokia, one time market leader, has been displaced by its competitors through marketing remix strategies.

Samsung came from almost nowhere and, gradually, but, systematically, positioned itself in the mobile phone market. It captured market shares from established players like Motorola, Sony Ericsson, and, finally displaced the market leader Nokia. Samsung first used marketing mix strategy, and, then employed marketing remix strategy. The company's primary focus was on product remix and pricing remix.

The Samsung story shows that marketing remix strategy can be used not only by the market leaders—as HUL, Cadbury and Bisleri did—but, also by NO. 3 or No. 4 challenger. In fact, the Samsung case clearly demonstrates that a challenger can very effectively employ a marketing remix strategy to establish its supremacy or leadership in the market.

The significance of marketing remix as a strategy is clear. Marketing mix makes the initial strategy which is essentially proactive based on analysis of the existing environment and market conditions. Market conditions keep changing almost continuously New products/brands, new competitors and innovations disrupt the past and the present. Maruti (Suzuki) came and shook up the sleeping Indian automobile market; Titan came and disrupted the Indian watch market and displaced the leader HMT; Sony brought with it a technological revolution in the Indian CTV market. Because of such developments, companies need continually resort to marketing remix as strategy which will be both proactive and reactive.

So, marketing remix, and, not one time marketing mix, is the right strategy to keep ahead of competition and secure and sustain competitive advantage.

THE LAW OF SERVICES

In Marketing Services, People are Marketed

Many feel that a service is just another product (though intangible), and a service should be marketed in the same way as a product. Nobody can deny that the basic tools (like advertising) for marketing services do not vary significantly from those for products. But, the method of application and people orientation in marketing should be very different.

This brings us to the fundamental difference between marketing a service and marketing a product. No one buying a service, not even the simplest service—say, dry cleaning—can know in advance what they will finally receive. In buying a product, no matter how complex—say a computer system—there is a reasonable chance of assessing well in advance what will be acquired. The customer cannot return a faulty service, but a product can be returned or replaced. Therefore, services need a different and more sensitive approach. The service system is a fine blending of tangible things (the office, the equipment, the telephone), and the intangible, sometimes invisible, service itself (speed, ambience, environment and, above all, people). It is a cliche, but true that services are a "people business" and no service is better or worse than the people who render the service.

But, people are not machines and quality of people output can vary even moment to moment. The smiling pleasant assistant at the airline check-in desk can suddenly turn into a snarling martinet after a clash with a customer. The garage mechanic uninterested in the middle-aged motorist with very real ignition trouble suddenly becomes a paragon of knightly virtue for the (apparently) helpless and attractive woman with an imaginary electrical fault in her car. The alternator functions in the same way for either car owner; but the mechanic does not. This means that in marketing services, people are marketed.

In services, therefore, the bulk of the marketing effort should take place in the pre-sale period—in training, orienting and motivating the service sellers. In many five-star hotels (Windsor Manor in Bangalore is a clear example), the restaurant manager holds a quick briefing session for the restaurant staff before the start of every lunch and dinner. This shows that service has to be marketed, many times, as much to its providers as to its customers.

How people oriented a service is has been best expressed by the Chief Executive of Scandinavian Airlines:

We don't seek to be one thousand per cent better at any one thing. We seek to be one per cent better at one thousand things. SAS has ten million passengers a year. The average passenger comes into contact with five SAS employees. Therefore, SAS is fifty million "moments of trust" per year. Fifty million unique ... opportunities to distinguish ourselves ... from each and every one of our competitors. My job is to manage (these) fifty million moments of trust!

IN CONCLUSION...

Ten marketing laws have been enunciated above. There can be more such laws. We have presented, which we consider are, the more important ones.

Some of the laws described above may appear, even at first sight, quite logical; some may even seem familiar or obvious. But none of the laws are to be presumed as axiomatic.

Some of the laws appear overlapping. For example, the Law of Subjectivity, the Law of the Mind and the Law of Impression. They do not really overlap. The Law of the Mind and the Law of Impression are extensions of the Law of Subjectivity and highlight two distinct dimensions of perception or positioning.

There can be exceptions to the laws derived from some company experiences. For example, the Law of Competition. Many companies may survive and even grow without knowing the competitors' plans. But this does not make the law meaningless or irrelevant. Observance of the law would have equipped the companies with a more comprehensive strategy—an outflanking or outwitting strategy—and they would have been generally better off. At any point of time, a company should be more successful in the marketplace by following these laws than otherwise.

It is always good to know a principle or a law even if we want to make an exception to it. This is a good thumb rule.

17 Major Marketing Sins

Like any other field of management, marketing is also evolving. New ideas or thoughts, plans and strategies are being floated. Implementations are taking place. Implementations are sometimes successful; but, sometimes they are not. So, are the results including turnover and profitability.

Marketing mistakes take place; you may call them marketing deficiencies. Kotler calls them "marketing sins." He has identified ten such sins. These are based on or the results of his association or working with Kotler Marketing Group which focuses on strategic marketing and works with companies like IBM, AT&T, Pfizer, McDonald's, Ford, Shell Chemical, SAS Airlines and others.

Some of these sins or deficiencies may not appear new. But, these require focus because they are on the drawing board. These also highlight the importance of the basics. Experience of many companies, and, marketing consultants, show that *basics re-emerge from time to time in new forms or manifestations*.

TEN MARKETING SINS AND SOLUTIONS

The ten marketing sins identified by Kotler are given below, but, not in the order in which Kotler has mentioned. This has been done to highlight the relative significance of these sins.

Real-time solution or strategy for correcting each marketing sin is also suggested for possible adoption by companies and marketing managers for correcting marketing sins in their companies.

The ten identified marketing sins are:

1. The company lacks sufficient market focus;
2. The company does not fully understand its target customers and is not customer driven;
3. The company is unable to properly define and monitor its competitors;
4. The company's product and service policies are loose;
5. The company's marketing plans and planning process are deficient;
6. The company's communication with customers and brand building are weak;
7. The company is not good at finding new marketing opportunities;
8. The company is not making enough use of technology;
9. The company is not well organised to execute "effective" and "efficient" marketing;
10. The company does not properly manage its relationships with stakeholders.[2]

THE COMPANY LACKS SUFFICIENT MARKET FOCUS

The company has not clearly identified the focus market areas for its products. This means, in other words, that the company has not correctly analysed the market in terms of target segments.

Major signs or symptoms of insufficient market focus are:

a. Incorrect or poor identification of market segments;

b. Inadequate prioritisation of market segments;

a. Incorrect or Poor Identification of Market Segments: In most companies, market segments are not uniquely defined or identified.

Here is an example. In Sears, the retail chain, top executives were asked the question: "who do you try to sell your goods?" The answer was: "We sell to everyone." Then, they were asked: "Do you get many teenagers coming for shopping at Sears?" The answer was: "Not as many as we would like" Then why should Sears try to sell to everyone and spend or block more resources? This points to poor identification of market segments.

Solution or Corrective Strategy: The company should go for more rigorous or focused segmentation like volume segmentation, value segmentation, benefit segmentation, and, deploy its resources accordingly.

b. Inadequate Prioritisation of Market Segments: Most companies identify different segments of customers, and, try to make packages or offerings for each segment. But, do they clearly differentiate the segments on the basis of their relative attractiveness? In other words, do they prioritise the sectors? Many companies do not. And, they may not allocate resources (market promotion etc.) for different sectors on the basis of prioritisation.

Solution or Corrective Strategy: If different segments have different relative attractiveness, which is mostly the case, prioritisation of sectors is essential. Prioritisation should be done on the basis of relative attractiveness of different segments so that the more important segments receive more attention and resources. For highly attractive segments, dedicated segment managers may be appointed or posted.

So, proper marketing focus boils down to correct or optimal segmentation criteria or strategy. The segmentation criteria should reveal a group of customers who are responsive to unique marketing campaigns or approaches. The group should be unique. If the group or segment is not unique, it cannot be considered as a focus category.[3]

THE COMPANY DOES NOT FULLY UNDERSTAND ITS TARGET CUSTOMERS AND IS NOT CUSTOMER DRIVEN

Understanding customers, or, more specifically, understanding target customers, is almost a perennial issue in marketing. Much has been said on this and much has been done, but, the issue persists.

In fact, the issue starts with the question: "Who is your target customer?" Has the company done sufficient market research or studies to correctly understand its target customers?[4] Many feel that the company's information or research on target customers is weak or incomplete.

A related question is: Is marketing policies and strategies of the company sufficiently customer driven?

Major signs or symptoms of not clearly understanding in customers:

a. The customers are not buying products of the company as planned or expected; they are buying more of competitors' products/brands.

b. Customer complaints and grievances are high;

c. The company has not created a customer culture.

a. The Customers are not buying products of the Company as Planned or Expected: The company should analyse or investigate into the reasons for shortfall in sales: it may be lack of penetrative customer profiling. It may also be that the company has not done correct competitor analysis—their product/brand offerings including pricing, discount and delivery strategy. Usually, it is a combination of both.

Solution or Corrective Strategy: The company should do more intensive customer profiling. It may review its distribution system, may form customer groups and also dealership network. A composite or comprehensive approach is necessary.

b. Customer Complaints and Grievances are High: This shows that the customers are neglected. The company has a mistaken thought that its offerings are good. Therefore, sales will come almost automatically. This means, in other words, that the company is not in regular contact with its customers and the prevailing market conditions.

Solution or Corrective Strategy: The company should improve its customer relationship management. It should implement CRM techniques and packages for better customer contact/relationship.

c. The Company has not Created a Customer Culture: The most glaring symptom of this is that the rest of the company thinks that dealing with customers is the job only of the marketing and sales departments. This is far from truth. In reality, customers have to deal not only with marketing and sales departments, but, also with company's logistics department, finance and accounts and sometimes, with PR and HR.

Solution or corrective Strategy: The whole company, including top management, should realise or remember what Ghandhiji has said: "The customer is the most important visitor on our premises. He is not an interruption on our work. He is the purpose of it...." This should become the company gospel. Then customer culture will prevail in the company.

THE COMPANY IS NOT ABLE TO PROPERLY DEFINE AND MONITOR ITS COMPETITORS

Every company has to deal with competition. Except in monopoly (which is rare), competition is inevitable. Every company has to sail through competition to survive and grow.

Many companies do not correctly identify its competitors and track or monitor competition systematically.

Major signs or symptoms of not identifying and tracking competition properly are:

a. The company focuses only on its nearest or immediate competitors and ignores emerging or potential competitors;

b. The company does not have in place an appropriate competitor intelligence system.

a. The Company focuses only on its immediate competitors and ignores emerging/potential competitors: This is a myopic view of competition. For example, McDonald's may consider only Burger King as its competitor. If the company takes a wider view of competition, it would also consider Pizza Hut, Subway and Taco Bell as its competitors.

Solution or Corrective Strategy: Take a total or complete view, and, not a partial view, of competition. This also means a long-term view. Prepare and make offerings to your customers better than those of your competitors. These are the best ways to increase sales and market share.

b. The company does not have in place an appropriate competitor Intelligence System: Most of the companies may not have an effective competitor intelligence system. If, for example,

Xerox has to bid against Sharp for 1,000 copiers, does it have enough information about the bidding policies and practices of Sharp? Does Xerox have sufficient knowledge about all the sources of information about the business practices of Sharp?

Solution or Corrective Strategy: Set up a dedicated office or manager for competitor intelligence.

The intelligence system should cover primary competitors, secondary competitors and also tertiary competitors. *Primary competitors* are the most immediate competitors in the *same product* category like Coca-Cola and Pepsi (soft drinks market). *Secondary competitors* are in the *substitute product category* like canned and packaged fruit drinks like Fruity, Lemon Soda. *Tertiary competitors* are distant substitutes like cold milk, butter milk, lassi, cold coffee.[5]

For primary competitors, the company should judiciously catch market signals given by such competitors. The company should also adopt the "ghost customer" approach to penetrate info some company's marketing/selling secrets. "Ghost customer" method is quite common in industrial products.

THE COMPANY'S PRODUCT AND SERVICE POLICIES ARE LOOSE

Does the company regularly/periodically review its product and service policies and offerings and take necessary corrective action(s)?

Progressive and well-planned companies like HUL systematically review its product portfolio and discontinue products and brands which have become unsustainable in terms of sales and profitability. HUL has discontinued its cash cow product like Dalda. But, many other companies do not do this.

Major signs or symptoms of the Company's loose product and service policies are:

a. The company has too many products and many are making losses;

b. The company is poor in cross-selling its products and services.

a. The Company has too many products and many are making losses: In many companies, a small percentage of products account for a large percentage of their sales. But, they have a large number of products in their portfolio which contribute very little to their sales. They continue these products/brands. They introduce new products and brands, but, do not simultaneously discontinue the losers. The profit centre approach is often not followed.

In the process of marketing/selling, many services are also offered free in the company's over-enthusiasm to sell.

Solution or Corrective Strategy: The company should adopt a profit centre approach to justify its portfolio of products and product operations.

The company should compulsorily establish a system of tracking non-performing or losing products/brands and phasing them out systematically avoiding market disruptions.

Here is almost a classic example from Unilever. Through their own internal survey or system, Unilever found that 50 of their total of 1600 brands accounted for 63 per cent of the company sales revenue. These are company's *power brands*. The company should strongly focus on these brands. The company worked on identifying its strongest 400 brands to be also called power brands. The remaining 1200 can be significantly reduced over time through 'sale, liquidation or combination." The company will finally concentrate on the power brands or money makers.[6] Companies like Nestle and P&G and such others are also refocusing on their power brands.

b. The Company is poor in Cross-selling its Products and Services: Companies which sell a large number of products and services are often poor in cross-selling, i.e., they do not make enough efforts to sell other products and services which go with the product already sold. For example, a dealer who sells a car does not make serious effort to sell car loan or car insurance.

Solution or Corrective Strategy: All companies should adopt a policy/strategy to maximise cross-selling. *Cross-selling is like generating additional sales or revenue without any additional cost or expenditure*. Only some extra effort is required. *More the effort, more is the success in cross-selling.*

Sales staff may not take serious interest in cross-selling because there may not be any incentive for them. This is a motivation factor. The company should motivate the sales people for cross-selling with extra commission or any other form of incentive. If the salespersons are sufficiently motivated, cross-selling will become more operational and effective.

THE COMPANY'S MARKETING PLANS AND PLANNING PROCESS ARE DEFICIENT

Marketing planning and plans are the starting point for implementation of the company's marketing policies and strategies. Its marketing planning or plans are deficient; implementation, even if efficient, will not produce the desired results. The marketing plan consists of budgets, targets, forecasts logistics and distribution, advertising, promotion etc. Deficiency can creep in any or more of these.

Major signs or symptoms of deficient marketing planning/ plan are:

a. Marketing plan/planning is not based on proper programming of plan components or activities;
b. The marketing plan/planning does not consider the alternatives or opportunity cost;
c. The marketing planning/plan does not include a contingency plan.

a. The Marketing Plan/Planning is not based on Proper Programming of Plan Components or Activities: Does the company ensure that all essential marketing activities occur in the right sequence, and, at the right time? Does the company clearly differentiate between activities which *must be organised sequentially* and activities which may be *treated parallel to each other*?[7] Does the company do correct workload (per week, per month) analysis for marketing/sales people for tracking productivity? Many companies do not do all these.

Solution or Corrective Strategy: The company should standardise system for proper sequencing of designated marketing plan components or activities in a defined time frame. The lag factor should be avoided. A programme or software can be developed for this.

SWOT analysis of marketing plan components should be undertaken to identity activities which require more immediate attention and action taken accordingly.

b. The Marketing Planning/Plan does not consider the Alternatives and Opportunity Cost: Does the company's marketing planning consider the alternatives foregone in terms of resources, sales forecasts, quota or allocations to different salespersons etc.? Does the company calculate or analyse the opportunity cost of the plan chosen? Are the marketers asked a question like: "What changes would you make in marketing/sales in terms of targets and achievements if you are given (a) 10% more budget or (b) 10% less budget?" In case of most of the companies, the answer will be "No."

Solution or Corrective Strategy: Choice of the final marketing plan must be based on evaluation of possible alternatives in terms of budgets, forecasts and achievements, i.e., opportunity costs.

Flexible budgeting, instead of fixed budgeting, may be a good method or strategy. Budget allocations may be linked to flexible sales targets to be given by marketing/sales managers. This is like 'voluntary pressure.' It is self-imposed. It works.

c. The Marketing Planning/Plan does not include a contingency Plan: Most plans, including marketing plans, are based on 'stability' assumptions—stability of economic or environmental conditions and market conditions. But, business environment and market conditions can change—sometimes suddenly as during coronavirus pandemic. The company needs a contingency plan for this. Is the company ready with this so that operational and strategic disruptions in marketing can be minimised?

Solution or Corrective Strategy: In progressive marketing, a 'Plan B' should always be ready if 'Plan A' faces hostile or adverse conditions because certain assumptions made in the plan are not valid any longer. Plan B will be based on revised budget/resource allocations, changes in product mix/offerings, discount/credit policy etc. to match the market dynamics.

THE COMPANY'S COMMUNICATION WITH CUSTOMERS AND BRAND BUILDING ARE WEAK

Communication with customers and brand building of a company are related to each other. A company tries to communicate with its customers through effective brand building with positioning and repositioning of brands. If a company can effectively communicate with its target customers through appropriate brand building, it becomes easier for the company to achieve its marketing objectives.

Major signs or symptoms of a company's weak communication with customer and brand building are:

a. Awareness of customers about the company and knowledge of its products/brands are poor;

b. The company's brand building process is ordinary; it does not show enough differentiation or any uniqueness.

a. Awareness/Knowledge of Customers about the company and its products/brands are insufficient/Poor: Brand building is not the only way to communicate with target customers. Intensive promotion and information-based channels and integrated distribution are equally important. Asian Paints is serving its customers through retailers with 84% efficiency—84% of orders are serviced within 24 hours. But, for vast majority of companies, the communication process/system is weak whether through distribution channels or brand building.

Solution or Corrective Strategy: The company should assess its methods or instruments of communication with customers and measure their effectiveness.

Various innovative methods of communication are 'exploding' around brands which provide communication—distribution synergy. Companies like Ceat, Titan, MRF, BPL and Singer are adopting such approach. Other companies should also resort to such innovative communication methods.

b. The Company's Brand Building Process is Ordinary; it does not show any Uniqueness: Ask your target customers the question: "Do you find our brand different or distinctive from the competitors' brands?" If the answer is "No", your brand building is weak. You have not developed uniqueness in its appeal and it will not succeed.

Solution or Corrective Strategy: Correct brand building is necessary for brand success. The company should develop the right method or strategy for brand success.

Four criteria are generally prescribed for success of a brand. The four criteria are:

(a) The brand should deliver benefits at the product level; (b) the benefits offered by the brand must be consistent with its personality; (c) the brand should offer some intangibles besides tangible benefits, and (d) the benefits offered must be relevant to the customer.[8]

Most companies which have achieved brand success satisfy these criteria—Lakme, Surf, Pantene, Ponds, Titan, Sunsilk, Honda, Cinthol, Lux, Sony and many others. Your company should achieve brand success though appropriate brand building.

THE COMPANY IS NOT GOOD AT FINDING NEW MARKETING OPPORTUNITIES

Opportunities are always there in the air. For marketing companies, opportunities exist in the market. But, how many companies locate, seize and exploit new marketing opportunities regularly? This is a pertinent question in modern marketing.

Major signs or symptoms of companies not able to identify new marketing opportunities are:

a. The company has not done well in finding new marketing opportunities in the recent past;

b. The company's initiatives in finding new marketing opportunities have largely failed.

a. The Company has not done well in finding new marketing opportunities: Companies like 3M regularly find and launch new products and services. In fact, the company's policy is to generate 30% of sales turnover during any year from products introduced during last five years.

But, companies like Coca-Cola and Procter & Gamble do not conform to such "newness" in product finding and new product introductions are more reactive for survival and growth than pre-emptive or new initiatives. For example, for Coca-Cola, the successful new beverages—bottled water, fruit juices and energy drinks—were introduced by competitors first. There are other examples.

Solution or Corrective Strategy: The company should set up a sound R&D unit and establish close link or communication between R&D and marketing. This is the best way to translate R&D results into new product innovations and introductions.

The company should not think that the industry is mature or the market is saturated and, therefore, there are no new opportunities. In reality, there is no such thing as a mature or saturated market. A company can always change the definition or structure of a market by introducing a new variant or brand. Starbucks, for example, did not consider the coffee market as mature or saturated.

b. The company's initiatives in Finding New marketing Opportunities have largely failed: The company might have taken some initiatives to find and launch new products. But the initiatives have mostly failed because the company has not gone through the new introduction process systematically or correctly. There may be lapses in concept development/testing, marketing planning, test marketing or commercialisation of the launch.

Solution or Corrective Strategy: Many initiatives, including good initiatives, fail because of poor new product management process. This should be taken care of by flawlessly integrating different stages from conception to marketing of new products.

Also new product concepts or initiatives should be innovative so that the chances of failure are minimised, or, rather, the chances of success increase.

One such innovative approach is lateral marketing.[9] *Lateral marketing* means thinking or relaunching your existing product linking it to another "product, service or idea." Examples are: snack bar (cereals + snack), protein bar (cereals + protein). Other good examples are: convenience store (petrol/diesel station + food store), cybercafe (cafe + computer) and walkman (audio + portability) Lateral marketing has good potential for success.

THE COMPANY DOES NOT MAKE ENOUGH USE OF TECHNOLOGY

Marketing of a company, to be modern, should be technologically sound or advanced. This involves use of the Internet (Intranet and Extranet) and other forms of automation in marketing and sales. These are essential for infusing speed and efficiency in the system and increasing marketing productivity. Companies which do not make proper use of technology fall behind in the marketing race.

Major signs or symptoms of company's lack of use of technology are:

a. The company makes very little use of the internet;

b. The company has not introduced any marketing automation.

a. The Company makes very little use of the Internet: Every company today makes use of the Internet in management and marketing functions. But, the issue is: does a company make enough use of the Internet in its marketing—planning, operations and customer management? Does the company go sufficiently beyond just establishing a website? Experience shows that many companies do not.

Solution or corrective Strategy: Make use of the Internet to the fullest extent possible. This makes marketing more technologically equipped and modern. Make the web site more functional and effective.

Utilise the Intranet for faster and efficient communication within the company. Use the Extranet for better communication with external stakeholders like suppliers, distributors/channel members and dealers. Focus more on e-market research. This opens up 'information highway.' Establish E-chatrooms for customers. In this way, make the Internet almost a pervasive tool in marketing.

b. The Company has not introduced any automation in marketing: Internet is not the only form of automation. A company can introduce automation in marketing in different other ways or forms. These include introducing programme softwares for replacing manual operations by automated systems. These can cover production-distribution-warehousing integration, sales force automation, CRM or e-CRM etc. But, very few companies adopt such marketing automation systems.

Solution or Corrective Strategy: All companies should introduce both market automation and sales automation—two vital components of marketing automation.

Market automation softwares can efficiently handle many routine/regular marketing decisions and operations including pricing. Many airlines use software programmes for yield-based pricing.[10]

Sales automation systems make the salespeople more organised and fast in sales execution. These include on-line communication/interaction with the sales manager/headquarters for instant decision making in the field on pricing, discount, delivery etc. to close a sale.

THE COMPANY IS NOT WELL ORGANISED TO EXECUTE 'EFFECTIVE' AND 'EFFICIENT' MARKETING

To achieve its objectives or to produce desired results, marketing should be both "effective" and "efficient". In an organisation, both effectiveness and efficiency depend on marketing leadership, performance skills and inter-departmental communication, coordination and cooperation. In the absence of these, both effectiveness and efficiency will suffer.

Major signs or symptoms of lack of effectiveness and efficiency in the marketing organisation are:

a. The marketing head may not be very effective;
b. The marketing staff lack contemporary marketing skills;
c. The relations between the marketing department and other departments of the company are far from healthy.

a. The Marketing Head may not be very Effective: Call this head of marketing, marketing leader or Chief Marketing Officer (CMO), the marketing head is the leader of the marketing team. The leader formulates policy, develops strategy and gives directions to the marketing team. The team's performance depends, to a very large extent, on how the leader leads. In many companies, may be by default, the marketing head is wrongly chosen. He is not effective, and, because of this, effectiveness of the entire team suffers.

Solution or corrective Strategy: The company should appoint, after weighing all factors, the most appropriate person as marketing head—dedicated, performing and effective. And, above all, he should be highly customer-oriented. Then, he passes the right message down the line.

Herb Kelleher, the co-founder of South West Airlines, US, shows the company's customer focus as this: "We don't have a marketing Department; we have a Customer Department." All Marketing policies and strategies follow from this. This may be the first and most important step towards making the marketing leader effective. This also makes the marketing team largely effective.

(b) The marketing staff lack contemporary marketing Skills: In most of the companies, marketing traditionally focuses on five skills: Logistics/distribution, market/marketing research, advertising, sales promotion and sales management. Very few companies go beyond this, and, acquire and adopt new marketing skills.

Solution or Corrective Strategy: Marketing and sales people should increasingly acquire and use/adopt new and contemporary marketing skills.

Companies are developing and using many such skills. Three important new marketing skills are: repositioning, market-driving skill and integrated marketing communication.

Positioning of a brand may not work any longer in the market, and, therefore, the brand needs repositioning. For example, Dettol toilet soap was initially positioned as a beauty soap. But, this was not in line with its core value—"germ Kill." The soap, therefore, had to be repositioned as a germ kill soap. Dettol was further repositioned as Dettol—"Protection from 100 illness causing germs." Such repositioning is required for many brands.

The genesis of market-driving skill is to invent new needs and new products. As Akio Morita, Sony's visionary leader, puts it: "Our plan is to lead the public with new products rather than ask them what kind of products they want." Many new products came into the market through market-driving skill—photocopier, mobile-phone, laptop.

Integrated marketing communications create impressions on the customers with different communications of a company in an integrated way. A salesperson's attire and personality communicate; company catalogue communicates; company's actions communicate; and, all these together successfully deliver company's products/brands to the customer.

(c) **The Relations between the marketing Department and other departments are far from Healthy:** In any company, marketing does not work in isolation. Its functioning is related to, and success depends on, number of other departments in the company particularly R&D, production, logistics and finance. But, in many companies, the attitudes of other departments are: "Marketing is the job of the Marketing Department." Such attitude is a major roadblock to marketing efficiency and success.

Solution or Corrective Strategy: The marketing department has to establish healthy working relationship with other co-related departments. The marketing department may have to do some "internal marketing" for improving inter-departmental cooperation.

Marketing and R&D should be regularly in communication about product modifications, new products or product innovations. Manufacturing has to implement these through production planning cost efficiency, inventory management etc. Logistic has to ensure smooth flow of products through the channels to the retailers or customers. Finance has to play its role in cost management, credit policy and planning and profitability analysis.

All these will make marketing both effective and efficient.

THE COMPANY DOES NOT PROPERLY MANAGE ITS RELATIONSHIPS WITH STAKEHOLDERS

A company has many stakeholders including its shareholders. Other important stakeholders are employees, suppliers, channel members and investors. Some of these like employees and channel members have a direct bearing on performance of marketing. We can call these stakeholders of marketing.

Major signs or symptoms of the company not managing its relationships properly with stakeholders are:

(a) The company's employees are not happy;

(b) The company's channel members are not managed well.

(a) The Company's Employees are not Happy: Employees are often considered the most important resource of a company. But, in many companies, they are not happy. Unhappy employees particularly in production, logistics, finance, not only slow down or disrupt operations, but, can sometimes even sabotage marketing.

Solution or Corrective Strategy: As a very important resource, all employees should be managed well. They should be paid well, respected, trained and motivated. They should be given the feeling that they are very valuable to the company. This will motivate them to contribute and increase their productivity. This will ultimately enhance productivity of marketing and the company.

(b) The Company's channel members are not managed well. The channel members—distributors, wholesalers and dealers—are a critical link in the marketing organisation of a company, and, they play a pivotal role in marketing efficiency and success. If they are not treated or managed well, as happens in many companies, performance of marketing will suffer.

Solution or Corrective Strategy: The company should attract the best channel members (those who have market reputation) and build and maintain best relations with them. Caterpillar, the renowned earth moving equipment company, view their dealers as their source of major competitive advantage. Most companies should follow the Caterpillar model for managing their channel members.

RESHAPING MARKETING

According to many, marketing is in bad shape today. Not only marketing theories, marketing practices are also being questioned. Analyses of ten marketing sins also point to the imperative need for reshaping marketing.

It is essential to correctly understand what business a company is really in to be able to play the marketing role properly. Here is an example. A friend of Andre Heiniger, Chairman of Rolex, asked him: "How is the watch business?" Heiniger replied: "I have no idea."

Surprising? The chairman of the world's most prestigious watch making company saying this. Heiniger clarified: "We are in the luxury business," i.e., luxury watch business.

This highlights the significance of understanding the uniqueness of a product/brand, the market and competitors—be it a mass market/product, a customised product or a niche product. This also indicates the need for analysing the changing market conditions, i.e., market dynamics. This may be environmental or competition-driven. The more a company understands the market dynamics, the better its marketing decisions are likely to be.

Marketing decisions and strategy may continue to evolve around or focus on right STP (segmenting, targeting, positioning/repositioning). But, these alone are not enough. These should be strategically combined with associated or correlated driving forces (new marketing skills) to secure competitive advantage in the market. This will be a sure step towards reshaping marketing.

A Marketing Epilogue

Many feel that, although marketing as a *management philosophy* is seen more and more as increasingly critical to organisational success, marketing, *as a management function*, is found wanting on many counts. CEOs are asking whether marketing is adding enough value to the corporation and its shareholders commensurate with its cost. All these indicate significant—some say structural—changes in the marketing function.

New marketing concepts, tools, and techniques are thrown into the marketing arena at regular intervals. Some of these are really new or innovative, but many are like old wines in new bottles. Many marketing gurus like Jack Trout believe that today's marketing concepts and tools will not be relevant for tomorrow because there is nothing inherently new or meaningful in those for people to hang on to. Those are just buzzwords. And, *buzzwords will come and go as will marketing gurus, consultants and practitioners.*

Buzzwords and mundane tools will not work. Mere extrapolation of the past is not enough. That only results in history repeating itself. Focusing only on the present is inherently myopic. It should be strategy for the future. Also, marketing should now focus on Total Value Proposition (TVP) as against the earlier emphasis on Unique Selling Proposition (USP). It is predatory marketing (call it "situational marketing", if you like) that will become the driving force. Inventive marketing will provide the strategy base for outwitting competition.

It is truly said that *fixed systems, checklists, and formats obstruct initiative and innovativeness*. And, intuitive skills thrive best under conditions of uncertainty, response time limitations, and insufficient database or information crisis. Only these skills and commensurate strategies may guarantee success in the marketing battle which has engulfed almost all countries today, be it in the domestic trade or in the global business.

The ubiquity of the Net may destabilise the four Ps of marketing. Yet, the marketing goal will remain the same: *delivering the right product to the right customer at the right price, time, and place*. The central theme of marketing would continue to evolve, as ever, around the three Ps (Product, Price, and Positioning) or three Bs (buyer need, buyer cost, and buyer management). The customer will remain the eternal truth. The customer as market 'operator' would finally dictate market shares and profitability of companies, whether in business-to-business, consumer goods or services.

Market and strategy only mediate between a company and its customer. But how successfully it is done, depends on the effectiveness of the strategy and would decide its ultimate success or failure.

If the strategy is ill-conceived and implemented, it can make a product like Milkfood Yogurt fail. But if it is brilliant in conception and execution, there is no limit to what marketing strategy can do. It can sell water for the price of milk in a poor country like India. Bisleri water beats DMS milk in price: Bisleri water was selling for ₹ 10 (per litre) and DMS milk for ₹ 8 at one time in Delhi.

So, strategy is the crux. Strategy should be developed innovatively as a dynamic process. Market dynamics should govern innovativeness. ***Marketing to be successful, should continue to evolve around the cycle of innovations.***

Section III

Selling

18

Why Salespeople Fail

Failure can occur in any sphere of life, personal or family life, business or selling. We can say that failure is almost a way of life (although we may not wish it) like success but, of course, with lesser frequency. Sometimes, and, for some people, failure and success alternate like darkness and light.

But, it is essential to understand the factors or reasons for failure, analyse them and take necessary corrective steps or actions and get back on course.

Factors behind failure in selling can be many. These factors or reasons can be classified into two categories:

A. Common factors for failure
B. Specific reasons for failure

A. COMMON FACTORS FOR FAILURE

Four major common factors behind failure of selling are:

1. Not following the basics
2. Lack of proper sales orientation
3. Not understanding the customer
4. Not analysing competitors.

NOT FOLLOWING THE BASICS[1]

In any art, discipline or profession, basics are very important. But, we often neglect them. And, this leads to many failures.

I narrate here a story of how forgetting the basics can result in a disaster. A newly married young lady wanted to cook a dish in her in-law's house. She bought a recipe book. She ceremoniously followed all the steps or instructions given in the recipe book. After she completed the cooking, she discovered that nothing was cooked. She wondered why. Then she found that she did not light the gas burner because it was not mentioned in the recipe book.

This may sound silly. But, it makes sense. This is a reminder of the bare basics.

Not following basics in selling can be in different forms. Five major forms are:

a. Not starting well
b. Not getting determined
c. Do not appear self-confident
d. Not prepared for initial struggle
e. Do not work within self-limitations

Not Starting Well

Many people who decide to become salespeople may not know anything about selling to start with. Some may not even know how to find a job in sales. But, many of them become successful salespersons. Of course, there are sloggers and there are failures. This is true of almost every profession. But, if you want to make a career in sales, get started well.

Plan before you jump into selling. Planning gives success. Prepare yourself. Preparation gives confidence. But, many salespeople don't do or follow this.

Not Getting Determined

This is an extension of not starting well.

Many salespeople take a wavering attitude before and during starting. *Wavering people always lose directions*. Think and decide. But, once decided, get determined and take the plunge. If you do not do this, you may fail.

Do not Appear Self-Confident

A salesperson should not only start determined, he(she) should also appear self-confident.

Externalities are also very important. This involves dressing well and posing well. Your outfit, posture and personality make the first impression. This is very vital in personal selling. This also might make the final impact. Many salespeople do not realise or remember this.

Not Prepared for Initial Struggle

If you want to make a career in selling, you should be prepared for some initial struggle.

Sales jobs, like all other jobs, are demanding. It is a new trade or profession for you and you have to develop the right traits for this. This means learning. And, learning may sometimes mean some initial struggle.

Joe Girard is the world's best salesman according to the Guinness Book of World Records. But, he did not become the world's best salesman automatically or overnight. If you look into his career growth, you will see many phases of struggle including the initial ones.

So, be prepared for some initial struggle. If you are not prepared for the initial struggle, you may not really take off.

Do not Work within Self-limitations

You may set high standard for yourself, but, be realistic in your approach towards goal achievement. This is what brings out the best in you.

If you only think in terms of how much money you can earn, you may soon reach a plateau, and, you may even lose directions. We all know that money or financial gain is the ultimate driving force behind everything. But, most of the time, earning is proportional to your performance and capability. And, you cannot overstress yourself too often. This can be counterproductive.

All of us have limitations. Even the best salesman in the world has his limitations. The best approach is to work within your limitations. This is a sure way to achieve the goal.

Once we enter the real world of selling, a new factor emerges. For the first time, our powers of persuation and our selling abilities are being judged. This can be intimidating; and, so we respond by convincing ourselves that we cannot sell, we do not know how to sell or do not want to sell. We then use these mental roadblocks to justify our lack of sales potential. If you wish to become a salesperson, do not fall into this trap.

If you fall into this trap, it shows that you are not following the basics.

LACK OF PROPER SALES ORIENTATION[2]

Many salespersons get into selling, but, they lack proper sales orientation. This is a basic shortcoming.

Your Sales Orientation

The best way to determine sales orientation is to use some quantitative indicator or measure.

Twelve simple exploratory questions are given below. Answer these in 'Yes' or 'No'. The answers will indicate your sales orientation.

	Tick(√) 'Yes' or 'No'	
	Yes	No
1. Is selling widely accepted as a key business philosophy in your company?	☐	☐
2. Have you taken to selling because of pressure or circumstances?	☐	☐
3. Have you chosen selling by your own choice?	☐	☐
4. Do you think you have the necessary skill for selling?	☐	☐
5. Do you have previous experience in selling?	☐	☐
6. Do you think you need some training to be a better salesperson?	☐	☐
7. Do you know the product well that you are selling?	☐	☐
8. Have you studied the market or territory allotted to you?	☐	☐
9. Are you clear about the price and discount policy of your company?	☐	☐
10. Do you know well your nearest competitor(s)?	☐	☐
11. Are you happy with the present compensation package offered to you?	☐	☐
12. Do you want to make a career in selling?	☐	☐

The answers to these questions are analysed as below:

Score (Total 'Yes')	Selling Orientation
10 or more	Excellent
8 to less than 10	Very good
7 to less than 8	Good
6	Average
Less than 6	Poor

If your score is between 7 and 8, your sales orientation is just 'Good' or OK. But, if the score is 6 or less, your sales orientation is definitely lacking. If these are the levels of your sales orientation, you are likely to more often fail in selling.

NOT UNDERSTANDING THE CUSTOMER

Customers are numerous and they are very diverse in their buying patterns and behaviours. Some say that the customer's mind is a "black box"; some say the customer is an "enigma"; some others say that the customer is a "puzzle" or a "riddle." These may be rightly so. Experience of many companies show that customer behaviour or the decision making process, on many occasions, is almost inexplicable.

DIFFERENT TYPES OF CUSTOMERS

So, it is almost obvious that there are many types of customers. Nine major customer types can be distinguished:

a. Discerning customers
b. Affiliative customers
c. 'Know-all' customers
d. Authoritative customers
e. Inhibited customers
f. Image customers
g. 'Value-for-money' customers
h. Credibility customers
i. Haggling customers[3]

MANY FACES OF A CUSTOMER

Another way to look at types of customers is in terms of various roles played by them. The customers commonly play six different roles:

a. Post-purchase feedback
b. Complaint feedback
c. Ghost shopping feedback
d. Focus group feedback
e. Trend type feedback

UNDERSTANDING THE CUSTOMER: SPECIFIC PERSPECTIVE

In addition to the general factors or perspectives mentioned above, salespeople also have to consider more specific factors for properly understanding the customer.

A salesperson operates in a particular region or territory. He(she) has to closely analyse the behavioural patterns, preferences and particular or special needs of customers in that region or territory.

A rural area or market is a special region. The rural customer is different from the urban customer. The rural customer's product/brand perception, buying behaviour or pattern, price expectation etc. have to be properly understood to sell in this region or market.

Also, if the customers in the region, whether rural or urban, are buying more of competitors' products, the reasons for this have to be clearly ascertained.

In short, a salesperson has to understand the customer in the correct perspective; otherwise, his(her) sales efforts will suffer or fail.

NOT ANALYSING COMPETITORS[4]

There is no selling without competition. Only in monopoly (one seller, many buyers), there is no competition. But, monopolies are rare. Under all normal market conditions, there is competition. So, if you are in selling, you have to face and deal with competition to survive and grow.

EXISTING COMPETITORS

Existing competitors of a company can be of three types: primary, secondary and tertiary.

Primary competitors are competitors in the *same product category* (with different brands) and are the most immediate ones; these are more clearly visible and easily identifiable. If we take the Indian soft drinks market, Coca-Cola and Pepsi are the most immediate or primary competitors followed by Thumps Up, Sprite, Fanta and Limca.

Secondary competitors are in the substitute product categories and are not so clearly visible. Again, if we take the soft drinks market, Lemon Soda, canned and packaged fruit drinks (like Fruity) and slush are substitutes for soft drinks and compete with different brands of soft drinks.

Tertiary competitors are more *distant substitutes* which are not easily visible or identifiable, but, those also compete with the product or brand. Tertiary competitors of soft drinks are cold milk/butter milk, lassi, cold coffee etc. During different times and conditions, consumers substitute them for soft drinks.

Therefore, any company in any business (product) must try to identity all its existing competitors—primary, secondary and tertiary—who always vie for part of the market or market share.

POTENTIAL COMPETITORS

Existing competitors are the most immediate threats to a company, and, potential competitors are potential threats. If potential competitors are not foreseen on time and dealt with properly, they can sometimes pose more serious problems than the existing competitors.

All existing competitors of today are potential competitors of yesterday. There are many examples of this in FMCGs and consumer durables: Titan to HMT; Maruti to Premier Padmini, Nirma to Surf; Canon to Xerox; Samsung to Nokia, etc.

COMPETITOR THREAT: FIVE FORMS

Threats from competitors, existing or potential, can come in different forms. Five major types of competitor threats are possible and are often seen in practice:

a. Threat from existing competitors
b. Threat from substitutes
c. Threat from buyers
d. Threat from suppliers
e. Threat from new entrants[5]

These five forms are depicted and elaborately explained in Porter's Five forces Model which is well known. Therefore, these are not explained here.

Before making marketing plans and strategies, it is essential for companies to analyse and assess the nature and magnitude of competition particularly the current competitors who are a constant threat to a company's business.

If you Ignore Competition

Most companies are busy with making their own marketing plans and strategies. Plans and strategies are made for both the present and the future—how to increase sales, market share and profitability. In this process, either they ignore competitors, or, do not consider or measure their full potential or impact. *This is one kind of marketing myopia.*

The outcome is: targets are only partially achieved or not reached at all. This has happened through decades. In the "70s," Raymond, Bombay Dyeing and Khatau (Voiles) ignored the emergence of Vimal fabrics; in the "80s", HUL (Surf) was overlooking the entry of Nirma and Premier Automobiles (Padmini) could not weigh the full impact of emergence of Maruti (Suzuki); in the "90s", HMT (Watches) could not measure the full impact of Titan; Weston, Uptron, Salora, Dyanora could not correctly anticipate the emergence of Sony, LG and Samsung; in 2000s, Nokia could not foresee the full measure of impact of Samsung; LG and Samsung could not clearly anticipate the market impact of Sony Led TV.

Some of the companies mentioned above have completely perished.

B. SPECIFIC REASONS FOR FAILURE

There can be many specific reasons because of which salespeople may fail. These are analysed below.

SIXTEEN REASONS FOR FAILURE[6]

Sixteen specific reasons for failure in selling are:

1. Lack of clarity of goals
2. Not being organised

3. Lack of commitment
4. Lack of motivation
5. Lack of openness/transparency
6. Absence of proper systems/procedures
7. Poor communication
8. Lack of coordination
9. Lack of monitoring
10. Over-confidence
11. Lack of confidence
12. Fear of rejection
13. Lack of proper training
14. Lack of team spirit
15. Too little follow-up
16. Too much follow-up

Lack of Clarity of Goals

"Lack of clarity of goals" may be the first reason or cause of failure in selling. The salespersons may not be clear about what is actually to be achieved—territories, products, customers—or which are the priorities.

Not Being Organised

"Not being organised" means not getting or going prepared for a sales presentation or meeting with a prospect.

Lack of Commitment

"Lack of commitment" and "Lack of motivation" are closely correlated. Lack of motivation causes lack of commitment. These two factors always cause salespersons to under-perform or fail frequently.

Lack of Openness/Transparency

"Lack of openness or transparency" imply ambiguity. The prospect may feel that the salesperson is trying to hide or conceal some information or details about the company or the product.

Lack of Proper Systems and Procedures

"Lack of proper systems and procedures" is another important factor. Salespersons might not be given clear or complete instructions or drills about allocation of territories, prospects/customers, discounts, etc. These may result in failure in execution of sales.

Poor Communication

"Poor communication" can be of two types; first, between the salespersons and the sales manager or headquarters, and, second, between the salespersons and the prospect/customer. Poor communication with the sales manager or headquarters may be in the form of incomplete brief, guidelines or instructions relating to a prospect/customer or sale. Poor communication with a prospect/customer may be in the form of non-supply of information or details about the product or offer or inadequate or incomplete follow-up with the prospect/customer.

Lack of Coordination, Lack of Monitoring

"Lack of coordination" is almost an extension of lack of communication. Lack of coordination is more often an issue with the sales manager/headquarters. This can also be with the prospect/customer. Lack of coordination with the sales manager also implies or includes "lack of monitoring". In lack of monitoring, the sales manager plays a more important role.

Overconfidence

"Overconfidence" of salespersons can be another cause of failure. Overconfidence can border on the thinking that the prospect/customer will come to them.

Lack of Confidence

Equally bad or damaging is "Lack of confidence". This is a psychological setback.

Fear of Rejection

Lack of confidence often leads to "fear of rejection".

Lack of Proper Training

Lack of proper training, particularly skill-based training, ill-equips the salespersons in selling. This more often becomes a reason for them to under-perform or fail.

Lack of Team Spirit

Salespersons may sometimes have to work as a team for selling certain products particularly consumer durables and industrial products. "Lack of team spirit" "in such cases may cause failure in execution of sales."

Too Little follow-up, Too Much Follow-up

Timely follow-up with the prospects is very important or essential for conclusion of a sale. But, too much follow-up may spoil the broth, i.e., sale. Also, too little follow-up may result in loss of sale. Both may be self-defeating or counterproductive.

FAILURE BECAUSE OF FOLLOW-UP FACTORS

There are a number of ways too little or too much follow-up can damage a sale or result in failure.

Too Little Follow-up

In actual sales situations, there are more reasons or causes for too little follow-up than for too much follow-up.

Ten common ways too little follow-up takes place are:

1. Laziness/Lethargy
2. Non-caring attitude
3. Habit of not pursuing or finishing the task
4. Lack of commitment
5. Overconfidence
6. Creating a big time lag for follow-up and then feeling embarrassed to call or follow-up
7. Taking a break or holiday in the middle of a pursuit.
8. Not keeping/maintaining regular diary
9. Not keen/conscious about target achievement
10. Feeling that they are chasing the prospect too frequently/ feeling that they are pushing the prospect too much

Too Much Follow-up

Six common reasons for too much follow-up are:

1. Too eager to sell/close a sale
2. Attitudinal problem: "I want to prove that I can close a sale faster than others"

3. Lack of patience
4. In a hurry to take a break
5. Too independent to follow proper norms or protocol
6. In a haste to receive a special reward

FAILURE IN SELLING AND BEHAVIOURAL PATTERNS[7]

It has been observed that salespersons with high rate or frequency of failure show certain common behavioural patterns. In other words, failure in selling and salespersons' behavioural patterns are closely correlated.

Eight observed common behavioural patterns are:

1. Salespersons with high rate of failure have an attitude problem;
2. Such salespersons have no clarity of goals;
3. Such salespersons mostly go unprepared for appointments or meetings;
4. They do not practice their sales presentations in advance;
5. They waste time in loose talks and gossips;
6. They think that prospects/customers will wait for them;
7. They generally suffer from overconfidence syndrome;
8. They are never proactive; they are always reactive.

So, the reasons or causes of failure in selling can be many and varied. To shield their failures, most of the salespersons try to shift the blame to the state of economic conditions in the country, environment or circumstances, the company, the sales manager, the product and, often their stars or bad luck. Shifting the blame to others, does not help your cause or solve your problems.

It is difficult to say which are the more important reasons for failure. These can be skill-related, attitude-related, behaviour-related or environment-related. These are usually not isolated set of reasons. These are more often a combination of them.

To ascertain the more important reasons, a salesperson should do self-analysis, and, also have reason or cause diagnosis sessions with the sales manager.

LINKAGE OF FACTORS BEHIND FAILURE IN SELLING

Common factors and specific reasons for failure in selling discussed above are not totally different or unrelated to each other. There can be, and usually is, linkage or relationship between the two sets of factors. See figure below.

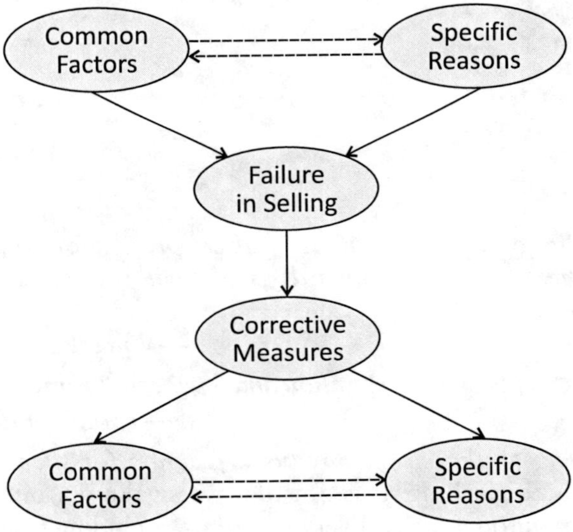

The linkage between common factors and the specific reasons can be easily explained. For example, if there is lack of proper sales orientation, there may be no clarity of goals, communication system may be poor, lack of motivation etc. If a salesperson does not understand the customer properly, there may be lack of follow-up, and, also overconfidence or lack of confidence. If he(she) does not correctly analyse competitors, he(she) may not be well organised, and, also may not follow correct systems and procedures, among others.

So, the common factors and specific reasons for failure in selling should be viewed in an integrated way to ascertain the factors or reasons in a total perspective. *This should lead the way for preventive or effective corrective measures for dealing with failure in selling.*

19
Success in Selling

The quality of a person's life is in direct proportion to their commitment to success, regardless of their chosen field of endeavour....

—Vince Lombardii

Success is 95 per cent perspiration and 5 per cent inspiration....

—Thomas Edison

There is no textbook or copy book formula for success in any field including selling. It is not that we swallow a pill and success comes automatically. Every one of us, including those in selling, has to work the hard way to achieve success.

But, we can learn from those who have achieved success. We can learn how to succeed. We can know essential qualities for success, laws of success, recipe for success or winning, adoption of role model etc. These are the factors which contribute or lead to success.

Various contributory factors or steps to success can be distilled into five more important ones:

1. **Roadmap for success**
2. **Recipe for Winning**
3. **Use of newer methods/technologies**
4. **Knowing the difference between effort and result**
5. **Adopting a Role Model**

ROADMAP TO SUCCESS

WHAT IS SUCCESS IN SELLING

Success in selling can be looked at or understood in different ways. Therefore, success can be defined or measured also in different ways.

We give below definition and measurement of success as commonly done:

Success is commonly defined or measured in relation to task, target or result. If a salesperson is asked to sell 100 units or pieces of a product, and he(she) sells all the 100 units, he(she) has achieved success.

There are two other related factors here; first, the cost or expenditure incurred to achieve the target and, second, the time period. The sales target should be achieved within the budget or resources allocated, and the prescribed time period.

Success, so defined, can be shown as below:

Success in Selling and Defining Constraints

Using these three factors, success can be measured as a weighted average or a composite index using a five-point scale. This way, success can also be rated. This is shown in table below:

Measurement and Rating of Success

Factor	Rating 1	Rating 2	Rating 3	Rating 4	Rating 5
Target achieved	5	5	5	4	3
Cost/resources	5	5	4	3	2
Time period	5	3	3	2	2
Total	15	13	12	9	7
Average	5.0	4.3	4.0	3.0	2.3

5.0: Outstanding, 4.5: Very good, 4.0: Good, 3.0: Average, 2.3: Poor

Based on the scores in the table, the level of success can be rated as follows:

Score	Level of success
5.0	Outstanding
4.3 – 4.5	Very good
4.0	Good
3.0	Average
2.3 or less	Poor or failure

The above scores and rating are hypothetical. In actual situations, scores and ratings by different companies would be different indicating different levels of success of salespeople.

ESSENTIAL QUALITIES FOR SUCCESS

One may be a leader in sales or a follower. But every salesperson must possess certain qualities to succeed.

The question is: which are the qualities or characteristics the salespeople should possess for success? Or, which are the essential qualities or attributes? This is an issue many sales analysts have been debating on, many companies have been seeking an answer to, and, often, sales managers and salespeople have been asking themselves. Is it qualification, knowledge, skill, training, ambition, aggressiveness or something else? All or some of these are definitely important, but which are the more important or essential ones?

Steeve Reeves, with 30 years of sales and sales management experience, offers an answer to this. According to him:

"Successful salespeople display the same characteristics in my experience, but those characteristics aren't the one most people would expect. They don't include ambitious, aggressive, gregarious, social, pushy or any of another 20 we might think of. But, they include the qualities we would look for when wanting to buy from somebody."

Reeves contends that every successful salesperson he has worked with, combines four qualities or characteristics in certain proportions. These are:

- Honesty: 30%
- Efficiency: 30%

- Empathy: 30%
- Luck: 10%

We may add skill to this. Then, the five qualities and their weights or proportions will be reworked as follows:

1. *Skill: 20%*
2. *Efficiency: 30%*
3. *Honesty: 20%*
4. *Empathy: 20%*
5. *Luck: 10%*

1. Skill: For success, salespeople must acquire or develop required skills for selling a particular product. Skills required for selling consumer goods, industrial products and services are usually different because of the nature of products and the target customers. Skill development can be done through proper training. Skill grows with experience and gets perfected over time.

2. Efficiency: *Efficiency is all about application, determination and perseverance.* These virtues are essential for success. Efficiency is also about delivery of products the customer wants at the right prices, quality, and on time with assured service. All these require high level of efficiency.

3. Honesty: Successful salespeople tell customers the truth—about their company, product and sales policy. They do what they say they will do. They also understand their customers well—their buying habits, likings, dislikings, emotions, etc. If a salesperson misleads a customer for buying something, he(she) can do it only once; and, his and his company's dishonesty may be established through words of mouth.

4. Empathy: Empathy, and not sympathy, is what customers want. *Empathy*, in a simple language, means understanding the customers in their own way. Customers want to buy from salespeople who understand the problems of deciding to buy, choosing whom to buy from and why. This way, they get inspired or induced to buy from salespeople who show the right empathy.

5. Luck: Every one of us needs a bit of luck in our life. So do salespeople. Some people may believe it or not, luck does play some role in success. It offers or provides that "extra something" which makes skill, efficiency, honesty and empathy produce result.

TEN LAWS OF SALES SUCCESS[1]

A recent Gallup poll on the honesty and ethical conduct of business professionals found that insurance salespeople and car salespeople ranked last. But it does not seem to be only the insurance salespeople and car salespeople who have a bad reputation. Bill Brooks of the Brooks Group estimates that more than 85 per cent of customers have a negative view of all salespeople. This perception may be generally true. This is primarily because of the way majority of salespeople present and conduct themselves in sales presentations and meetings with customers.

To change this perception, salespeople need to learn and develop right skills and techniques which may make customers think differently about the selling process. And, this would increase the success rate in selling significantly.

Len Foley suggests ten principles—he calls them "tactics" or "laws"—which prepare salespeople better for success. These ten principles or laws are:

Law 1 Talk less and listen more: This is particularly important during the first few minutes of the sales meeting/interaction with the prospect/customer. It is true that the salesperson wants to introduce himself (herself) to the prospect/customer. He(she) likes to tell his(her) name and the purpose of his(her) visit (phone call). But, he(she) should not try to talk much about the product or service. At this point, the salesperson does not have any clear idea about what he is offering is of any interest to the prospect. So, the salesperson should talk less and listen more to find out the prospect's interest and need.

Law 2 Sell with questions, not answers: Instead of immediately trying to sell the product or service, the salespeople should focus on understanding what or why the prospect wants to buy. To do this, the salespeople should try to get close or intimate with the prospect. They need to ask carefully phrased questions to know more and more about the prospect's mind and thinking.

Law 3 Pretend that you are on a first date with your prospect: Salespeople should try to get curious about the prospects/ customers by asking about the products and services they are presently buying. Are they happy with those products? Sometimes, customers buy products, but they are not really happy with it. They use them because of lack of suitable alternatives. Therefore, salespeople should try to find out what they really need or are looking for.

Law 4 Speak to your prospect just as you speak to your family or friends: Salespeople should try to create an air or atmosphere of informality and move/proceed slowly. They should not quickly switch to sales mode with formal sales talks. They need to avoid exaggerated tones. Instead, they should speak normally and, of course, appropriately to let the sales points or issues emerge automatically or spontaneously.

Law 5 Pay close attention to what your prospect is not saying: In selling, we normally expect the salespeople to pay close attention to what the prospect or customer is saying. That, of course, is important. But what is equally, or may be more, important is to pay enough attention to what he(she) is not saying, but is trying to express through his(her) mood or visual revelations. Is he(she) looking upset or agitated? If this is so, the salesperson may ask: "Is this a good time to talk? Or we should meet some other time or day?" Very few salespeople do this. Most salespeople are so occupied with what they are going to say next that they forget to pay enough attention to the mood, posture and possible reaction of the prospect.

Law 6 If you are asked a question, answer properly but briefly, and move on: If a prospect is asking questions, it generally means that he(she) is showing interest in the salesperson's approach or talk. The salesperson has to reply to the prospect's query to his(her) satisfaction and move on. He should not get stuck in that question, even if it is a tricky or difficult one. The art of answering, and not avoiding, difficult questions comes into play here.

Law 7 Correctly assess the needs of the prospect, then you make your offering: Product offering should not be made in a haste; salespeople may end up in wrong offering. It is, therefore, essential to correctly assess the prospect's requirements, and then make the product offer. This enhances the chances of concluding the business.

Law 8 Refrain from making a very long sales presentation: In industrial products, sales presentation can be little long because it involves greater details on product features, performance, maintenance, etc. But, for consumer goods (except for consumer durables to some extent), talks or presentations should be short and precise. Individuals and households do not generally like long presentations. The salespeople should focus on those points or aspects which have a direct bearing on the prospect's thinking, and liking and the particular situation. This also includes the positives or benefits of the offering.

Law 9 Ask the prospect if there are any barriers to taking the next step: After the salespeople have gone through the first eight steps, they should have a good understanding of the prospect's needs in relation to the company's products or service. The salespeople would have also developed mutual trust and belief. They should now be in a position to bridge the gap between the prospect's needs and their offering, or, find out from the prospect if some gap or barrier still exists. They are now actually getting ready for Law 10 (closing).

Law 10 Invite your prospect to take some decision or action: This means that conventional closing techniques are not necessary because the salesperson is not trying to close the sale, but inviting the prospect to do so. The ball is in the prospect's court. And, he or she has to take the final view or decision. The salesperson should lead him(her) to that. If the salesperson can successfully lead or guide the prospect to the decision, he(she) is well on his(her) way to becoming a successful or even outstanding salesperson.

RECIPE FOR SUCCESS

Here is a known recipe for success:

Right/Proper goal setting

+ Great attitude/mindset

+ Correct planning

+ Appropriate sales strategy
+ Hunger for result
+ Proper implementation
+ Determination to succeed
= **Success**

This is recipe and not formula for success. The recipe gives the direction or roadmap for success.

Follow the laws of success as far as possible. Remember and put in practice the recipe for success. Hurdles with come. Work hard. Try to cross the hurdles.

You have to perspire. Success will come your way—if not today, by tomorrow. Keep hope. You will succeed.

RECIPE FOR WINNING

Success means winning. To succeed is to be a winner. All of us want to win. And, we want to win always. This is more true of salespeople, because, every time they win, they secure an order or business, and, they win some reward.

If you are tired of your mediocre performance, try winning. Also, if you want to explore your potential to the full, try winning. Trying to win means doing more than the next person (your colleague). Trying to win means pushing yourself a little harder, a little further and little longer than you have done before. You can start by finding out what winners do and how they do.

THE WINNING ATTITUDE

We should also remember another truth about winning. This is about the winning attitude. *The difference between winning and losing, many times, is not your company or resources or your position or your customer or your competitor, but your mindset or attitude.*

Winning Attitude: A Self-evaluation

Every salesperson can make a self-evaluation of his (her) winning attitude. Here is a self-evaluation exercise. Twenty statements are given below, each relating to winning. Read each statement carefully and assign scores/values of 1 to 5. Assign

1 if you 'strongly disagree' with the statement; assign 2 if you 'disagree'; assign 3 if you 'agree'; assign 4 if you 'quite agree'; and assign 5 if you 'strongly agree' with the statement. See the statements below:

	Statement	Score
1.	I always expect to win	—
2.	I plan to win	—
3.	I have a plan for today, this week and this month	—
4.	I know exactly what I must do to win	—
5.	I have developed a formula for winning	—
6.	I prepare to win	—
7.	I believe that I am so important that I should win	—
8.	I work hard enough to win	—
9.	I have the will to win	—
10.	I refuse to lose	—
11.	I never allow myself to make excuses for not winning	—
12.	I never allow others to make excuses for me when I do not win	—
13.	I pay the price to win	—
14.	I do not allow routines like car problems or traffic problems or any others to delay the start of my day	—
15.	I consider the costs as well as the benefits of winning	—
16.	I would not be surprised if I win a national sales contest	—
17.	I increase my will to win if others win national or other sales contests	—
18.	I can accept failures to finally emerge winner	—
19.	For winning, I am able to summon all my resources	—
20.	I want to make winning a habit	—
	Total Score	—

You add up all the scores (total score) to evaluate or ascertain your winning attitude. If total score is 80 or above, you have a strong winning attitude; if the score is between 50 and 80, you have a positive winning attitude; if the score is below 50, you have a losing or defeatist attitude.

Once you know your winning attitude or orientation, you can work on this to improve and prepare yourself for winning.

SIX CS FOR WINNING

Also know the six Cs for winning.

Adopt six Cs for practising and developing winning as a habit. The six Cs are: clarity, competence, communication, character, courage and conviction. These are made clear below:

1. *Clarity*: Clearly spell out objectives or goals.
2. *Competence*: Possess/acquire required skill and capability to sell.
3. *Communication*: Develop persuasive skill and the ability to convince prospects.
4. *Character*: Show integrity and determination even during setbacks.
5. *Courage*: Demonstrate braveness to move ahead fighting failures.
6. *Conviction*: Make your belief anchored in the organisation and profession.

The six Cs are made more focussed with the diagrammatic presentation:

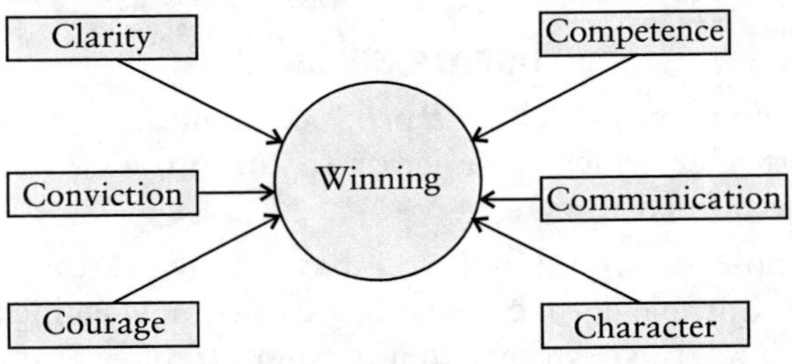

Keep a photocopy of the diagram in your pocket. This is your recipe for winning.

The six Cs mostly complement each other and can be viewed as integrated Cs. Develop the six Cs and try to reach perfection in them.

USE OF NEWER METHODS/TECHNOLOGIES

For success or winning in a sustainable way, salespersons should adopt more unconventional techniques and newer methods and technologies.

CROSS-SELLING, UP-SELLING AND COMBINATION SELLING

Salespersons are often stuck with conventional ways of closing sales, and do not make extra efforts for cross-selling, up-selling and combination selling to boost total sales.

USE CROSS-SELLING

Cross-selling means selling other products/brands from your company after the sale of one product/brand has been concluded.

An example of cross-selling: you have gone to a bank for opening a savings account. After opening of the savings account is over, the bank official, a smart salesperson, gets into action. He(she) tries to induce you to avail of other services of the bank like recurring deposit, term deposit, safety locker, etc.; and, he(she) successfully sells one or more of these services or products. This is cross-selling.

Every cross-selling generates additional sales or revenue.

USE UP-SELLING

Up-selling means selling a product or model or brand to the same customer which is superior to the product/model/brand originally offered for sale.

Example of up-selling: you have finalised the sale of a consumer durable like a car or motorcycle or a washing machine. Then, you tell the customer that he(she) can have extra features or a superior model by spending a small additional amount. You say: "Sir/madam, you don't make an investment on such products often. By spending a small extra amount, you can get more utility and satisfaction." This is up-selling.

Like cross-selling, every up-selling generates additional sales or revenue.

USE COMBINATION SELLING

In certain situations, depending on the nature of response or body language of the prospect/customer, you can use a combination of cross-selling and up-selling.

Example of combination selling: As you are selling a colour TV, you can offer a CTV with HD property or feature (up-selling). Once you have sold this, you can also offer a microwave from your company (cross-selling). If you can achieve both, you have done combination selling. This gives you more than additional sales or revenue. *It is like hitting a sixer.*

More and more use of cross-selling, up-selling and combination selling give greater success to salespersons and the company. This is particularly important and recommended for companies with a big range of products in consumer electronics and automobiles.

USE MORE M-COMMERCE

Mobile commerce (m-commerce) is a large area of activity comprising transactions connected with or delivered through different mobile devices—mobile phones, communicators, palm size computers, tablet computers, PDAs (personal digital assistants), etc. M-commerce is a logical successor of e-commerce.

Increasing Use of M-Commerce

Technological developments have helped mobile commerce. Wireless technology is facilitating increased use of mobile commerce and its applications. Wireless technology enables companies or sales managers to develop mobile applications for their sales force. The sales force can communicate, and, more importantly, integrate their information inputs with organisational database while they are on the move. This enables them to create a cohesive data bank for decision making in the field.

Mobile phones, iPhones, tablet PCs and PDAs support or sustain mobile communication anywhere any time with wireless network. Mobile commerce has made it possible to close sales faster and better. This is almost like a mini revolution in selling.

New horizons are emerging for mobile commerce. These will make possible sales planning, order booking, sales management, and, also sales closure on the same platform through hand-held or mobile devices. Newer dimensions and possibilities are developing.

In the days to come, mobile computing will emerge and this will introduce new platform and enable salespersons to perform their functions faster with greater precision and accuracy.

M-Commerce is the Future

The key drivers of m-commerce service adoption are ease-of-use and convenience keeping the security issue intact. The challenge is to implement a simple, secure and fast working commerce module.

This is happening. M-commerce is coming of age. FMCG majors like Hindustan Lever (HUL), Procter and Gamble (P&G) and also ITC are making more use of m-commerce for increasing their sales. Many other companies are doing the same. Some more to follow.

Today is the age of sales force automation. M-commerce is one of the important ingredients of this.

Enter this field if you have not already entered. Use the technology. Use this to your advantage and grow in this field.

Be modern and make more use of mobile commerce for selling. You can supplement your conventional methods of selling with mobile commerce selling. This will help you to increase your total sales, and, may also improve your success rate in selling.

VIRTUAL SELLING[3]

Virtual selling is a new, in fact, one of the latest innovations in selling technology. The transition to virtual selling is in process in many countries. In countries like the US, this has already gained enough ground.

What is Virtual Selling?

In simple terms, *virtual selling* may be defined as: *How to get a purchase order (PO) or make a sale without being there.*

In extended terms, *virtual selling* may be defined as: "Running a sales process where you can take many months to do it; you got phone calls, proposal presentations, and, even the contracting process; and, all of that, or 95% of that, is done virtually", i.e., without being there in person.

Till recently, it was thought that it is not possible to get a PO without some sales presentation in person. But, things are changing; this is because of changes in buyer behaviour. All buyers do not insist that you have to be there in person. They accept you not being there. This signals transition to virtual selling.

How to Make Virtual Selling Successful

Selling is not easy. Virtual selling is also not easy. Companies or salespersons have to acquaint themselves with the ways virtual selling should be conducted or concluded. Certain tools or techniques are available for virtual selling. These have been used by companies who have been successful in virtual selling. Some call these tips or guides or techniques for winning the virtual selling game.

Ten proven tips or guides are mentioned below:

1. Choosing right tools.
2. Alignment with marketing.
3. Ensuring Internet speed.
4. Setting the video.
5. Setting the sound system.
6. Remembering that the sales process is important.
7. Client's questions are important.
8. Sales process should be educational for the prospect/customer.
9. Wrapping touch points.
10. Tracking performance of virtual selling or outcomes or sales results.

A number of tools or techniques are now available for virtual selling. These are essentially video conferencing software. These include Zoom, Microsoft teams, Skype, Go to Meeting and WebEx. Some of these softwares are tested and proven tools for virtual selling. A number of new softwares are also emerging.

A company or salesperson needs to choose a particular tool or tools based on features, cost and suitability to the organisation. Choice of an appropriate tool is important. This is almost the first step in successful virtual selling.

With the sales process under way, the next logical step is to plan out every single touch point within the sales process which wraps around the virtual meetings. Touch points include phone calls, video calls, text messages, sales-generated e-mails, follow-up e-mails and, any other documents used with the prospects.

By properly designing the wraparound touch points and, making them distinct in the communication process, a company can differentiate itself from the competitors. The touch points exercise can help a company to shorten the sales cycle and increase close rates or closing ratios.

Try to develop virtual selling skill. Your company should adopt virtual selling as a corporate policy and support you with necessary tools and facilities. This will give another avenue for selling, and, an edge over other salespersons and also your competitors.

IMPROVING SALES AUTOMATION SYSTEM

M-commerce and virtual selling are very important sales automation systems. There are also other ways to improve sales automation or use of technologies in selling.

A number of routine marketing and sales decisions can be better handled by technology—sales softwares—than manually. The salespeople make better decisions and the company saves cost. A good example of softwares beating human decisions is IBM's Deep Blue software. This software beats world's greatest chess champion Garry Kasparov.

With appropriate software programmes, determining display positions of brands on retail shelves can now be done better than before. Kratf manages cheese positioning in shelves for many years. The software determines optimal mix of cheese brands and shelf-positioning of brands in low, medium and high income areas.

For better results or more success, salespeople should be equipped with the latest sales automation techniques or systems. The automated system should enable salespeople to deal with questions or objections in the customer's or prospect's premises, interact with the sales manager (as required), and, make instant or spot decisions and conclude a sale. This is an extension or complete application of M-commerce. Some highly skilled or trained salespeople in progressive companies like GE are already doing this.

KNOWING THE DIFFERENCE BETWEEN EFFORT AND RESULT

Salespeople may use unconventional approaches, newer methods and technologies. But, these are not end of the road to success. These only mean that you are making good efforts. But, we should clearly understand that efforts, howsoever sincere, do not always guarantee success.

Efforts should produce results, and results mean success. The relationship between efforts and results is like input-output relationship: efforts (input) produce results (output).

We must also remember the fundamental truth: results are rewarded, but, efforts are not. This is true in every sphere of life including selling. But, this is not always clearly understood. Salespersons have to accept it, face it and prepare for it.

DIFFERENCE BETWEEN EFFORTS AND RESULTS

Let me give some live examples of this. These are facts or truths of life.

Example

In a race, whether national competition, Commonwealth Games or Olympics, ten to twelve runners run (after initial screening). All of them put their best efforts according to their abilities. But, only three runners are rewarded: first (gold medal), second (silver medal) and third (bronze medal).

This is how results are rewarded, but, efforts are not. ***Results are visible; efforts are not.***

EFFORTS AND RESULTS IN SELLING[4]

The company or the sales manager assigns you monthly, quarterly, half-yearly or annual targets. The targets are usually in terms of territories, products and customers. The achievement of the targets is a test of your selling skill and capabilities; in other words, a test of the difference between making efforts and producing results.

If you cannot achieve the targets, you are an under-achiever or have produced poor results. If you achieve the targets, you are a good achiever or have produced the desired results. If you have overshot the targets, you have produced excellent or outstanding results and you get suitably rewarded financially or otherwise.

In every case, you have put enough efforts. But, if you are an under-achiever, you lack the ability or capability to produce results. The company may not appreciate your efforts because you have failed to produce the result they wanted. You should have now understood the difference between effort and result and reward. You have to work on yourself to improve.

A Case in Selling

Let us take a case or situation or test in selling. Your company have a bad territory. But, they want to sell there. They have tried two salespersons earlier, but, they have failed to penetrate. The competition is very high. It is difficult to sell there.

The company feels that you are a good salesperson. They have assigned you the territory. The sales manager has given you necessary guidelines, instructions and strategy to be adopted. But implementation is in your hands. You can use your training, skill and capability to produce results. This depends entirely on you. Nobody is going to help you in the failed. You have to sell all by yourself.

If you can achieve the target/goal, you have understood the difference between efforts and result. The company will reward you adequately. But, if you cannot produce the result, you have still to work on it and move towards the result or goal.

SPECIAL ATTRIBUTES/CHARACTERISTICS FOR RESULTS

To convert efforts into results and rewards, you need to possess or develop some special attributes or characteristics. Six such attributes or characteristics are:

1. Burning desire to produce result
2. Self-motivation to succeed
3. To be passionate about results/success
4. Belief in yourself
5. Desire to improve/be perfect
6. Pride in result/success

These six attributes or characteristics are prescriptive, and, not necessarily conclusive or exhaustive. Some other sales trainers or sales experts may suggest some alternatives or additional attributes or characteristics. But the spirit of these attributes are important.

Keep these on your agenda for self-improvement. ***Self-improvement is a continuous process.*** It does not end with one result or achievement. Keep regularly reminding yourself about such attributes. These are imperatives. These should drive you every moment or everyday.

In most of the actual sales situations, you have to successfully combine efforts with selling skill or acumen to cross the margin or fence to achieve the goal. ***You may call it the marginal booster dose.***

If you have done or achieved this, you have fully understood the difference between effort and result. Then, you have also approached your goal.

ADOPTING A ROLE MODEL

Almost every person in a profession adopts a role model or tries to adopt a role model. It may be cricket, football, athletics, acting or management. It can apply to selling also. You should also try to adopt a role model.

Cricketers think of adopting a role model like Don Bradman or Sunil Gavaskar or Kapil Dev or Sachin Tendulkar. Footballers try to adopt a role model like Pele, Maradona or Messi. Film actors may like to adopt a role model like Amitabh Bachchan. Managers wish to adopt a role model like Y.C. Deveshwar (Chairman, ITC) or Indra Nooyi (CEO, Pepsi), R.C. Bhargava (Chairman, Maruti-Suzuki). Entrepreneurs and salespersons dream of adopting a role model like Dhirubhai Ambani. There can be many others.

TRY TO BENCHMARK YOURSELF[5]

Adoption of a role model should start with benchmarking yourself.

What is Benchmarking?

Benchmarking may be understood as a comparison with and *adherence* to prescribed norms or standards or practices in a business.

A functional definition of benchmarking is given below:

> Benchmarking is a process of identifying, understanding and adopting outstanding practices from the same organisation or from other businesses to help improve performance.

The objective of benchmarking is to emulate or adopt any good practice or the best practice in the same business or any other business or industry. This can apply to selling and salespersons also.

So, by benchmarking, you set a standard for yourself. This is a step towards adopting a role model and improving your performance.

WHO SHOULD BE YOUR ROLE MODEL

Your role model should be ideally a person who is in selling. He(she) may be in your company or in some other company whom you know. He(she) may be selling the same product(s) or any other product.

Your role model should be a person who is known to be performing well or outstandingly, i.e., a high performer. The person has certain attributes or characteristics which attract you and you want to emulate. He(she) is unique in his(her) own way. He(she) sets examples.

Your role model should be one who has attributes or characteristics you do not possess. It may be his(her) commitment or dedication or discipline or hunger for success. You wish to acquire or develop these to reach his(her) level of performance. He(she) is usually senior to you in terms of age and experience. You feel that you can learn from him(her).

CHOOSE YOUR ROLE MODEL

Given these attributes or factors, you try to choose your role model. You may have some alternatives open before you, i.e., more than one personality known to you or in your view. The person you choose should be one who inspires you. This is important.

The person need not necessarily be from your company. He(she) can even be from your competitor company.

You should ideally consider or look for the following factors in choosing your role model:

1. He(she) is a high performer.
2. He(she) is a self-starter.
3. He(she) is a self-motivated person.
4. He(she) likes challenges.
5. He(she) is not afraid of failure.
6. He(she) has a hunger for success.
7. He(she) believes in himself(herself).
8. He(she) is loyal to his(her) organisation.
9. He(she) is not a rolling stone, i.e., he(she) does not switch job frequently.
10. You know him(her) for sometime.

You may or may not find all these virtues or attributes in one person. But, the person should be possessing most of them. Overall, he(she) should be a proven or accomplished or outstanding salesperson. He(she) should be your role model.

SET GOALS FOR YOURSELF

To move closer to your role model, you have to set certain goals for yourself. *Goals give you a sense of direction.* Goals drive you to be result-oriented and focussed on accomplishment or achievement.

Goals lead to targets. A professional and result-oriented salesperson sets goals or targets as time-bound plans. Time frame can be broken into different time zones or horizons. Time zones can be:

1. Monthly 2. Quarterly	→ Very short-term
3. Half-yearly 4. Yearly	→ Short-term
5. One year to three years	→ Medium term
6. More than three years/up to five years	→ Long-term

Beyond five years, it should be a *rolling plan*, i.e., at the end of five years, plan should be prepared for the next five years and so on. This gives the right long-term perspective.

In rigorous planning, monthly targets should be broken into weekly and even daily targets.

Remind yourself of your daily targets every day in the morning. **Plan your targets one week in advance.** Any shortfall in daily target should be made good the next day or during the week. Daily fluctuations cannot be ruled out. But, it should be balanced by the end of the week.

Implementation and results of monthly, quarterly, half-yearly and annual plans should be reviewed regularly for any course correction. Keep the milestone always in view. This facilitates goal achievement.

MOVE TOWARDS YOUR ROLE MODEL

Goal setting and achievements will take you closer to your role model.

Through the process of goal setting and achievement, you will gradually acquire the ten virtues or attributes mentioned above. You may already possess some of them. Learn or develop new ones. These will lead you closer to your goal.

Your goal achievement should match your role model in the medium term. Short-term may be too ambitious or unrealistic.

If not in the medium-term, you must accomplish your goal in the long-term.

If you are determined for goal achievement, you may one day become a role model yourself. *Keep that as your dream.*

CONCLUSION: MOVING TO SUCCESS

Five critical factors discussed so far are complementary to and reinforce, each other; and, these factors may be mostly in logical sequence for stepwise progression to the target/goal or success starting with roadmap:

Roadmap for Success

→ Recipe for winning

→ Use of newer methods/technologies

→ Knowing the difference between 'effort' and 'result'

→ Adopting a role model

→ Achievement of target

Determining the relative roles of different factors or prioritising them is difficult. It largely depends on the salespersons concerned, company position and market conditions. Relativity of the factors will remain. The best way to understand and implement the complementarity is as a package for success. We may also call this a reinforcing 'booster' package.

Above all, we must remember that

Success (in selling) demands singleness of purpose

—Vince Lombardi

This is the most important factor.

Section IV
Entrepreneurship

20 Entrepreneurship and Business Success

Dictionary of Economics and Business defines an *Entrepreneur* as "the decision maker, risk-taker and organiser in a commercial enterprise. His functions are to supply risk capital, decide on what to produce at what scale of production with what combination of inputs, to manage the enterprise, and, to bear the risks."[1]

"Entrepreneurship is regarded as the fourth factor of production together with land, labour and capital with profit being its reward. It is assumed that the entrepreneur aims to maximise profit, although in practice, he may not always act with this sole aim especially in the short-run. The entrepreneurial spirit, however, is essential."[2]

WHO SHOULD BE AN ENTREPRENEUR

The definition of 'entrepreneur' shows that he(she) should be an organiser, a risk-taker and a decision maker with the objective of making profit. He(she) has a strong intent and determination. All these also imply many challenges he(she) has to face and hurdles he(she) has to cross or overcome.

If you want a routine easy life, you should be an office goer because you lack the entrepreneurial spirit. I never wanted to be an entrepreneur. Many others like me don't. Rightly so.

Entrepreneurial Spirit

The entrepreneurial spirit is in-born or inherent in a person—this cannot be inculcated. The entrepreneurial spirit is the *burning desire* to do something new and challenging and creative. In other words, it is the passion or dream to create a new business. The legendary Dhirubhai Ambani is one of the greatest examples of this. The realisation or fulfillment of the dream give you return, i.e., profit and, of course, lot of satisfaction.

To be an entrepreneur is obviously not for everyone. It has been correctly said that, if everyone becomes an entrepreneur, the whole world will be self-employed. In reality, "ninety-nine per cent of the people should be working for somebody." You should be in one per cent of the people to be an entrepreneur possessing the right characteristics or virtues.

You may like to go into business because you are "sick and tired of being told what to do"; or, you want more "freedom"; or, your work is "unappreciated or undervalued" in your company. These are definitely not the reasons for becoming an entrepreneur. These are very sweeping thoughts and the decision may be impulsive. You may be lacking the intent, commitment and skill to be an entrepreneur. It may also mean that you are trying to run away from your present job. One day, you may run away from your business also.

But, this does not mean that somebody who is in a job should not or cannot become an entrepreneur. There are many instances where people have successfully switched over from job to entrepreneurship. They had the intent and entrepreneurial zeal in them. It was a matter of waiting for the opportune moment and deciding the timing.

Mark McCormack, founder and President of IMG, is one of the best examples. The success story of his company has been taught as a case study in Harvard Business School. McCormack was a lawyer with a prestigious Cleveland firm. But, he did not want to spend the rest of his life in building a career. He would rather spend his energy in a venture of his own. McCormack observes: "starting a business is a financial and professional commitment. But, even more, it is an emotional one."[3]

The desire to make lot of money or become rich is the motivation for some people to become an entrepreneur. This becomes a strong motivator for success. This drives them almost relentlessly. Such dreamers (with their foot on the ground) are willing or prepared to take the risks involved, face the challenges and cross the hurdles to reach their goal. Many highly successful entrepreneurs with extraordinary growth belong to this class—rags to riches stories. Examples: Henry Ford (Ford Motor Company) Bill Gates (Microsoft), Michael Dell (Dell Computer), Akio Morita (Sony), Dhirubhai Ambani (RIL), Karsanbhai Patel (Nirma) and such others.

Age for an Entrepreneur?

Is there an age factor for starting a business? Generally not, but, considering the factors involved—uncertainty, risk taking and the possibility of loss or failure—the age group 25-45 may be the most appropriate or ideal. During this age, social or family commitments are less and, one can always take some risks. This also gives an entrepreneur the necessary building period for a business. Also, *this may be the best period for nurturing a dream.* Most of the successful businessmen became entrepreneurs during this age group.

There are, however, some people who venture into entrepreneurism at a late age. One of my former colleagues (and a present friend) can be mentioned as an example. He is a highly qualified (B.Tech, IIT Kanpur and MBA, IIMC) professional. He was in corporate job for many years including senior positions. One day he decided to start his own enterprise. He pursued this for some years, then gave up because he did not taste much success. According to me, this is half-hearted entrepreneurism. He might not have given his 'full'—may be the age factor (60±). This does not give success. You should be: *Lage Raho Munna Bhai* (stick to the entrepreneurial passion) for success. Success never comes the easy way except for the most lucky.

STARTING A BUSINESS

Starting of a business should generally follow the conventional norms, systems and procedures. Unconventional or path-breaking entrepreneurs may not follow the established models. They may develop and ride through unconventional methods. They may charter their own course (Chris Gayle, Kapil Dev, Virender Sehwag in cricket).

Generally speaking, however, if it is a manufacturing unit, site or location of the plant/equipment, applicable taxes or tax exemptions, available incentives, local regulations, financing (risk capital)—all have to be considered. For service products, location of the business/enterprise may not be so important or vital except for 'cluster' advantages (silicon Valley, Bengaluru etc.)

Books on entrepreneurism lay down all the systems/guidelines. Some business schools also offer courses on entrepreneurism which teach such things. I shall not delve into the details of established methods or practices for starting a business. I shall, instead, focus on the important issues, factors and situations which are confronted with or learnt through real life applications and experiences.

For starting a business, in addition to complying with the necessary "setting up" conditions, an entrepreneur should pay heed to seven important factors:

1. Think or aim big
2. Ask yourself some hard questions
3. Start small and keep it simple
4. Commitment: first and foremost
5. Be prepared for the risk
6. Know your competition
7. Fear of failure

Think or Aim Big

To be an entrepreneur, you should be a dreamer who does. You should think or aim big. That will give you the inspiration and excitement of an entrepreneur—to do something new.

One of my students in XLRI (Jamshedpur) had decided to be an entrepreneur after completing his MBA programme. He told me: "I wish to become a big and successful entrepreneur. I am so excited." I told him: "Go ahead and keep up your excitement."

Ask yourself some Hard Questions

You may foster your dream, but, you must keep your feet firmly on the ground. To balance these two, you should ask yourself some hard questions before you embark. Four important questions are:

(a) Have I chosen the right product—'hard' product (merchandise) or 'soft' product (services)?

(b) Have I chosen the right time?

(c) Are the resources (financing/risk capital) in place?

(d) What is the 'doability quotient'?

The doability quotient, in simple terms, is the feasibility of the project in terms of matching risk, resources, implementation (including the lag factor) and return.[4] If the doability quotient is low, the project should be reworked to improve the quotient; higher the quotient, more are the chances of success.

You should seek answers to other questions from yourself, do your homework (i.e., project study) and, once you are satisfied, start or proceed.

Start Small and Keep it Simple

If you start small, it is easy to control the predictables (they are few) and also deal with unpredictables. Risk elements are also less. You build the base and build further on this to grow.

Michael Dell, McCormack, William Lever, Akio Morita, Dhirubhai Ambani, L.N. Mittal (Arcelor Mittal) B.M. Munjal, all started small—with capitalisation of less than $ 1000. They all demonstrated that small is good to grow big later.

If the business is small, it is also simple and easy to manage. Management problems, and business complications, start creeping in with size—as the business grows larger and larger. By that time, you have acquired the necessary skill and expertise and developed the experience to deal with management of size.

Commitment: First and Foremost

To accomplish or achieve these, you should be fully committed. You have to get over hesitancies and distractions. It should be total commitment—commitment to life, commitment to business, commitment to quality, and, foremost, commitment to the self.

In the initial or formative stage, many people get easily distracted, disillusioned and lose heart, and they give up. It has been rightly said that "most people fail not because of lack of ability or intelligence but, because of lack of desire, direction, dedication and discipline (in other words, commitment)."[5]

So, if you want to start a business, give 100%. Many things will fall in place. You can take off.

Be Prepared for the Risk

Uncertainty, risk and profit go together. If there is no risk, there is no profit (windfalls excluded). So, if you wish to start an enterprise and make profit, be prepared for the risk—risk of a new venture.

If it is a mundane product others are selling in the market, the risk may be less, profit may also be less. But, if it is a new or highly innovative product, the risk is more, and, the return or profit is also likely to be high. So, *the risk quotient (and the profit quotient)* is largely determined by the product you have chosen.

Whatever be the product, the risk element cannot be altogether eliminated. There is nothing like a sure success business. But, preparedness for the risk enables you to handle the risk or absorb the sock better.

For the more enterprising entrepreneur, risk taking almost becomes a habit.

Know Your Competition

Competition is concomitant with business except in pure monopoly which is rare.

Japanese entrepreneurs know, better than others, how to live and grow with competition. Akio Morita says: "The glory and nemesis of Japanese business, the life blood of our industrial engine, is good old-fashioned competition. It is a severe kind of competition, and, sometimes, it is so severe that I am worried about its export to other countries."[6]

Know your competition at all levels—primary, secondary and tertiary. Pay maximum attention to primary competitors who pose the most immediate threat, next secondary competitors and then tertiary competitors. Analyse and decide your competition strategy. Keep an eye on potential competitors also.

Try to find a Japanese entrepreneur friend or develop one for useful competition tips.

Fear of Failure

Many of those who have been entrepreneurs for years think that "Fear of failure is at least as common as the desire for success" among those who wish to start a business. This is a worrying phenomenon.

Fear of failure is more a mental attitude and has less to do with the feasibility of a business.

It is more a matter of difference between positive attitude and negative attitude. If the fear of failure haunts you, you cannot go for a venture.

A typical recipe for failure is like this:

Poor (negative) attitude
→ Poor values
→ Poor planning
→ Poor action/implementation
→ Frustration
→ Out of business (failure)

The general attitudinal prescription for choice between success and failure is:

(a) Hope for success > Fear of failure
→ Go ahead and do the business

(b) Hope for success = Fear of failure
→ you are a fencesitter; you need advice or counselling for attitudinal change

(c) Hope for success < Fear of failure
→ Don't proceed; entrepreneurship is not for you; you are doomed to fail.

I wish to narrate here the classic "half-full"/"half-empty" story. A glass half filled with water can be described in two ways: half-full or half-empty. If you say 'half-full', you are half way though to success; if you say "half-empty," you are half way to failure.

This is what attitude means in life and business.

So, always start a business with hope for success and not with fear of failure.

BUILDING A BUSINESS

If you adhere to the seven factors for starting a business, and, guard against the possible pitfalls, building a business may be comparatively easy. The challenges will, however, remain.

McCormack observes about building a business: "A lot of building a business is listening to your own common sense, then taking necessary steps to turn the theories into practice."[7] How many theories should be put into practice and how many theories should be ignored (because those are not applicable) would depend on the nature of the product, risk, investment involved and expected return.

For successfully building a business, one should reckon with six factors:

1. Business first, organisation later
2. Management philosophies may not work
3. Decision making
4. Manage with confidence
5. Motion, mistake, accomplishment
6. Don't hesitate to hire expertise.

Business First, Organisation Later

For building a business, you require an organisation—organisation of people, organisation of a team. Smaller the business, smaller may be the organisation; larger the business, larger may be the organisation. But, a business organisation is essential.

Ideally, both business and the organisation should be developed together—one supporting the other. But, if one has to prioritise, which should come first? *Business First, Organisation Later.*

Some people get busy organising their team. Business gets less attention and it suffers. The team is important, but, focus should not shift from business.

Many successful entrepreneurs like Dhirubhai developed their business almost single-handedly. The organisation was built gradually. Sometimes, it follows from the business itself. Kiran Mazumdar-Shaw (Biocon) selected and developed her own team and the organisation dedicated to her venture.

Management Philosophies May Not Work

Based on his own experience, McCormack says: "Most management philosophy that you read in a book or learn in a classroom is going to have limited effectiveness. Once you factor in human beings—egos and personalities—even the most sensible theories begin to fall apart... Management philosophies and management theories are always topped by Real Life."

"The only management philosophy that does work is the one that acknowledges what none of them does: be flexible and strive for consistency."

Most successful entrepreneurs including Akio Morita, Dhirubhai Ambani, L.N. Mittal, BM Munjal did not follow published/traditional management philosophies and systems. They did not go to business schools also (except Morita). They developed their own systems for building business.

Two factors are, however, important: flexibility and consistency. *Flexibility* means adjusting the methods and systems for building the business. Flexibility also means rethinking the business approach or process for achievement of result. *Consistency* means consistency of performance—building the business at a steady space rather than going for unbalanced or lopsided growth. We can say: *flexibility is the means and consistency is the end* for building a business.

Decision Making

Decision making is the key in business—right decision at the right time. The time factor is very important. You must act on time; otherwise, you may miss the bus, I mean business.

During the process of building business, almost every situation demands a decision, be it small or big—small operational decision or some major strategic decision. Decision making models may be taught in business schools. They may also simulate decision-making situations. But, the actual art of decision-making exists in real life. This is learnt and practised on business as the situation demands—be it product line, funds flow or making a sale or transaction. These decisions are mostly intuitive or guided by the entrepreneur's judgement.

Some feel that, for good decisions, one needs lot of facts or information. Once all the facts are in place, decision making becomes easy. It is true. But, in real life, all the facts are hardly in place. So, decision making has to be almost always based on incomplete data. This is where the role of intuition or judgement comes into play. In fact, most of the decision makers in business are intuitive decision makers with some back-up facts. Some decisions may go wrong, but, more often, they are right.

Manage with Confidence

This is because they mostly decide and act with confidence. This enables them to come back quickly from wrong decisions. Not only this, implementation of decision also requires lot of confidence.

Confidence in decision making implies managing the business with confidence. *Hesitation or double mindedness has no place in business management*. Confidence also gives satisfaction.

I know a young entrepreneur who runs a small enterprise. He is always full of confidence. In fact, it is in the genes. He told me: "confidence is my asset." Confidence is truly an asset in business.

But, overconfidence is bad; it is counterproductive.

Motion, Mistake, Accomplishment

In course of decision making and managing business, mistakes can occur. In fact, risk, initiative, innovativeness and mistake often go together. It has been correctly said by management experts that, if you have not made any mistake in business and life, you have never taken any initiative to do something new or big. Almost all successful entrepreneurs have proved this.

Once you are in motion as a self-employed, you don't always know how many hours you should put in a day. Some entrepreneurs feel that number of hours you put in has meaning only in terms of what you do with these hours, i.e., those should be productive hours, and, you have to define yourself the "productive" hours.

A successful entrepreneur observes: "Most successful entrepreneurs spend twenty four hours a day either working or thinking about their business. But, it is how they fill those hours that makes the difference between success and failure. The cliche is, 'Don't work hard, work smart.' The truth is 'Work hard, work long *and* work smart.'"

During the process of working "hard, smart and long," an entrepreneur may make some mistake. One should learn from the mistakes, correct them and get in motion again. This is the path to accomplishment.

Don't Hesitate to Hire Expertise

One may have the entrepreneurial spirit or zeal. He might have identified the product which has prospect or market. He can also line up finances or risk capital. But, he may not possess the expertise for making and marketing the product. He need not lose heart. If he is determined, he can hire the expert or expertise.

Established entrepreneurial practices show that expertise can be hired in two ways: first, as a collaboration or partnership on profit sharing basis; second, hiring the expertise on salary or compensation basis. The choice is with the entrepreneur. He may like to retain the enterprise with him and hire the expertise on compensation basis for as long as he likes. According to me, this is true entrepreneurship.

Partnership has its own problems of understanding, operations and management. Many partnerships have fallen apart.

Aditya Birla Group has a policy of hiring expertise on the basis of pay role compensation (tenure appointment) or as a consultant or advisor. Once they internalise the experience, they may dispense with the services of the consultant/advisor. I was hired as Advisor by the Group company, Hindalco Industries (Copper Unit) for a number of years till their copper business was established. We then had a separation package.

GROWING IN BUSINESS

It is difficult to say, where "building a business" ends and, "growing a business" begins. In reality, these two may be overlapping or complementary. Anyway, let us not get into semantics. That is for the theorists.

The purpose of building a business is to prepare the base, bring consistency and stability in business. Growth takes place on this base. For more dynamic entrepreneurs, the base may keep changing. They build growth on changing base. We can also say they achieve *growth on growth*. L.N. Mittal is one of the best examples of this. He built his steel empire by building growth on growth almost at an accelerated pace.

For growing in business, eight factors are pertinent:

1. Grow slowly and steadily
2. Work for profit
3. Manage unconventionally
4. Decide growth strategy
5. Identify growth constraints and fix them
6. Strive for sustainability
7. Continually seek SCA
8. You should be lucky

Grow Slowly but Steadily

It is almost a foregone fact that, in business, you cannot stay the same size. This may lead to stagnation. You may even be trending backwards. To avoid this, you have to plan to grow.

But, the pertinent question before an entrepreneur is: grow slowly or grow fast? There are arguments for both the choices.

But, one point is clear. It you grow slowly and steadily, you will have more control over your business and growth. If you grow fast, you take more risk. If may be a test of your risk taking ability and making growth fast and continuous. Laxmi Mittal could have done this. But, many others may not be able to handle this.

So, the more viable prescription or advice is: grow slowly, but, maintain the growth momentum. This may give long-term sustenance.

Work for Profit

The complete prescription is: grow steadily and keep reaping profit. Growing fast may have higher chance of profitability, but, the risk of a setback or loss may also be high.

Few entrepreneurs like Kiran Mazumdar-Shaw may be exceptions. Kiran Mazumdar says: "The fast buck and greed element has to go away. One has to work for the joy of creating something."[8] But, the vast majority of entrepreneurs are profit seekers. Rightly so. *Profit is the oxygen for growth*. It sustains growth.

Sometimes, entrepreneurs and companies are shy of making profit. Appears strange; but, it is true. Companies do not see profit that is there. They are not sure of what the market or customers can bear. The leader-entrepreneur has to show them the way.

When Maruti Udyog (now Suzuki Motors) introduced "Maruti 1000," this was the first Indian 3-Box car with modern technology. Maruti's Marketing Group was not sure about its pricing. R.C. Bhargava, CMD, told them: "Price what the market can bear, and, not just a mark-up on your cost." Maruti 1000 was priced at ₹ 4 lakh breaking conventional pricing norms. The market absorbed it. Maruti made big profit.

So, look for every opportunity for profit, seize and exploit it. Then plough it back into business. This *way, profit may bring more profit*.

Manage Unconventionally

Most of the successful entrepreneurial ventures are run or managed unconventionally. They don't follow formal organisation structures or management systems. Informal management largely prevails. These entrepreneurs more often break rules. "You also have to be consciously, actively and aggressively punching holes in the company's conventions and conventional wisdom." This is entrepreneurism at its best. You sustain this; break new grounds; you succeed.

This is how IBM developed its Peanut computer. The company picked up some of its brightest brains, put them in an environment outside the existing organisational structures and rules, and, entrusted them the work on the project for developing a novel computer. Their accountability system was different. The outcome was Peanut computer.

It has been observed that, almost every time entrepreneurs are profiled or written about in a business magazine, their "success is attributed to breaking the rules, not following them, for encouraging employees, departmental and divisional independence..."

So, manage unconventionally. Use your wisdom. Do not wait or look for opportunities; create them. Aggressively pursue change. Make managing unconventionally almost a habit, if not obsession.

Decide Growth Strategy

Entrepreneurs have to decide their strategies for growth. Many growth strategies are available. There are two broad types of strategies: organic growth strategy and inorganic or diversification strategy. Diversification strategies are of two types: related diversification (also called horizontal diversification) and unrelated diversification (also known as vertical diversification).

Organic growth strategy is the simplest. Business will grow on existing product lines, technology is known, expertise already exists and risk is also less. It is assumed that market exists for bigger business. Diversification has comparatively more risk. Related diversification is closer to the present product lines. Unrelated diversification means venturing into entirely new business, technology will be new, expertise has to be acquired or hired, and, the risk element is also likely to be higher. So, also may be profitability. We will not go into much details on this. A vast literature exists on this in books of strategic management.

Henry Ford decided to go for organic growth strategy. William Lever went for related diversification. Michael Dell had gone for organic growth. Akio Morita went for related diversification. Dhirubhai Ambani embarked on unrelated diversification (from yarn, fabrics to petrochemicals). Laxmi Mittal opted for organic growth (mostly through acquisitions). BM Munjal also pursued organic growth (in cycles), and, then ventured into related diversification (some may call it unrelated diversification)—from cycles to motorcycles. Kiran Mazumdar Shaw preferred organic growth in her specialised product group. There are other examples also.

These examples show that, for an entrepreneur, the choice of growth strategy depends on various factors—business dream or vision, opportunity visible, resources available, risk element, revenue growth and profitability. Every entrepreneur has to choose his(her) growth strategy based on analysis of these factors, their relative prioritisation and the probability of success. This is very important. The venture has to succeed.

Identify Growth Constraints and Fix Them

During implementation of their plans and strategies, most entrepreneurs face hurdles or impediments. They need to identify the growth constraints and fix them early. L.N. Mittal did this timely and boldly. Kiran Mazumdar overcame many impediments and sailed through successfully. So, also did Karsanbhai Patel and other successful entrepreneurs.

Growth constraints can be of two types: internal and external. Internal constraints relate to planning, implementation and management issues in the company—production bottlenecks, logistics, marketing/selling problems etc. These can be handled more easily.

External constraints relate to business environment, government policy, regulations etc. Business environment can change suddenly. Recession may grip the economy/market (like the coronavirus pandemic, 2020-21). Recession leaders or champions like Dell Computer and Procter & Gamble have demonstrated how to use recession as opportunity. Kiran Mazumdar had hit many roadblocks in her journey for establishing biotechnology and Biocon in the prevailing Indian environment. But, she dealt with those in her own inimitable way.

Sometimes, government policy can be exploited not to fix a growth constraint, but, to be used as a growth engine. Dhirubhai exemplified this. The government of India had announced High Unit Value scheme. Through this scheme, polyester yarn (raw material) could be imported against export of nylon fabrics (finished product). Dhirubhai fully exploited this opportunity with shrewd business acumen. His company achieved more than 60% of export under this scheme. This meant a big growth in business. Handsome profit was also made.

So, fix the growth constraints or exploit the growth drivers. Both will produce the same result—contribution to growth.

Strive for Sustainability

Growth should be sustainable, i.e., it should be growth with stability. There may be occasional or short-term instability or fluctuations caused by business cycles (economy, market, environment), but, in the long-term, growth should be stable. This is sustainability.

Growth strategy should be oriented towards this. Strategy formulation should always keep the long-term sustainability of business in view. This requires product modification or rationalisation, constant promotion, enough knowledge of competitors' strategies, etc.

Entrepreneurs like Michael Dell have demonstrated how sustainable growth can be achieved even during periods of business fluctuations or recession.

Continually Seek SCA

Sustainability should lead to sustainable competitive advantage (SCA) in the market or over competitors.

Objectives of entrepreneurs/companies with respect to SCA should be twofold: first, how to develop sustainable competitive advantage over competitors; and, second, how to neutralise SCAs of competitors. Some possible SCAs, as has been shown by businesses in practice, are low cost of production, reputation for quality, strong resource base, early entrant in the industry etc.

Some entrepreneurial companies have secured SCA. It does not depend on the size of the company. The essential point is that every entrepreneurial company should continually search for SCA and eventually secure some SCAs to increase sustainability of its growth.

You should be Lucky

Some believe in destiny. Some do not. I believe in destiny. I have experienced this.

McCormack also believes that luck has a role to play in growth and success of business. He says: "Be smart enough to know when you're lucky." One may have to be an astrologer or soothsayer to know when he(she) would be lucky. But, the point is made. Luck should be with you.

Some talk of the 80 : 20 principle of success: 80% hard work and 20% luck. There can be debate on this. But, I subscribe to something like this.

Most of the slips between the cup and the lip are explained by luck and nothing else. So, let us all wish that luck is with us. Let luck be with all entrepreneurs.

STARTUP ENTREPRENEURS

Good startups thrive in bull markets. Great startups thrive in bear markets. The best startups thrive in any market.

—Andrew Gazdecki

Every billion dollar startup began with zero revenue, zero funding, zero press, zero customers. Keep going

—Andrew Gazdecki

Startup entrepreneurs are the order or trend of the day. In keeping with the trend, government of India has recognised (on June 3, 2021) 50,000 startups across India[9]—623 districts in 30 states and union territories, Maharashtra, Gujarat, Karnataka, Uttar Pradesh and Delhi being the leading ones. All registered startups enjoy simplified compliance structure, fiscal and infrastructural support including tax exemptions, among others.

Startups are flourishing. The Pandemic has not dampened their spirits. The slogan is:

If you want to become your own boss, be a startup entrepreneur

If you are aiming to be a startup entrepreneur, take the following steps:

1. *Evaluate your abilities*: Decide that you can do it;
2. *Take your family's support*: This gives you encouragement and confidence;

3. *Make a Financial Plan*: Identity the cost elements and prepare a budget;
4. *Seek Expert Support*: Find a mentor or someone in the industry who can guide you;
5. *Get the Timing Right*: Prepare yourself for the drive (do not act in haste).

Fail, Learn, Succeed[10]

You may follow the steps, but, the entrepreneurial journey is not easy. It is saddled with roadblocks, struggles, failures. Success may ultimately come. So, is with startup entrepreneurs.

Jeff Bezos (the founder of Amazon which started in a garage), the world's second richest person, once said: "Nine times out of ten, you're going to fail. But, every once in a while, you'll hit a home run that, in business terms, is more like one thousand runs. Given a ten percent chance of a one hundred times payoff, you should take that bet every time." This tells a lot about how startup founders learn from their failures.

Three recent stories of startups—challenges, failures, learnings and successes—are presented below:

Story 1: "Decide, Act, Move on"

The story is about one of the latest service products: Online education.

With pandemic and home confinements, online education is catching up. This is the opportune moment to hit the market. This is what upGrad founders Mayank Kumar and Phalgun Kompalli and their team have done.

Mayank and Phalgun had their shares of challenges and failures. Some of the important lessons they learnt from their failures were how to convince the people about online education, how to convince the market on price points, determining the right experience for an online audience, and, deciding the right team at different stages of growth of the organisation.

These are some of the challenges. There are other challenges. Mayank and Phalgun observe: "We operate in such evolving times that, in order to stay relevant, we have to be prompt and decisive to make the right choices at the right time. Also, giving ownership to the right team and letting them handle is critical to drive the business correctly."

Mayank and Phalgun handled the challenges and pressures boldly and successfully. For them and the upGrad team, the mantra for success is: "Decide, Act and Move on." There is no looking back; only looking ahead.

Story 2: "Believe in Yourself and Anything is Possible"[11]

This is the story of Ram Patidar—story of journey from a humble painter to a real estate expert and a successful builder.

At a very young age, Ram migrated from his village to Indore for a livelihood. He started working as an ordinary painter. But, Ram's dream was to become an entrepreneur. He was slowly building the foundation for that.

Soon, he was working as a contractor with a small office and team of his own. Business started flourishing and Patidar soon set up a multi solution advertising agency. His creative mind and passion for more success propelled him in soaring higher. In 2011, he was emerging as one of the fastest growing entrepreneurs in the city.

Real estate sector was booming in those days. Ram wanted to exploit the opportunity. He entered the profession with the same enthusiasm and dedication to succeed and worked as hard as ever to establish himself in the new venture.

More than a decade later, today, Ram Patidar owns a construction company called 'Nev Construction' in Indore. A team of highly qualified professionals works under him. He has fully established himself in the new business. Today, Patidar is known as one of the most successful building contractors and developers around Indore.

Patidar believes that *success lies outside the comfort zone*. If one has to earn, he also has constantly to learn, and, translate the learnings into practice through hard work. Patidar always gives his 100% into every project or task he and his team undertakes.

About his success, Ram Patidar says: "Our mantra for success is our consideration of the feelings of our clients. ...

We believe in understanding their dream and come together to create a collective dream." Fulfillment of the dream is Patidar's goal and the road to business success.

Story 3: The Lion Roars in the Sunrise Industry[12]

This is the story of Yatin Gupta, passionate entrepreneur, MD and chairman of Wardwizard Innovations and Mobility—manufacturer of electric two wheelers located at Vadodara.

Driven by the constant quest for innovation, Yatin's Wardwizard started with a team of just five people in a 500 sq.ft. office in 2016. It had zoomed to 5,000 sq.ft. office with more than 2000 employees in June 2020. It has also created history by getting listed in BSE under the EV manufacturing sector.

Yatin says: "I follow a simple logic. The moment you feel the whole world is against you, that's the moment one must realise you are knocking on the right doors." This philosophy is the driving force behind Wardwizard's thumping success.

Wardwizard started with manufacturing electric bicycles in 2016. The company has come a long way with its motorcycles—Joy e-bikes. Joy e-bike is an electric vehicle with 4+ low speed bikes and 5+ high speed bikes. In just five years, Joy e-bike has become a brand to reckon with in the Indian market. Yatin shares: "Joy e-bike clocked a record increase in sales in April (2021) with environment-conscious people wanting smart mobility."

In fact, the overwhelming sales were achieved within just four months of inauguration of the company's OEM (original equipment manufacturer) plant in Vadodara in January 2021. This is one of India's largest electric OEM plants with full capacity of producing 3-4 lakh vehicles annually. This is significantly contributing to PM's "Make in India" vision.

Wardwizard's mission has always been to create a mode of transport which is "flexible, efficient, easily integrated, clean and safe." The company is confident of achieving this with its core values of teamwork, empowerment, customer satisfaction and sustainable growth.

The vision and tenacity of Yatin Gupta have earned him several accolades. The Economic Time awarded him "The Most

Promising Business leader of Asia 2020-21"; and, Joy e-bike got recognised as the Best Brand in the category of "Fastest Growing Electric Two-wheeler company in India" by the Economic Times in the 3rd edition of the Best Brands 2020.

LEGENDARY ENTREPRENEURS AND *MANTRAS* FOR BUSINESS SUCCESS

All the legendary entrepreneurs mentioned so far are exemplary and unique in their own distinctive styles and methods of business management. They have created histories and are models by themselves. Some of these names are: Henry Ford, Konosuke Matsushita (National Panasonic), William Lever, Michael Dell, Bill Gates, Sam Walton (Walmart), Akio Morita (Sony), Dhirubhai Ambani, Jeff Bezos (Amazon), L.N. Mittal (also known as Arcelor Mittal), B.M. Munjal, Verghese Kurien (Amul), Karsanbhai Patel and Kiran Mazumadar Shaw.

All these entrepreneurs come from diverse backgrounds. Most of them are without any business background. They have ventured into diversified products with different technologies, risks and challenges. Some have jumped into unknown territories with more risk and uncertainty. These entrepreneurs are pioneers or path breakers in their fields. The diversity of products or businesses developed by them include automobile, electrical appliances, consumer goods, desktop/laptop computer, software applications, retail trade, consumer electronics, petrochemicals, e-retailing, steel, bicycles/motorcycles, diary milk, detergent powder, biotech products etc.

Underlying these diversities, there are some common mantras which the legendary entrepreneurs have followed in their business pursuits. These are reflected in their visions, building of business and achievement of goals. Ten distilled *mantras* are:

1. Have a dream
2. Be a dreamer who does
3. Formal education is no bar
4. Funds will flow
5. Roadblocks and setbacks are challenges
6. Self-motivation is the best motivation

7. Don't follow conventional wisdom
8. Make your own management system
9. Keep the customers in perspective
10. Believe in yourself

All aspiring entrepreneurs should follow these *mantras* for business success.

PART B

LESSONS FROM WHAT THEY DON'T TEACH AT BUSINESS SCHOOLS

Twenty Lessons from What they Don't Teach at Business Schools

The management lessens presented below are like "distilled" conclusions or findings from the text.

My business or professional career has taken me to private corporate sector, public sector with institutional interludes, and, back to private sector. During this long search or career, I have come across diverse managerial personalities, situations, management practices, decisions, improvisations or innovations. I have also been involved in many of these. All these lead to certain important conclusions on career making, management and organisation. These have also influenced or moulded the distilled conclusions or lessons.

Twenty important lessons are presented below.

1. THE ABCD PRINCIPLE

The ABCD Principle is very basic or fundamental to man agerial and organisational functioning. A, B, C, D in the Principle stand for:

A	:	Assimilation
B	:	Boss Management
C	:	Centre stage
D	:	Depart

Assimilation means assimilating yourself in the company or organisation you are joining. Every company/organisation is unique in terms of its functioning, work style, culture etc. You should try to settle or fit into this environment as soon as possible. This is the first requisite in career making. It helps or adds to your performance or productivity. If you cannot assimilate, you can not function properly.

We had recruited some MBAs from IIMA and IIMC in MMTC. They thought they were much above the "average manager" in the company. They should be involved only in policy and strategy making. With such notion or bias, they could not settle down in the company. They became misfits. They did not know that, for any meaningful policy or strategy making, you must first know the organisation well. In such situation, you hardly contribute anything to the organisation and no organisation needs such people.

Boss management is the most conventional or significant principle. You can be successful in a company if you are able to manage your boss well. Much has been said and written about this; I need not elaborate. The experts' advice is: "Swim with the boss." You must remember that the boss is always right (although the boss may sometimes be wrong). Never question the boss.

Centre stage means occupying the central place in your department or company.

Through your work or performance, you should become very important to your seniors and boss. In other words, you should try to become an indispensable manager. This sustains and promotes you in the organisation.

Depart means departing or leaving the company. If 'A', 'B', 'C' fail, 'D' comes into play.

You try to assimilate in the company, you try hard to manage your boss, and, you do almost everything to occupy the centre stage. But, in spite of all these, i.e., your best endeavours, you may not feel settled down or happy or comfortable. This means that the organisation does not suit you. It may happen after you have worked for sometime in the company. There may be various factors (cross-currents) at work. May be the boss has turned against you because of some new developments. May be, you are not getting the due or expected promotion. All this signals that it is time for you to leave the company.

2. DO NOT COMPLAIN AGAINST YOUR JOB AND KEEP STICKING TO IT

This follows from or is an extension of 'D' of the ABCD Principle.

You may not be happy with your present job, and keep complaining about it. Don't do this. It neither helps you as an individual or professional nor you contribute to the cause of the company. Your productivity becomes nil or negative. This is a lose-lose situation. Neither you like the company nor the company wants you. Do not keep sticking to the company. Do not rot. It is high time you leave your present job and look for better pastures.

We know that it is not always easy to change a job. You may have the qualifications and also experience. But, you may still have to wait for a chance or opportunity. Many of us have experienced this.

Bid your time in the present job till you leave. Bid your time as usefully as you can. This may be the best way. Time also may pass quickly.

3. DO JOB HOPPING FOR CAREER GROWTH

It is well recognized in the corporate world today that job hopping is essential for career building or growth.

Recent studies by the US Bureau of labour Statistics show that the average American have more than 8 different employers between the ages of 22 and 32. A study by the Danish Social Science Research Council found that the average person in Denmark will have at least 12 different employers by the time they reach the age of 60. Australian Human Rights and Equal Opportunity Commission established that 42 per cent of the country's workers change jobs at least every two years.[1]

In India, the frequency of job switching may not be so high, but, job hopping at managerial level is a foregone conclusion.

It is difficult to grow fast in the same company. Even if the management recognizes your merit or performance, there are different constraints (like peer comparability) to put you on the fast track. *Loyalty may be recognized, but, it may not often be rewarded.* To get over all this, job switching is the way.

20s and 30s are the best times for job hopping. During this period, you are relatively unencumbered. You can take some risk for career building. According to me, a manager should change 3 to 4 jobs till the age of 40. This may enable you to optimize or maximize your career growth.

4. THAT ORGANISATION IS THE BEST WHICH SUITS YOU MOST

Which is the best organisation to work with? This is the question which roams in every manager's mind. And, every manager is in search of such an organisation.

Is a high performing company the best organisation to work with? Is a highly professional company like Hindustan Lever (HUL) the best place to work? is ITC the best place? Are Procter & Gamble, Godrej, L&T, Infosys the best organisations to work with? We can add the names of many more good companies.

The pertinent question is: which criterion should be used to determine the best organisation? The criterion should be subjective and not objective. Taking all aspects into account, it is the individual manager's perception, assessment and experience of the company which should be the determining factor and not the world view. A company may be high performing or professional, but you may not get along with it. As an organisation reviews or assesses the performances of a manager, the manager should also be able to perceive the suitability of the organisation to his(her) functioning and expectations. Peter Drucker has said that you should work for that organisation which serves you better. I only echo his view.

According to me, there is no good or bad organisation. Every organisation is good (in certain respects) and bad (in certain respects). But, that organisation is the best which suits you most.

5. GROWTH IN AN ORGANISATION DEPENDS ON PROFESSIONAL EXCELLENCE, RELATIONSHIP WITH THE BOSS AND LUCK IN THE RATIO 50:30:20

Success or growth in an organisation does not depend on professionalism or hard work alone. If some manager thinks it does, he(she) is mistaken.

Professionalism and hard work increase productivity, give a manager visibility and may be also more acceptability. But, all this should be recognized and appreciated by the boss. Such recognition and appreciation depend largely on the equation or relationship with the boss. My experience has shown this enough number of times. Along with performance and equation /relationship with the boss, you also need some luck so that there is no slip between the cup and the lip.

More precisely, we can say that growth of a manager in an organisation depends on three factors: professional excellence, relationship with the boss and luck in the ratio 50:30:20. The actual weights or ratios may be debatable, but, the relative roles or significance of the three factors may not be debatable.

So, do not run after only performance or hard work. If you do so, sometimes you may be doing only donkey's job. Ensure that you are at the same waive length with your boss. Destiny should also be on your side.

6. ALL SUCCESSFUL MANAGERS MAKE COMPROMISES

Philosophers say that life is full of compromises. Management analysts/experts contend that a manager has to make many compromises. SVS, one of MMTC's most successful chairmen, once told me (I had mentioned this earlier also): "Nag, we have to make many compromises. Even as a Chairman, I make compromise everyday."

If a chairman has to make many compromises, what about lesser mortals? I mean the managers. To compromise is to sacrifice or barter your ego or self-esteem. A manager may have to do this for his(her) success or growth, if not survival. You may make compromise to save or resolve situations, maintaining relationship (with boss, peers and also sometimes subordinates) or getting things done.

You have a difference with your boss—a professional difference. You think you are right. But, you agree with boss's view: you compromise. One of your subordinates often comes late but, he is a good worker and one of your confidants (he also sometimes sits late if required). You do not like to rub him on coming late and digest it: you compromise. It is about 6 pm. You are about to leave office. Your peer steps into your room and wants to discuss a point with you. The peer is known to be close to the boss. So, you do not want to tell him that you can discuss the point next morning. You sit late with him: you compromise. You have been asked to entertain a customer by going out of your way. You think it is unethical. But, you do it: you compromise. One of your suppliers/vendors is close to your boss. But he does not give you enough recognition and respect. You still have to deal with him with a smiling face: you compromise. In course of your functioning, you have to make many such compromises.

If you aspire to be a successful manager, you should learn to be a compromising manager. This is a necessary condition for success, although may not be a sufficient condition.

7. SUCCESSFUL MANAGERS DON'T DO DIFFERENT THINGS; THEY DO THINGS DIFFERENTLY

Peter Drucker, in his book *The Effective Executive*, has said: "Effective executives don't do different things; they do things differently." The same can be said about successful managers.

"Effectiveness" and "success" are closely related. "Effectiveness" is plan-output relationship—how much of the plan has been fulfilled or realized. Effectiveness, therefore, focuses on contribution to the target or result. Success means result. Therefore, all effective managers are likely to be successful managers.[2] There may be some difference of degree.

To "do things differently" is the art or skill or technique of execution. This differentiates the successful managers from others. "To do things differently" may mean doing things in a way which is very clearly visible; it may mean doing things in a way which the boss wants; it may mean doing things in a way which produces result; it may mean doing things in a way the situation demands; it may mean doing things in a way the customer wants; and, so on.

In summary, all successful managers do things differently, i.e., the way success demands.

8. PROFESSIONALISM DOES NOT GUARANTEE SUCCESS, IT ONLY GUARANTEES YOUR JOB

A professional is an upholder and follower of his profession—guided and governed by the basics, conduct rules, methods, techniques and prognostications. A professional is governed by the codes of his profession; these set the domain for his functioning.

There is also a paradox: Multinationals (presumably with professional management) have succeeded; they have also failed. Family enterprises (even small ones) with essentially entrepreneurial, and not professional, culture have succeeded. So, professional management is not the answer or therapy for success. A company requires something more.

Professionals are mostly governed by the rule book. But, for success, you may have to look beyond the rule book.

Success often requires entrepreneurial skills or abilities—initiative, aggressiveness, innovativeness. Professionalism does not embody these tenets. But, professionalism trains you for disciplined and good work. This protects or preserves your job.

But, for success, you may have to look beyond pure professionalism.

9. MANAGERIAL EFFICIENCY IS ONLY 50% INPUT-OUTPUT RELATIONSHIP; BALANCE 50% IS BOSS'S PERCEPTION

Some say that efficiency norms are motherhoods. But, that may not be true.

More than two decades ago, a management expert observed: "Our knowledge about what makes for efficiency is still limited; so, there is plenty of scope for disagreement"[3] on this. The observation holds good even today.

In quantitative terms, efficiency is defined and measured as input-output relationship—how much of output has been produced with how much of input. We also call this productivity. There are measurement problems in this.

We learn from the Japanese (who originally learnt from the Americans) that the key to higher productivity is in working better (quality) rather than working more or faster (quantity). So, the emphasis on quality is vital.

This means that, for determining managerial efficiency, quality efficiency is as important as quantity efficiency. But, who determines or decides quality efficiency? It is the boss; it is a purely subjective view or assessment.

So, we may put quantity versus quality efficiency as 50:50. Dogmatic bosses may perceive "quality" to be a more important criterion or factor.

To conclude, assessment of managerial efficiency has no escape from high level of subjectivity.

10. MANY BOSSES CANNOT DO GOOD TO SUBORDINATES; BUT, ALL BOSSES CAN DO ENOUGH HARM

Bosses can be of different kinds or types. Some rule with an iron hand; some have a professional style; some have weak personalities. Some are good leaders; some are bad leaders. Some are positive; some are negative. Some are benevolent; some are vindictive. These are the predominant characteristics or styles.

Whatever be the style, all bosses have their own powers to do good or bad to the subordinates. For some bosses, the power to do good may be limited. This may happen if they are themselves not rated well or highly by their bosses. But, the same bosses or boss can do bad or harm to subordinates if he is not happy with particular subordinates. He may turn vindictive and give adverse report to a subordinate. Good reports can sometimes be ignored; but, adverse reports are difficult to ignore. This is the basic truth about appraisal systems. *A stroke of pen can do many things.*

Things can be worse if you try to disagree with the boss. The professionalist's prescription is: Don't disagree if it is a matter of opinion, but, disagree if it is a point of principle. But, in reality, this hardly works. Most of the bosses are intolerant particularly if they are negative or vindictive types. And, this is common knowledge that it is easier to harm somebody than to do good.

So, beware of a bad or vindictive boss. He may spoil your career prospects.

11. INFORMAL MANAGEMENT PLAYS A SIGNIFICANT ROLE IN COMPANY FUNCTIONING AND MANAGEMENT

Most of us, particularly senior managers, almost regularly adopt informal management practice without often being consciously aware of it. This plays almost as significant role as the formal management system in running of business and companies.

In every company, there is a formal organisational structure and reporting system. This is shown in the organisation chart. But there is also an unwritten informal system. The formal system and the informal system run parallel to each other.

In informal management, a decision is taken by a senior/top executive and it is given the disguise or form of a formal decision.[4] This means that the informal system undermines the formal systems or it prevails over the formal decision making system.

Informal management system operates in every organisation with difference of degrees. Formal management is mostly bottom-up; informal management is mostly top-down. Higher the level of management, more is the use of the informal management practice, the maximum being at the highest level, i.e. the CEO or the CMD.

If we closely analyze the day-to-day functioning of companies, the role of informal management vis-a-vis formal management may be more clear. Whether informal management is good or bad for organisations may be a matter of difference of opinion or debate. But, that does not change the reality.

Informal management practice exists both in the public sector and the private sector, but, more in the public sector because of rigidity of the formal system.

12. "LINE" AND "STAFF' ARE TWO SIDES OF AN ORGANISATION; THEY REINFORCE EACH OTHER AND THE ORGANISATION

Much has been said and written about "Line" and "Staff" and their relationship. It is possibly also true that many of the difficulties and frictions found in the daily life of an organisation is because of "line" and staff" problems. Misconception and lack of clear understanding of what "line" and "staff" are may be the source of many bickering, conflicts, disunity, duplication and loss of production or sales even in companies which are generally known to be well-run.

But, all this is changing. The proverbial mother-in-law (line) controlling and daughter-in-law (staff) serving have also almost lost its relevance.

Conceptually or conventionally, "Line refers to those functions (like production, marketing, sales), which have direct responsibility for achieving the major objectives of the company, and, 'staff' relates to those functions of the organisation which help the line in achieving the primary objectives, i.e., activities which are indirectly related to the major objectives.

This line of thinking is being debated today if not challenged in the modern management system. With manufacturing and selling as the two core line functions, most of the functional growth has been in the staff departments. It may not be correct to say that all staff functions are auxiliary in nature. Functions like HR (in the extended sense) and budgetary planning are definitely mainstream functions. In general, it can be said that staff functions are gaining more focus and control today.

A comparative study of a number of industrial organisations in different European countries points to a possible inter changeability of 'line' and 'staff' in connection with span of control. In some of the organisations studied, staff managers have been used to relieve 'line' managers to widen the span of control. In practice, they may work as an intervening level of management, although this is rarely shown in the organisation charts.

Also, experience of many companies has established that "to-day's" "staff" is "tomorrow's line". Dr. Ashoke Ganguly started as a Research Scientist in Hindustan Lever and was changed to 'line' and moved upto Chairman of HLL (HUL). I began in staff cadre in MMTC and was later moved to line function. In Birla Copper (Hindalco Industries). I was again in advisory (staff) role. This makes a complete circle. This also shows that staff-line movement cuts across public and private sectors.

All these clearly establish that "line" and "staff" are like two sides of a coin; they reinforce each other and the coin—the organisation. For the organisation's interest, this is the best way to view the relationship.

13. THE GENERAL MANAGER IS BOTH A GENERALIST AND A SPECIALIST

Hanry Ford once said: "When a person becomes a General Manager, he hires the specialist and forgets about the details." Many other management practitioners and analysts support the view. The logic is: as an operational manager progresses from functional management to general management, his administrative and general management skills become more important than technical knowledge and ability. As captain of the team, he becomes a "fixer" in management of the team or department. Let specialists play their roles.

This sounds logical, but, it may not mostly hold good in practice. My experience as GM, RO, Bombay, MMTC showed that a General Manager should be both a generalist and a specialist. It is true that as a GM, I had to take administrative and management responsibilities for running the RO, but, simultaneously, I had to play the role of a specialist. I had to do this as a specialist in non-ferrous metals.

The same applies in the fields of production, marketing and sales. GM (Production) is responsible for planning, scheduling and monitoring production. But, he should be simultaneously ready to attend to or solve any problems in the production process which may arise from time to time. Similarly, GM (Marketing) has to organize the marketing department/team, but, at the same time, be prepared to offer solutions to marketing issues or problems the marketing managers may come up with. The same applies to GM (Sales). He has to organize and man the sales team and assure its smooth/efficient functioning, but, should also be able to offer specialist service/advice to sales manager and also the sales force as required.

Therefore, to say that a general manager should be a generalist may, to a large extent, be out-of-date perception today. *The modern GM[5] has the challenging task of combining the generalist's job with that of the specialist.*

14. MAKING MISTAKES IN MANAGEMENT IS NOT A CRIME; ON THE CONTRARY, IT REVEALS CERTAIN SPECIAL CHARACTERISTICS OF MANAGERS

A common perception is that making mistakes in management goes against professionalism. This is far from truth. Mistakes can and do happen in professional management.

Peter Drucker had said: "I would never promote a man into a top-level job who has not made mistakes.. ... otherwise, he is sure to be mediocre. Worse still, not having made mistakes, he will not have learned how to spot them early, and, how to correct them ..... The better a man, the more mistakes he will make—for the more new things he will try".

Another way to interpret Drucker's statement or observation is: the fact that a manager has never made a mistake shows that he has never taken initiative, showed boldness and innovativeness in management and decision-making. These are the special characteristics of a result-seeking and progressive manager.

In a professional or a progressive company, the CEO may give his managers some freedom or authority to take decisions and make some mistakes. How much freedom the managers should be given is CEO's choice or decision and a difficult one. It also depends on how progressive and result seeking the CEO is. But, the fact that the managers should be given some minimum freedom to take decisions and make mistakes is indisputable. Otherwise, the performing managers tend to get frustrated or fall prey to indecision. The top management/CEO has also the challenging task of correcting the mistakes of managers and guiding them for the future and encouraging them to get on with their job. This also assumes a favourable organisational environment.

Some managers suffer from mistake-avoidance complex. Their approach to their job is passive or often negative: don't take a decision, and, therefore, don't make a mistake. The fear of a mistake haunts them with the result that they hardly perform. Some say that such people remain supervisors all their life. But, the organisation does not want that. As and when in managerial cadre, they must be counselled or trained to come out of their shell or shyness and start performing, and, making some mistakes if performance warrants or involves such mistakes.

In public sector, very few managers make mistakes because they don't take decision. Decisions are pushed to as higher level as possible (this is management by obstruction). The accountability system discourages managers from taking decisions and making mistakes even if they are honest ones.

In conclusion, we can say that initiative, drive and innovativeness in decision making and mistake go together. They are mostly inseparable. But, they all conform to professionalism.

15. SITUATIONAL MANAGEMENT IS KEY TO SUCCESSFUL MANAGEMENT

Modern management is not static. It is dynamic. The same method or strategy does not work every time. Situations are changing. Therefore, to be effective or successful, there is need for situational management techniques.

Different managers in different organisations during different times face different situations which require different solutions. Old wine in new bottle does not work. You require new wine in new bottle, i.e., new or evolving methods and strategies.

Carlisle, in his book *Situational Management*, gives a comprehensive account of situational analysis and techniques. In growth phase of a company, it requires one strategy; if the company is in break-even point/situation, it needs a different strategy; if the company is stagnating or loss making, it requires still another strategy. Even during growth phase, it can be high, medium or low growth; strategies required in each of these three situations would be different. Break-even situation can quickly/suddenly change to loss making one; then the company requires change of strategy. Then there are intervening situations.

There can also be situational shocks because of sudden change of government policy (like very recent demonetization) or environmental changes. All these call for differential situational response strategies. Improvisation of strategies may be required.

In situational management, the focus is on leadership because the leader leads the company and the managers. Some situations call for leaders who are visionaries; some call for leaders who are outstanding planners and decision makers; some for leaders who are expert organizers; some for leaders who are best human resource developers; some for leaders who are specialists in implementation, monitoring and control; some for leaders who thrive during crises; and, so on.

We have many stories of successful situational leaders—leaders who have seized situations, exploited situations and thrived during particular situations. Krishnamurthy (SAIL), Luther (DVC) and Gujral (Coal India) are some examples.

In reality, there can be as many different situations as can develop in companies. For success in all such situations, a leader with only particular traits cannot succeed. We need a situational leader and not a traitist leader.

We can also call it the situational cult.

16. CORPORATE ETHICS IS A FLOATING PHENOMENON

An ethics realist has said: "It is not the crook in modern business that we fear, but the honest man who does not know what he is doing". This summarises the growing concern for corporate ethics today.

Blanchard (management consultant) and Peale (moral consultant) voice the concern of millions about deteriorating ethics: "Everywhere we turn today, there are signs of ethical deterioration. In business, bright young people have made immoral millions by using insider trading information. In government, hardly a day goes by without some public official being involved in an ethical dilemma."

Business schools are teaching or preaching ethics. But, business houses are diluting it or discouraging it directly or indirectly. Managers are either falling a prey to it or are taking advantage of it.

Even the best managed companies can stray. Take Johnson & Johnson, a company known for its integrity in business. Its "credo" urges managers to be "just and ethical", and, is, says Ralph Larsen, the company's Chairman, "the most important thing we have in this company." But, that did not stop wayward employees from shredding papers to hinder a federal probe into the company's marketing of an ache cream. "There was no excuse", says Larsen.

Arun Monappa, in his study on Ethical Attitudes of Indian Managers, has found that the majority of business managers believe in good ethics, but, circumstances often prevent them from putting their beliefs into practice. The managers surveyed constantly reiterated the importance of company policy influencing ethical action. A manager's personal code of conduct was given only second place.

This has also been confirmed by a survey by the All India Management Association (AIMA) conducted among more than 300 managers at top management, senior management, middle management and junior management levels. The result of the survey is summarized as: 83% of the managers agree that "managers resort to practices which are considered shady but appear necessary in today's rat race."

In most of the organisations today, the manager is left to make a conscious choice. He(she) can either master the rules of the career game (with a high pay-off for ethics), and, start climbing towards the top of the power pyramid; or, he can join the multitude of competent but, anonymous office non-politicians who support the corporate structures on their backs. This has almost become a global syndrome.

All this proves that corporate ethics has become a floating phenomenon today. Companies and managers can take their picks.

17. CORPORATE CORRUPTION IS MORE TOP-DOWN THAN BOTTOM-UP

If corporate ethics is a floating phenomenon, corporate corruption is either endemic or epidemic. According to me (and may be many others), it is more epidemic than endemic.

Does corporate corruption begin at the top? or, to put it in another way: is corporate corruption more top-down than bottom up? It is most often top-down.

An odd manager may indulge in some corruptive practice. If he does this all by himself without the support of seniors, he may soon be caught and punished including dismissal. But if he does this with the support of the boss or bosses, he may survive, and, may continue to do so.

Even better, if he does it as part of a chain starting at higher levels, he is secure. And, if it starts at the top, he is more secure, but, not, however, completely safe. We know that many ministers and bureaucrats do not openly indulge in corruptive practices, but, do it through their designated agents or middlemen. The same is true about top managers or CEOs. In many companies, Heads of the departments or even CEOs have their designated managers or agents.

Once a manager in the procurement department in a company was caught taking bribe. Having no way to escape, he confessed/ pleaded that he had done this at the instance (instruction?) of the Head of the Department. When the Head of the Deptt. was approached he denied it. The poor manager was sacked and out of sheer shame, he committed suicide. There are many such innocent suicides taking place in the corporate world. This is the irony of the top-down corporate corruption story.

In spite of this, corruption continues or perpetuates. Some middle/junior level managers survive and others become victims (leading to dismissal/suicide) of this. But, because of involvement of the top management, the corruption system gets sustenance. If it is bottom-up, corruptive practice is not sustainable. As in management, bottom-up proposal or strategy sustains only if it receives enough support upwards which often does not happen.

So, the way corruption is becoming widespread in the corporate sector (both public and private), one is almost made to conclude that corporate corruption is more top-down than bottom-up.

18. THE DIFFERENCE BETWEEN THE PUBLIC SECTOR AND THE PRIVATE SECTOR IS BUREAUCRACY

Ever since the creation of the public sector, an issue or debate which has cropped up from time to time is: what is the difference between the public sector and the private sector? It is not the constitutional difference or shareholding pattern that we are talking about. We are concerned with the management systems and the managers in the two sectors.

The moment we talk of the management difference between the public and private sectors, the Jagirdar System immediately comes to the mind. Sharu Rangnekar has analysed the jagirdari approach in the private and public sectors and its effect on the respective management system. The Jagirdari system in industry and management started with the family system. A business or industrial enterprise was managed like a jagir with family members holding and managing key positions. Management hierarchy and changes in that generally depended on family pulls and pressures. Business/industrial expansion was often initiated or undertaken to satisfy the need for or to accommodate family expansion.

During the industrial evolution process in India, a stage came when government entered the industry. This was in pursuance of the constitutional provision/objective of the socialistic pattern of society. The Indian economy became a mixed economy. The government entered Industry in two ways: first, by nationalizing some of the existing enterprises in sectors or industries like steel, and, second, almost simultaneously, setting up green field projects. The public sector was born.

As government entered the industry, new jagirdars from the civil service emerged in the industrial field. The family members in industrial enterprises were replaced by the clan of civil servants. The management jobs or managerial positions in the public sector were decided and valued in terms of different grades in civil services.

Over a period of time, public sector companies introduced their own pay scales and compensation packages. But, this was old wine in new bottle. The pay scales or salary systems were drawn from those of bureaucrats and made fully compatible with those to ensure that the public sector managers did not take a march over the bureaucrats. Bureaucrats also exercised control over the functioning of the public sector. This was, and, is also done today through the administrative ministries.

So, it is clear that the way public sector management has taken shape or been moulded is due to dominance of the civil service or bureaucracy. We can say that the fundamental difference between the public sector and the private sector is bureaucracy. All other differences between the two sectors follow from or are the results of this with some sectoral modifications.

This is the reason why the public sector model is closer to the government sector model than the private sector model.

19. THERE IS NO DIFFERENCE BETWEEN THE EFFICIENCY LEVELS OF THE PUBLIC SECTOR AND PRIVATE SECTOR MANAGERS: IT IS THE SYSTEMS WHICH MAKE THEM APPEAR DIFFERENT

Efficiency level of public sector managers is often a matter of discussion or debate. In fact, public sector managers are generally considered to be less efficient than private sector managers. But, this is not a well-founded perception or observation. As we will see soon, it may, in fact, be otherwise.

Efficiency is defined and measured as input-output relationship—output produced by an input or a factor of production. This is same as productivity of the input or the factor. Some studies have shown that efficiency or productivity in the public sector has been observed to be higher than in the private sector.

Bakul Dholakia (Director, IIMA), based on a detailed study of productivity trends in the public and private sectors, concludes that "the performance of Indian public sector enterprises, judged by the criterion of total factor productivity, has generally been distinctly superior to that of the corresponding private enterprises especially during the more recent years. While the private enterprises may have performed much better than the public enterprises in terms of net profitability, their performance in regard to improvement in total factor productivity has been rather unsatisfactory. In fact, it can be easily shown that, if private enterprises had performed equally well on the total factor productivity front, the overall performance of the Indian economy would have been much better than the one actually observed during recent years."

The study further observes that "the severe criticism of the management of Indian public enterprises exclusively on the basis of their low profitability is, to a large extent, misleading in as much as it represents only a partial view of the overall performance; and, does not necessarily find adequate support when we apply some of the other, and, perhaps, more relevant as well as comprehensive criteria of evaluating the performance of these enterprises."

Managerial productivity or efficiency in public and private sectors should be viewed or compared in this perspective or background. Efficiency level of managers in the public sector may appear lower because their productivity gets diffused or lost in the multiplicity of goals or objectives and output is never focused. The accountability system also dilutes productivity in the public sector. The accountability system can be summarized as: a manager is never punished if he does not take any initiative. But, a manager is definitely punished if he takes initiative to do something and makes a mistake. In the private sector, in contrast, a manager's productivity or efficiency is judged by results, and, not by a mistake or mistakes he has committed for achievement of his target.

So, the efficiency levels of managers in public and private sectors should be assessed in relation to the corporate objectives and management systems in the two sectors, and, not in absolute terms or in isolation.

20. CORRUPTION EXISTS IN EQUAL MEASURE IN BOTH PUBLIC SECTOR AND PRIVATE SECTOR

A common perception is that public sector is corrupt. There is truth in it. But, what is not commonly known is that the private sector is equally corrupt. There may be difference of degree.

There is a reason why the public sector is more commonly known to be corrupt than the private sector. The reason is the management/procedural systems in the two sectors and resulting from this, publicity or otherwise of corruptive actions.

There is distinction in visibility or publicity of corruptive practices in the public sector, and, the private sector, and, the way such practices or cases are handled by the respective managements. In the public sector, there is noise about corruptive practices. A full fledged Vigilance Department exists, and, this is often headed by a director. Once a case of corruption is known, it is referred to the Vigilance Department. A Memo is initially issued, then a charge-sheet is prepared and served on the manager (junior or senior), enquiry is held, and, then punishment is awarded. This is a long process like the process of law in our country. This becomes a public matter both inside and outside the organisation. Newspaper reporting is quite common.

In contrast, in the private sector, once a corruptive practice comes to the notice of the management, the manager in warned and let off if it is not a serious offence. But, if the level of corruption is high or very serious, the manager is straightway dismissed.

This is what happened to DDJ in Birla Copper (now Hindalco Industries). He was sacked for his corruptive practices in the Group company he was working before Birla Copper.

Such and similar cases keep occurring with regular frequency in the private sector. But, most of such cases do not get media exposure. So, the community at large do not come to know about it. But, it does not mitigate the incidence or intensity of corruptive activates in the sector. The public sector, on the other hand, is thought or known to be more corrupt because of high media exposure or publicity.

If every corruption case in the private sector would go through the same process of investigation, and, resulting publicity, it would be easy to establish that *corruption exists almost in equal measure in both public sector and private sector*. The only distinction is: one happens in silence, the other occurs with sound; one remains a "private" affair, the other becomes a "public" matter.

PART C

THE EPILOGUE

The Epilogue

The epilogue is an integral concluding part of what has been said or written in the text. This makes some important observations or reflections on the missing links in *What They Don't Teach at Business Schools*.

Business education is under attack all over the world today.

In the US, the process had begun as far back as 1959 when the Ford Foundation had issued a landmark report on the state of business education in the country. The report came to the drastic conclusion that graduate business education in the US was "a fraud, the students were second-rate, (and) the faculty third-rate."

If ever such a study is undertaken in India, the conclusion could well be that management education in this country is "a business, the students first rate and the faculty fourth-rate."[1] The more temperate might say "students first-rate and the faculty third-rate." We may also add the course dimension and say: "students first-rate, faculty third-rate and the courses second-rate."

These statements or observations may appear hyperbolic, but, all the same, these show enough concerns about the state of business education in the US, India and many other countries.

KEY ASPECTS OF BUSINESS EDUCATION

Three pertinent aspects of business education today are discussed below:

1. Industry-Institute interface
2. Business school faculty
3. Course curriculum

In view of the latest developments, one more aspect or factor is also discussed:

4. Digitalisation of business education

At the end, we make some concluding remarks about the future course of management education.

INDUSTRY-INSTITUTE INTERFACE

Management institutes synthesise the students, the faculties and the courses, and, therefore, lot depends on the institutions. Management institutes are booming like mushrooms in India today next only to computer centres or computer course centres. And, when there is mushrooming growth, quality is always the casualty. At the apex or top, we have the IIMs (among them also there are quality differences at least of degrees if not of order), and, at the bottom, tiny institutes housed in a room or two including long-distance or correspondence course institutes. The fall is almost heaven to hell. No wonder, there is complete commercialisation at the bottom level.

A Global Debate

A global debate which also hots up in India from time to time is: is the industry-institute interface good enough to make management education effective and deliver the goods, that is, prepare the students properly for real time industry jobs? Do business schools give enough priority to this vital factor? How to improve or optimize the interface?

According to me, the present level of interface between industry and most of the Indian business schools is far from satisfactory or optimal. This observation is based on my experience both as an industry person (ORG, MMTC, Hindalco Industries (Copper Unit), Nihon Ispat and as a management faculty (BITS, XLRI, IIT, IIFT), and also my interactions with both industry people and management faculties.

It is not enough to send the students to industry for a summer project (in some cases, it almost becomes a ritual), or call occasional speakers from the industry, or, teach some cases. The whole system has to be much more interactive and real life oriented.

Present B-schools in India can be broadly classified into two categories; first, management centers or departments which are extensions of the existing universities, and, generally follow the traditional university model even in management education, that is, mostly academic in approach; second, autonomous or private business schools (IIMs, ISB, MDI, XLRI etc.) which have been specifically set up for management education, and, which definitely have a much better interface with the industry. There is a third category of business schools which have sprung up allover the country which are purely commercial (management education can be good business now). These institutes neither follow the university model nor the autonomous B-school practices. They have their own ways (call them systems?) of imparting management education and generating cash flow or revenue which is their prime objective. These institutes have the least interface with the industry.

Interface Gaps

Even in the regular B-schools (autonomous or private), interface with industry is still not strong enough to go deep into real life situations or problems. Let me try to illustrate this. Let us take marketing. A regular customer of a company is snatched away by a competitor (often happens in business-to-business marketing), and the company's marketing intelligence or market surveillance fails to foresee this for pre-emptive or timely action. The marketing manager is at a loss as to what to do. What does B-school education has to say on this? Let us take finance. In courses on finance or financial management (core or elective), students are taught about various instruments of payment including letter of credit (LC) which is a very vital instrument in both national and international business. Does

B-school education say how often LCs are dishonoured and banks (including nationalized banks) refuse payments on some pretext of discrepancies in the LCs? Managers of tomorrow should know what are the risk factors involved even in an apparently safe instrument like LC.

Let us take business ethics. Many B-schools offer courses on business ethics. Students are taught about professional ethics and value ethics or personal ethics and ethical standards. But, are they told about the changing definition of ethics in today's value system, and, also different ethical connotations in public and private sectors? Private sector companies believe in results, and, a manager can not defend himself (herself) for non-performance on grounds of ethics or integrity. I am not saying (and, nobody says) that a manager should be corrupt. I am only talking of realistic ethics, and, ethics or ethical reasons not becoming an hindrance to performance too often.

Does B-school education emphasize this? We can also give plenty of examples from HR or general corporate governance or strategy. Almost decades ago, Mark McCormack had lucidly stated *What They don't Teach you at Harvard Business School*—the ifs, buts, ponderables and imponderables of business. I don't think there has been any significant change in the B-school education focus even today.

Industry exposure of students should increase in a more direct way. An industry interaction programme should be worked out for final year students through which *each student or a group of two or three students should spend full working day with managers in different functional areas observing their working process*—disposal of papers, telephones, various issues, handling subordinates, peers, seniors, pressures and tensions—all that a manager goes through in a typical day. This would enable the students to position the potential industry job and class room learning, and think how best they can bring compatibility or complementarity between the two.

Finally, we can have appropriate organisations to promote the interface. The Institute for Corporate Learning (IFCL) at Leeds is one such organisation. IFCL is considered to be a bridge between academia and the corporate world—it provides a platform for partnership between business and B-schools. Such organisations can be very useful catalysts for effective interface between industry and the management institutes.

Interface and Stakeholders

Proper industry academia interface or collaboration can benefit all the three stakeholders—the industry, business schools and the students. The industry will get better managerial inputs; business schools will have better branding and placement and students will receive more realistic business education. All these will also benefit the fourth stakeholder—business education.

We shall talk more about industry—institute interface in the concluding section.

BUSINESS SCHOOL FACULTY

Faculty quality has been squarely blamed for the crisis in American management education today. "... A major cause of inertia in management education remains its all too often insular and narrowly trained faculty.[2] Very few American faculty members have substantial experience as managers, let alone leaders. Specialists, however, abound on business school faculties. Faculty members with the breadth of business experience and long-term perspective that is required to develop today's business manager and leaders have become rare in the United States, They might have become rare in many other countries also. Most of the business school faculties today, one must painfully say, are the second-best or the third-best.

There are good reasons why the faculty is second-rate or third rate, particularly in India. To begin with, our academic institutions do not attract the best talent as faculty, that is, top performers in universities, institutions of management and technology do not generally come to the teaching profession essentially because of low compensation. In the compensation structure for jobs, institutions are quite lowly placed. The first attraction is from multinationals and the private corporate sector generally, and, closely followed by or simultaneously, from the civil or administrative services. The IIMs (and few other management institutes) may offer good packages with consultancy cash flow etc., but, even these incentives do not outweigh the best private sector jobs, the top brass of the civil and allied services.

Faculty Selection

Let us take faculty selection or recruitment. It is true that, in advertisements for faculty recruitment, most of the B-schools, particularly the leading ones, do mention about industry experience. But, enough weightage is not given to this factor during selection and, if we see faculty composition in most of the institutes, we would find that more than 50 per cent of the faculty do not have industry experience. I do not consider doing consultancy with industry as industry experience. Only if a person has worked in a business unit, he (she) knows what exactly management in practice means. And, when he (she) teaches a course to the students, industry orientation or flavour comes almost spontaneously through his (her) lecture. Faculties without industry experience may be quite capable or brilliant, but they may not be able to infuse the necessary industry orientation or inputs to make B-school education closer to industry requirements.

With initial faculty input not of very high order, the lack of sufficient internal development of faculty adds to the woe. One fundamental factor often missed in HRD Phobia or obsession for training is that people who train others also need to train themselves. As a postgraduate or an MBA has to be appropriately trained for a particular managerial position or responsibility after the acquisition of basic qualifications, the management faculty also has to be oriented through suitable faculty development programmes. Faculty development must keep pace with development of training. There are some faculty exchange programmes in IIMs and IITs leading to exchange of faculties with foreign countries, but, these are negligible compared to total faculty development needs. There are also some ad hoc or crash programmes here and there, but, there has been no policy approach to faculty development programmes at least in India.

Faculty Development

Besides general development programmes, a good way of faculty growth could be through feedbacks from MDPs. In almost all training programmes, there is an evaluation session. In fact, it forms an integral part of every MDP. Through such sessions, evaluation can be done of a topic, a particular training session or slot, a trainer or faculty, a training course or a programme or a training institute. Many interesting works have been done on evaluation of training—individual components as well as a total training programme. If some of these component evaluations are done in conjunction with others, and, with objectivity and positiveness, this can lead to all round faculty development.

But, unfortunately, the evaluations or feedbacks are at best used, only half-heartedly, for faculty correction, and, not for growth and development. The management or training institutes do not use, with enough objectivity, and seriousness, feedback processes as instruments for improving faculty quality. In other words, faculty development through feedback systems, has not yet been institutionalised in many countries including India. This has remained more a ritual.

Management institutes hinder faculty development (with respect to training) also in an indirect way. In any management institute, staff college, or business school, a middle or senior level faculty has to generally perform three functions, namely, to serve as faculty for MDPs, to participate in consultancy work—individual or institutional, and to undertake research—fundamental or applied. Depending on the professional standing of the faculty in his field of specialisation, demand for time on consultancy and research would vary.

Each faculty member should be allotted only as many sessions as he can satisfactorily undertake having regard to consultancy assignments, research works and some minimum free time for preparation of course materials and improvement (including innovations) in teaching. If this is not done, faculty quality will suffer.

Some management institutes take on many more courses than what the faculties can bear (partial commercialisation) and, the quality of management education becomes the casualty. A leading training college in South India runs as many as 120 MDPs in a year (for different levels of business executives, administrators and bureaucrats); that is, on an average at the rate of 10 programmes a month. Is this number not too high considering that all programmes are heterogeneous in character? Overcrowding of programmes will always retard development of good faculty.

COURSE CURRICULUM

Course curriculum in business schools is deficient in many ways. The course structure or curriculum design needs closer examination or scrutiny for determining its suitability to appropriate business school education.

First, in the AICTE business school curriculum, there are many general courses, which, in terms of utility, can almost be made redundant. For example, a course like "Legal Procedures or Management" or a course on "Research Methodology." Some institutes also teach a course on "Knowledge Management." These can, at best, be made optional, and, not compulsory or mainstream courses.

Course Correction

Instead, more useful course like "Development of Management Thought" can be included. In post-graduate course in Economics, there is a course on "History of Economic Thought." Similarly, the course on development of management can deal with how management thought has evolved over time to its present form.

In addition to such curriculum changes, some new element can be introduced to give the course more industry orientation. In every course that is taught whether in general management, HR, marketing, finance, IT or E-commerce, there should be some lectures or talks on actual industry experience. A manager middle, senior or top level—should take these sessions to analyse his(her) experience in the particular functional area with reference to handling some situation or problem solving. Pedagogy or teaching style should ensure this to illustrate how real life situations support or modify text book principles or models.

Course curriculum and examination-linked business education can have more dimensions. This is described below.

Recent developments in management education owe much of their origin to Prof. Charles Handy's *The Making of Managers*. This report is a clear, concise and extremely thoughtful study that reviews the study of management education, training and development in the United States, West Germany, France, Japan and the U.K. It also makes useful recommendations for reform.

Professor Handy's recommendations may be summarised as below:

"The most straightforward way to put more system into the present plethora of arrangements for early business education and experience, ... would be to move to a two-part qualification scheme on the professional model with periods of early study leading up to a preliminary examination followed by work experience interfaced with study leading to a full qualification. Though qualification could never be mandatory, for management should not be a closed profession, but, in time, the preliminary examination should become a customary requirement for all aspiring managers whether they be in industry, government or any other sector and the second level of study and qualification a desirable way for individuals to certificate their early training and acquire a credential."[3]

The first phase is tentatively designated as MBA Part I, Business Diploma, or Business Certificate. Preparation for this qualification could be accomplished through a variety of in-house and/or external arrangements and would consist of successfully completing an examination (or being granted a waiver) in economics, accounting, finance, statistics, organisation behaviour, marketing, production, and corporate strategy. The first qualification would be a prerequisite to the MBA Part II which would be offered through the universities or polytechnics. The MBA Part II as proposed, is to be a specialised, application-based qualifications directed towards immediate and practical usefulness.

DIGITALISATION OF BUSINESS EDUCATION

Digitalisation of business education has been forced by the pandemic. Some call it new model. Some call it alternative MBA.[4] This seems more appropriate.

Pandemic and lockdown have, among many other things, led to reimagining the way business education is delivered across the globe. Digitalisation is the new way. Significant transition in specialised training programmes is taking place in the digital era. According to some estimates, more than 1.2 billion students are out of classroom. These students are urged or prompted to adopt the digitalised system. MBA education in the digitalised system is focussing on data sciences, digital marketing, artificial intelligence and technology learning.

With the growth of new-age technologies, there is widespread adoption of Internet of Things (IoT). IoT is pervading many fields. Many students and professionals are identifying programmes for upskilling and taking up challenging roles. It is anticipated that digital social media, data sciences and IoT will change the MBA education landscape.

Alternative MBA

As per the guidelines of New Education Policy (NEP 2020), students enrolling for MBAs are now sceptical of the institutes' commitment to provide required placement assistance. On the other hand, alternative MBA institutes have cut their trimester and course duration to manage completion of the curriculum online. This means, in other words, that there is reduction in imparting knowledge in the alternative MBA programmes. This is a drawback or shortcoming of the present digitalised system.

Almost every professional company today is chronicling its operations as per changing consumer behaviour and business conditions. To deal with the market dynamics, organisations are preferring to hire managers based on knowledge and exposure rather than pure qualification. They are looking more for 'profession-ready' candidates.

This poses a challenge to alternative MBA compared to traditional MBA programme. Alternative MBA programmes, however, have an edge in updating and upskilling in digital social media, digital marketing, data sciences and the IoT.

FUTURE COURSE OF BUSINESS EDUCATION

Digitalisation is a technology. Technology and innovations will have to play their roles in making business education more contemporary and giving it more industry orientation.

This indicates structural reforms in business education. In fact, the process has already begun.

In the U.S., one of the most recent studies on the state of business education was commissioned by the American Assembly of Collegiate School of Business (AACSB), the principal business accrediting body in the States. The study is based on visits to 60 schools of business and management, interviews with 200 executives and surveys of nearly 9,000 educators, managers, and business school students and alumni. A major finding of the study is that past rapid growth and market success caused business educators to be complacent about their traditional business school model. But, the traditional model is ill-suited to the needs of the next century. The authors of the AACSB study state: "In our opinion, if any single element of organisation culture ideally should characterise the US business schooling the next decade, it should be an ingrained, embedded, and spirit of innovation. If this occurs, society will be a winner."[5] But, if that is to occur, most business schools will have to undergo sudden and dramatic change.

Alternative Model

Porter, Muller and Rehder have suggested an alternative model[6] of school of management with a fundamental shift in the objective, design and development. The emphasis is on changes or transformations in terms of strategy and vision, (culture philosophy, values, goals), human resources, organisational structure, and management systems. The model could provide opportunities for students to broaden their perspectives, to integrate theory and practice and to develop judgements, habit of critical thinking, practical know-how and interpersonal and communication abilities. "We are in desperate need of an antidote to the narrow technical curriculum orientation that now characterise the traditional school of business" observe the authors.

The AACSB study has made some penetrating observations. Porter, Muller and Rehder model purports to be a more complete approach to a new system. This should provoke more discussion and debate for reforms and generate newer strategies to eliminate routine and institutionalised obsolescence in present management education.

Simultaneously with general course corrections in the management institutes, individual companies, specially the large ones, can also consider what Brian Bowden, Personnel Director of Shell, UK, is striving at. Shell, UK has a problem of developing the best and brightest of its young managers: it would like them to have some formal business training at key moments of their careers, but, it cannot afford to send them for two-year MBA programmes.

Bowden is now considering an MBA programme comprising in-house courses tailored to meet Shell's specific needs along with general courses to be taken in academic institutions like business schools.

The Manchester Business School recently went into a huddle with eight companies to discuss the introduction of a modular MBA course in two parts. The first part involves doing course at Manchester on a part-time basis spread over three years. The second consists of credits reflecting the training and experience gained by managers in their companies.

Role of Industry

Time has come for industrial organisations in various other countries to work on similar modular MBA courses for their managers in collaboration with management schools. The concept of in-house training programme has already gained ground, and, many management institutes are conducting in-company training programmes on specific requisitions. But, what is imperative is development of a complete modular course as mentioned above. Under such scheme of things, the end-products (MBAs) will be more in line with the requirements of the users and closer to organisational realities.

Developments are taking place in India also. Some business schools are trying to make innovations. The pandemic seems to have opened up new avenues and possibilities.

According to many, the pandemic can be used as an opportunity to review archaic curriculum and introduce contemporary relatable courses. For example, soft skills are becoming important in the field of management as the ability to collaborate and build trust and relationships is the call of the day. "It has become increasingly evident that 'soft skills' embodied in self-awareness, ability to work in diverse teams and 'first principles' thinking have a major role in the modern day curriculum. To this list of expectations is added the ability to adapt to technological disruptions and yet conceptualise sustainable business models."[7]

These changing realities have "led to a lot of changes in the curriculum across top business schools. Courses on self-awareness—as an individual, as a member of a team, and, finally, as a transformational leader have found a way right in the initial stages of coursework."[8]

Industry interaction of business schools has also significantly increased. Because senior corporate professionals are now not able or required to travel, they are quite willing to find and commit time to engage with students. The practice or model is to engage small groups with senior professionals, organise one-to-one mentoring and more short-term industry projects.

Paradigm Shift

As per NEP, 2020, UGC and AICTE may be merged and new institutions like Higher Education Grants Council (HEGC) and Professional Standard Setting Bodies (PSSB) may be formed. These institutions are likely to come up with new course structure which may make the present MBA largely redundant in future years. New or alternative MBA—with appropriate blending of traditional MBA and digitalised courses—may become the optimal programme structure.

If all these happen, there may be paradigm shift in management education. Then, the gap between *What They Teach at Business Schools* and *What They Don't Teach at Business Schools* can be bridged significantly.

Notes and References

Chapter 1: Decision Making at Corporates

1. M.H. McCormack, *What They Don't Teach You at Harward Business School*, Fontana/Collins, 1989.
2. H.R. Horton, *The CEO Paradox*, American Management Association, 1992.
3. M.H. McCormack (1989), p. 227.
4. A. Nag, *The Management Refresher* (2nd Edn.) Vikas Publishing House, 1994, p. 36.
5. H.R. Horton (1992), p. 43.
6. *Ibid*., p. 51.
7. Akio Morita, *Made in Japan: Akio Morita and Sony*, Fontana Collius, 1987, p. 198.
8. *Ibid*., pp. 198-99.
9. "Corporate Dossier", *The Economic Times*, March 21, 2003.
10. *Ibid*.
11. R.T. Pascale and A.G. Athos, *The Art of Japanese Management*, Warner Book, 1982, p. 46.
12. A. Nag, *The 100-Minute Manager*, Vikas Publishing House, 1997, p. 83.

Chapter 2: Line-Staff Relationship

1. H. Mulla, "The Line-staff Link," *Business India*, June, 1989, p. 12-25.
2. R. Stewart, *The Reality of Management*, Pan Books Ltd., London, 1967, Ch. 2.

3. T. Haimann, *Professional Management: Theory and Practice*, Eurasia Publishing House, 1966, Ch. 14.
4. A. Nag, *The Management Refresher* (Second Edition), Vikas Publishing House, 1997, Ch. 4.
5. "HR Not Backroom Department, It's Vital Cog for Success," *The Times of India*, December 15, 2021.
6. *The Times of India*, December 15, 2021.

Chapter 3: Informal Management

1. C.N. Parkinson and M.K. Rustomji, *Realities in Management*, India Book House, 1984, p. 213.
2. These structural forms are discussed in detail in A. Nag, *Strategic Management: Analysis, Implementation, Control* (Second Reprint), Vikas Publishing House, 2013, Ch. 12.
3. C.N. Parkinson and M.K. Rustomji (1984), p. 215.
4. A. Nag, *In Search of a Career* (Unpublished), 2020, Ch. 22.
5. A. Nag (2020), Ch. 22.
6. C.N. Parkinson and M.K. Rustomji (1984), p. 215.

Chapter 4: Management by Obstruction

1. J.F. Harrison, *Management by Obstruction or How To Save Your Organisation from Needless Efficiency*, D.B. Taraporevala Sons & Company, 1979.
2. *Ibid.*, (1979), p. ix.
3. *Ibid.*, (1979), p. 63.
4. *Ibid.*, (1979), p. 137.
5. A. Nag, *In Search of a Career: Lessons from Companies* (Unpublished), 2020, Ch. 23.
6. *Ibid.*, Ch. 23.

Chapter 5: Managing the Boss

1. R. Stewart, *The Reality of management*, Pan Books Ltd., London, 1969.
2. P.F. Drucker, *The Practice of Management*, Allied Publishers, New Delhi, 1985, pp. 139-43.
3. R.R. Blake and J.S. Mouton, *The New Managerial Grid*, Jaico Publishing House, 1985.
4. N. Maluste, "Disagreeing with the Boss," *Business India*, December 26, 1988-January 8, 1989.

5. N. Maluste, *op.cit.*
6. N. Maluste, "Delicate Art of Delegating," *Business India*, February, 6-19, 1989.
7. D.P. Sinha, "Managing the Boss," *Business India*, May 20-June 2, 1985.
8. D.P. Sinha, *op.cit.*
9. These are major categorisations given by Mary Abbajay, Washington-DC based career expert, reported in "ET Panache", *The Economic Times*, February, 24, 2021.
10. "ET, Panache," *The Economic Times*, February 24. 2021.
11. Adapted from ten steps suggested in Gorick Ng, *The Unspoken Rules: Secrets to Sharing Your Career Off Right* reported in *The Economic Times*, February 16, 2021.
12. *The Economic Times*, February 16, 2021.
13. I. Ghosh, "A Step Down from the Lofty Pedestral" *The Economic Times*, January 4, 1992.
14. I. Ghosh, *op.cit.*

Chapter 6: Climbing the Ladder

1. Mark McCormack, *What They Don't Teach at Harvard Business School*, Fontana/Collins, 1989, p. 73.
2. Mark McCormack (1989), pp. 81-82.
3. A. Nag, *The Management Refresher* (Second Edition), Vikas Publishing House, 1997, p. 15.
4. Walter Vieira, "Workplace Politics," *Business World*, August,16-29, 1989.
5. S.K. Tarafder, *How to Become an Efficient Manager*, Atlantic Publishers & Distributors, 2009, p. 26.
6. Mark McCormack (1989), pp. 68-69.
7. "ET Panache," *The Economic Times*, October 14, 2021.
8. C.N. Parkinson and M.K. Rustomji, *How to Get to the Top without Ulcers, Tranquillisers or Heart Attacks*, Macmillan India, 1983.
9. T.R. Horton, *The CEO Paradox*, American Management Association, 1992, p. 23.
10. T.R. Horton (1992), p. 54.

Chapter 7: How to Be a Successful Manager

1. The Management writer is Rosemary Stewart. Rosemary Stewart, *The Reality of Management*, Pan Books Ltd., London, 1967, p. 51.
2. Michael Le Boeuf, *The Greatest Management Principle*, Jaico Publishing House, Bombay, 1987, p. 74.
3. Kenneth Blancard and Spencer Johnson, *The One Minute Manager*, William Collins, Willow Books, Glasgow, 1983, p. 20.
4. For the GMP story, refer Boeuf, op.cit., pp. 58-59.
5. Peter F. Drucker, *The Effective Executive*, Pan Books Ltd., London, 1979, p. 2.
6. George S. Odiorne, "The Activity Trap," *Management by Objectives*, 1973, p. 2.
7. For details of "BW-MARG Poll on India's best Chief Executives, refer *Business World*, 29 March-11 April, 1989.
8. W.J. Reddin, *Effective Mbo*, Management Publication, London, 1971.
9. Peter F. Drucker, *Managing For Results*, Pan books Ltd., London, 1967.
10. An unpublished (and undated) talk which Professor Argyris gave at the Graduate Business School of Columbia University. For the present reference and Drucker comments, see Drucker, op. cit., p. 22.
11. S.K. Tarafder, *How to Become an Efficient Manager*, Atlantic Publishers & Distributors, 2009, Ch. 48.
12. S.K. Tarafder (229), pp. 116-17.

Chapter 8: Corporate Culture and Values

1. C. O'Reilly, "Corporations, Culture and Commitment: Motivation and Social Control in Organisation," *California Management Review*, Summer, 1989, p. 10.
2. R.M. Lala, *The Creation of Wealth*, IBH Publishing House, Mumbai, 1981, p. 198.
3. A. Nag, *The Management Refresher* (Second Revised Edition), Vikas Publishing House, 1997, p. 140.
4. A. Nag, (1997), pp. 141-42.
5. S. Rangnekar, *In the World of Corporate Managers* (Second Edition), Vikas Publishing House, 2012, pp. 166-67.

6. C.N. Parkinson and M.K. Rustomji, *Realities in Management*, India Book House, Bombay, 1984, p. 43.
7. A. Nag, (1997), p. 142.
8. P. Jha, "Be Alert to Erosion of Trust at Workplace to Stem Attrition," *Times Ascent*, June 20, 2022.
9. A. Monappa, *Ethical Attitudes of Indian Managers*, All India Management Association (AIMA), 1980.
10. S. Ghoshal, "The Value of Values," *The Economic Times* (Supplement), March 5, 1999.
11. Partly based on J.C. Collins and J.L. Porras, *Built to Last: Successful Habits of Visionary Companies*, Harper Business, New York, 1994.
12. Refer T.R. Horton, *The CEO Paradox*, American Management Association, 1992, pp. 103-04.

Chapter 9: Man Management

1. A. Nag, *The Management Refresher* (Second Edition), Vikas Publishing House, 1997, p. 11.
2. S. Covey, *The 7 Habits of Highly Effective People*, Simon & Schuster, New York, 1989.
3. Also refer C.N. Parkinson and M.K. Rustomiji, *Excellence in Management*, India Book house, 1985, Ch. 16.
4. Refer A. Levit, *They Don't Teach Corporate in College*, New Age International Publishers, 2006, p. 175.
5. A. Nag, *Success in Selling: Thirty Valuable Mantras*, Atlantic Publishers and Distributors, 2022, pp. 92-93.
6. P.N. Singh, "Corporations, Cows and HRD," *Business World*, March 14-27, 1988.
7. C.N. Parkinson and Others. *The Incredible Japanese*, Macmillan India, 2000, Ch. 20.
8. "Should You Face up to the Office Bully," *The Times of India*, May 15, 2022, p. 22.
9. P.S. Viswanath, *Times Ascent*, July, 20, 2022.

Chapter 10: Managing Time

1. A. Nag, *Success in Selling: Thirty Valuable Mantras*, Atlantic Publishers and Distributors, 2022, Mantra 23.
2. A. Nag, The *100-Minute Manager*, Vikas Publishing House, 1997, p. 63.

3. T.R. Horton, *The CEO Paradox*, American Management Association, 1992, pp. 62-64.
4. Thomas R. Horton (1992), p. 60.

Chapter 11: Leadership: Ins and Outs

1. Frank Goble, *Excellence in Leadership*, Tharaporevala Publishing Industries Private Ltd., Bombay 1978.
2. Harry Levinson and Stuart Rosenthal, *CEO: Corporate Leadership in Action*, Basic Books, Inc., Publishers, New York, 1984.
3. Rensis Likert, *The Human Organisation*, McGraw-Hill, New York, 1967.
4. Levinson and Rosenthal, op. cit.
5. Warren Bennis, "Four Traits of Leadership" in John N. Williamson, Ed., *The Leader-Manager*, John Wiley and Sons, 1986.
6. Goble, op. cit., Ch. 13.
7. Napoleon Hill, *Think and Grow Rich*, Fawcett Publishers, Inc., Greenwich, 1958.
8. Norman Jaspan, "Why Employees Steal," *New and World Report*, 3 May 1971.
9. A.H. Maslow, *Motivation and Personality*, Harper and Row, New York, 1954, pp. 203, 207, 257.
10. H.M. Carlisle, *Situational Management: A Contingency Approach to Leadership*, Taraporevala Publishing Industries Private Ltd., 1981.
11. Pradip N. Khandwala, "Two Routes to Turnaround," *Business World*, 12-25 April 1989.
12. Khandwala, op. cit.
13. N.R. Narayana Murthy, "Life Lessons from Dhoni: Corporate India can learn much about Leadership by just Watching his Matches," *The Times of India*, August 17, 2020.
14. These are based on Chetan Bhagat, "Ten Practical Leadership lessons: Congress offers a crucial Management Case Study: What Not to do as a Leader: *The Times of India*, August, 29, 2020.
15. Biplop Banerjee has suggested some methods. Refer "Times Assent," *The times of India*, October 28, 2020.

Chapter 12: Crisis Management

1. S. Fink, *Crisis Management: Planning for the Inevitable*, AMACOM (American Management Association), 1986, p. 15.
2. S. Fink (1986), p. 1.
3. S. Fink (1986), p. 30.
4. A. Nag, *In Search of a Career: Lessons from Companies* (2020), Ch. 21.
5. Those interested in more details, may refer "MMTC": Managing Strategic Change" (Long Case 2), A. Nag, *Strategic Management*, Vikas Publishing House, 2013, pp. 436-443
6. A. Nag (2020), Ch. 21.
7. "A Guide to Disaster Management", *The Economic Times*, April 27-May 03, 2022.

Chapter 13: Many Management Styles

1. A. Nag, *The Management Refresher* (Second Edition), Macmillan India, 1997, p. 138.
2. Refer A. Nag, "Public Enterprises: Performance Evaluation" *The Economic Times*, August 8, 1986.
3. A. Panagariya, "Private Enterprises Unlimited," *The Economic Times*, February 22, 2012.
4. Within the Eastern World also, there are differences in the patterns of management. We have the Arab management, the Korean management, the Thai management, the Indian management etc. We can also talk of an ASEAN (Association of South East Asian Nations) management system.
5. R.T. Pascale and A.G. Athos, *The Art of Japanese Management*, Warner Books, New York, 1982. This is one of the best books on the contrast between American management and Japanese management.
6. R.T. Pascale and A.G. Athos (1982), p. 91
7. Akio Morita, *Made in Japan: Akio Morita and Sony*, Fontana Paperbacks, 1987. This book gives a fascinating account of Morita's association with Sony and his reflections on Japanese management.
8. Akio Morita (1987), pp. 179-180.
9. "Corporate Dossier," *The Economic Times*, March 21, 2003.
10. Management thought and philosophy of Morita are contained in his celebrated book (1987).

11. R.T. Pascale and A.G. Athos (1982), p. 76.
12. S.N. Chary, *Business Gurus Speak*, Macmillan India, 2002, p. 162.
13. S.N. Chary (2002), p. 65.
14. S.N. Chary (2002), p. 41.
15. S.N. Chary (2002), p. 77.
16. "Times Business," *The Times of India*, September 11, 2020.
17. "Times Business," *The Times of India*, July 26, 2021.
18. "Brand Equity," *The Economic Times*, November 25, 2020.
19. "Times Business," *The Times of India*, September 30, 2020.
20. "ET Panache," *The Economic Times*, February 11, 2021.
21. *The Times of India,* June 29, 2021.
22. *The Times of India,* January 30, 2022.

Chapter 14: Excellence in Management

1. C.N. Parkinson and M.K. Rustomji, *Excellence in Management*, India Book House, 1978.
2. T.J. Peters and R.H. Waterman, Jr., *In Search of Excellence: Lessons from America's Best-run Companies*, Harper & Row Publishers, 1982.
3. S.K. Bhattacharyya, *Achieving Managerial Excellence: Insights from Indian Organisations*, Macmillan India, New Delhi, 1989.
4. S.K. Bhattacharyya (1989), p. 80.
5. P.F. Drucker, *Managing for Results*, Pan Books Limited, London, 1967.
6. P.F. Drucker (1967).
7. A. Nag, *The Management Refresher* (Second Edition), Vikas Publishing House, 1997, p. 116.
8. "Business Impact Awards 2022". *The Economic Times*, February 25, 2022.

Chapter 15: Marketing Myopia

1. T. Levitt, "Marketing Myopia," *Harvard Business Review*, 1960.
2. J.S. Panwar, *Marketing in the New Era*, Response Books, 1997, p. 33.
3. P. Kotler, *Ten Deadly Marketing Sins*, Wiley India, 2004, p. 23.
4. Doug Hall, *Jump Start Your Business*, Brain Brew Books, 2001, p. 3.

5. P. Kotler (2004), p. 4.
6. Nirmalya Kumar, Director, Centre for Marketing, London Business School, quoted in "Brand Equity," *The Economic Times*, November 19, 2003.
7. A. Nag, *Marketing Successfully: A Professional perspective*, Macmillan India, 2001, p. 132.
8. A. Nag (2001), p. 132.
9. "Brand Equity," *The Economic Times*, August 4, 2004.
10. "Brand Equity," *The Economic Times*, November, 19, 2003.

Chapter 16: Important Marketing Laws

1. Ries and Trout give an excellent exposition of marketing laws. Refer AL Ries and Jack Trout, *The 22 Immutable Laws of Marketing*, Harper Collins Publishers, New Delhi, 1996.
2. A. Nag, *Success in Marketing: Know the Mantras*, Atlantic Publishers and distributors, 2023, Mantra 8.
3. All Ries and Jack Trout, *Positioning: The Battle for Your Mind*, McGraw-Hill, New York, 1981.
4. A. Nag (2023), Mantra 18.

Chapter 17: Major Marketing Sins

1. Kotler actually calls these "Deadly Marketing Sins." Refer Philip Kotler, *Ten Deadly Marketing Sins*, Wiley India, 2006. How deadly these marketing sins are may be a matter of discussion or debate.
2. Philip Kotler (2006), p. 10. The order of the ten deadly sins has been changed.
3. Gerard Earls and Patrick Forsyth, *Making Marketing Work*, Wheeler Publishing, 1995, p. 36.
4. We should clearly understand the difference between "consumer" and "customer." "Consumer" is the universe; "customer" is a sub-set of this. Customers are always understood with reference to a market, company or product. For example, customers for Hindustan Lever (HUL)s' Lux toilet soap or Surf detergent powder.
5. A. Nag, *The 100-Minute Marketing Manager* (Second Edition), Macmillan India, 2010, p. 90.
6. Marketing Leadership Council, *Stewarding the Brand for Profitable Growth*, Corporate Executive Board, Washington, D.C., December, 2001, p. 179.

7. For example, booking of advertising space and preparation of advertising content can run parallel to each other.
8. A David, The Handbook of Brand Management, Random Century House. :London. 1992; also YLR Moorthi, *Brand Management: The Indian Context*, Vikas Publishing House, 1999, pp. 78.
9. Philip Kotler and Fernando Trias de Bes, *Lateral Marketing: A New Approach to Finding Break through Ideas*, John Wiley & Sons, 2003.
10. Philip Kotler (2006), p. 138.
11. The difference between "effectiveness" and "efficiency" should be clearly understood. 'Effectiveness' is plan—output relationship—how much of the plan bas been achieved; "Efficiency" is input-output relationship—how much output has been produced per unit of input.
12. Philip Kotler (2006), pp. 108-121.

Chapter 18: Why Salespeople Fail

1. A. Nag, *Success in Selling: Thirty Valuable Mantras*, Atlantic Publishers, 2022, Mantra 4.
2. A. Nag (2022), Mantra 2.
3. A. Nag, *Marketing Successfully: A Professional Perspective*, Macmillan India, 2011, Ch. 12.
4. A. Nag (2022), Mantra 12.
5. For Porter's Five Forces Model, refer books on strategic marketing or strategic management. Refer, among others, A. Nag, *Strategic Marketing* (Second Edition), 2008, Ch. 12.
6. A. Nag (2022), Mantra 13.
7. S. Khera, You Can Sell (New Edition), Bloomsbury Publishing India, 2018, Ch. 28.

Chapter 19: Success in Selling

1. A. Nag, *Success in Selling: Thirty Valuable Mantras*, Atlantic Publishers, 2022, *Mantra* 24, pp. 152-55.
2. A. Nag (2022), *Mantra* 25, pp. 158-161.
3. A. Nag (2022), *Mantra* 19.
4. A. Nag (2022), *Mantra* 20, pp. 124-25.
5. A. Nag (2022), *Mantra* 29, pp. 193-94.

Chapter 20: Entrepreneurship and Business Success

1. S.E. Stiegeler, *Dictionary of Economics and Business* (Second Edition), 1985, Gower Publishing Co., England, 1985, p. 129.
2. S.E. Stiegeler (1985), p. 130.
3. M.H. McCormack, *What They Don't Teach You at Harvard Business School*. Fontana/Collins, 1989, p. 236.
4. By assigning scores or weights to the critical factors, a 'doability quotient' for a project can be worked out in quantitative terms.
5. Shiv Khera, *You Can Win*, Macmillan India, 2000, p. ix.
6. Akio Morita, *Made in Japan*, Fontana/Collins, 1987, p. 203.
7. M.H. McCormack (1989), p. 161.
8. S.N. Chary, *Business Gurus Speak*, Macmillan India, 2002, p. 20.
9. "Times Business," *The Times of India*, June, 4, 2021.
10. "Power of the Crowd," *The Economic Times*, April 16, 2021.
11. "ET Newsmakers," *The Economic Times*, May 31, 2021.
12. "Et Newsmakers," *The Economic Times*, May 31, 2021.

Twenty Lessons from What they Don't Teach at Business Schools

1. A. Levit, *They Don't Teach Corporate in College*, New Age International Publishers, 2006. p. 12.
2. We are not going into the finer distinction between "Executive" and "Manager" which some people would like to make.
3. Rosemary Stewat, *The Reality of Management*, Pan Books Ltd. London 1967, p. 51
4. For more explanatory details, refer text (Ch. 3.)
5. In modern time, the designation might have changed from 'GM' to 'VP', but, the functional logic remains the same.

The Epilogue

1. P.N. Singh, "Mis-managing Education," *Business World*, 3-16, August, 1988.
2. J.L. Porter, H.J. Muller and R.R. Rehder "The Making of Managers: An American Perspective," *Journal of General Management*, Vol. 14, No. 4, Summer, 1989.
3. C. Handy, *The Making of Managers, National Economic Development Office*, London, 1987.

4. "Education Times," *The Times of India*, November, 2, 2020.
5. J.L. Porter, H.J. Muller and R.R. Rehder (1989).
6. Poter, Muller and Rehder (1989).
7. "Paradigm Shift in Management Education," *The Economic Times*, October 29, 2021.
8. *The Economic Times*, October, 29, 2021.

Index